Further Praise for

The Leaving Season

"[Kelly] McMasters' writing shares some of its DNA with Leslie Jamison and Rebecca Solnit. . . . *The Leaving Season* is a candid, often wrenching account of a relationship's slow, inexorable crumbling and a survivor's attempt to climb from the ruin and build a new life. Kelly McMasters is a graceful, fluid writer, and though the subject matter of her memoir is anything but easy, the rewards of sharing her company on the page are undeniable." —Harvey Freedenberg, *Bookreporter*

"[McMasters] rhapsodically renders the experience of living at one with the natural world. . . . [*The Leaving Season*] is told with candor and grace." —*Kirkus Reviews*

"McMasters shares a wise, honest, and completely absorbing memoir of marriage and motherhood that is particular in the details but universal in a way that will resonate with many readers." —*Booklist*

"McMasters's masterful, moving memoir of her journey from the city to the country to the suburbs makes an excellent case for taking the time to figure [out who you are], no matter how frightening it seems."

—*BookPage*

T0036271

"A profound and beautiful book. . . . Never have I encountered a memoir that explores motherhood and marriage with such warmth, intimacy, and wisdom. This is a book that will forever change the way you see your world—and yourself. If you loved Cheryl Strayed's *Wild* or Claire Dederer's *Love and Trouble*, you must read *The Leaving Season* immediately."

—Joanna Rakoff, author of *My Salinger Year: A Memoir*

"*The Leaving Season* is an astoundingly gorgeous memoir of life, love, and leaving. With devastating insight, Kelly McMasters paints a delicate portrait of love, home, and what happens when it all falls apart. *The Leaving Season* is about how endings are beginnings and beginnings are things of beauty. With an eye for detail and empathetic, deeply human portraits of the communities she inhabits, McMasters has created a soul-deep work of aching beauty and stubborn hope. Written with lush prose and an expansive heart, both gentle and gut-wrenching, beautiful and profound, *The Leaving Season* is a work of wonder."

—Lyz Lenz, author of *Belabored: A Vindication of the Rights of Pregnant Women*

*The
Leaving
Season*

The
Leaving
Season

A MEMOIR IN ESSAYS

KELLY
McMASTERS

W. W. NORTON & COMPANY
Independent Publishers Since 1923

For information about permission to reproduce selections from this
book, write to Permissions, W. W. Norton & Company, Inc., 500 Fifth
Avenue, New York, NY 10110

For information about special discounts for bulk purchases, please
contact W. W. Norton Special Sales at specialsales@wwnorton.com or
800-233-4830

Manufacturing by Lakeside Book Company
Book design and illustration by Ellen Cipriano
Production manager: Lauren Abbate

Library of Congress Control Number: 2023952271

ISBN 978-1-324-07605-6 pbk.

W. W. Norton & Company, Inc., 500 Fifth Avenue, New York, N.Y. 10110
www.wwnorton.com

W. W. Norton & Company Ltd., 15 Carlisle Street, London W1D 3BS

1 2 3 4 5 6 7 8 9 0

for anyone who has ever left,
or wanted to

The heart of another is a dark forest, always, no matter how close it has been to one's own.
—WILLA CATHER, *THE PROFESSOR'S HOUSE*

With our pack of memories
Slung slack on our backs
We venture into the circle . . .
—JOY HARJO, "MEMORY SACK"

You think this happened only once and long ago?
—MARIE HOWE, "YOU THINK THIS HAPPENED ONLY ONCE AND LONG AGO"

Contents

Home Fires

*W*HAT SHOULD WE SAVE, MAMA?

Every year, my children come home asking the same question after the annual fire safety assembly at their elementary school: What should we save if the house is on fire? We make plans, the three of us, for what to grab, how to get out, where to meet.

We'd come together at the fire hydrant in front of our apartment, they decide, its glossy red head a beacon of safety to them. I don't explain that we likely wouldn't be able to get close to the hydrant because the fire truck would need that space, thinking that if the kids made it to the hydrant and I did not, someone would collect them and keep them safe. We won't have a fire anyway, I reassure them. This is all just precaution.

Pre-caution. Care taken in advance. A kind of controlled burning.

But then, this winter, there are two house fires on our street. Both at night, both kitchen fires, a few weeks between them, both houses with children in them. The sirens bring the neighbors out into the middle of the street and we huddle and remark, point from afar. No one is hurt, donation pages are created. One house is quickly taped off and under reconstruction within a few weeks, puffs of damaged insulation curling over a dumpster in the driveway like yellowed cotton candy. The other house sits quiet and dark, broken windows covered with plywood, circulars piled on the stoop like wet leaves.

The neighborhood children claim the property, climbing the single tree in front of this house day after day, hanging from its limbs in front of the sagging façade, intuitively understanding that this house has been abandoned, long before the adults realize. The children have no appetite for nostalgia; preciousness can't compete with their craving to turn the tree into their own *Roxaboxen* kingdom. They quickly forget their friends who used to live there, what cars belonged to this driveway. The home's history washes away; the fire, the family only as real as the sound of a song that just ended.

In her book *The Future of Nostalgia*, Svetlana Boym calls nostalgia "a longing for a home that no longer exists or has never existed." There is romance inherent in loss and longing. In order for humans to move on after loss, collective memory shifts and binds together, agreeing on a shared memory of the past or of a place, a new beauty. Boym cautions us against believing in the truth of our nostalgia. We are lulled into trusting that this new beauty, this lie, is safe to believe because access—to the past, to home, to a place, to a person—is impossible.

There is no fact-checking for nostalgia.

———

Years ago, when the boys and I lived with their father in an old farmhouse in the middle of the woods, I obsessed over fire safety. I kept a go-bag packed. I tucked fire ladders under the beds, stationed a fire extinguisher in the kitchen and another near the woodstove. I was so focused on preventing fires inside the house, I was unable to see until it was too late that our family had been consumed by a less spectacularly dramatic catastrophe. Marriage, after all, is just one long exercise in controlled burning.

Each time we do this annual safety exercise, my sons' answers change about what they would save. This year, at the assembly, the kids were told to choose a pillowcase and fill it with a flashlight and soap, bottled water and a first-aid kit. But they don't care about those things, and our flashlight's battery is dead. They stuff their cases with toys, a tae kwon do belt, candy.

The boys never ask me what I would save. In our apartment, this small space that holds the three of us quietly at the dead end of a tree-filled suburban street, I feel insulated. Perhaps a better word is inoculated, immunized by whatever calamities we've already experienced or escaped. And whatever steel trap we may yet be marching toward, I feel somehow confident that a house fire is not part of those scissored jaws.

Still, as I quietly kiss my sons goodnight, their sleeping heads become flames of burnt umber in the streetlight's shine through their window, and I play along in my mind. I think of the robin's-egg blue box tucked high in my closet with the crusted twigs of my children's umbilical cords, soft nosegays of baby hair from their first haircuts, the nubby flannel blankets they came home in from the hospital. I think of my grandmother's dainty wedding ring

tucked inside the faded purple Shalimar clamshell box in the basement. I think of my journals.

I also think of all the things I'd leave behind, the things I
would let burn.

There are so many.

Intrepid

THE NAVY AIRCRAFT CARRIER USS *Intrepid* feels a bit like the island of Manhattan itself: a floating slab of metal that is a feat of engineering, dependent upon a complex set of social and mechanical systems that, should they fail, would condemn its inhabitants to death. The ship is a kind of skyscraper on its side, its body pushing against the sparkling water like a listless grey whale.

The aircraft carrier docked on Pier 86 of the Hudson River on Manhattan's West Side is the fourth Navy ship to bear the name. The *Intrepid* was the eleventh carrier commissioned by the United States; of the first ten, one other was turned into a museum, three were scrapped, and six were sunk in various battles, or, in the *Saratoga*'s case, as a nuclear test target in Bikini Atoll. After coming online in 1943, the *Intrepid* churned in the seas during World War II, the Cold War, and the Vietnam War, as well as working as a recovery vessel for the Gemini and Mercury space missions, plucking astronauts out of the water after they'd just rained down from outer space. The ship was decommissioned in 1974 and turned into a museum eight years later.

I first saw the *Intrepid* in 1999. I knew nothing of its history at the time, just that it was the site of that evening's work party. I'd moved to the city after college the previous year; my plan to move to California fell through when I was offered a job as a corporate legal assistant at a law firm down near Wall Street instead. I'd been working summer and part-time gigs since I was fourteen, but this was my first full-time job, and with my new position a sense of adulthood bloomed. The acceptance letter came to my campus mailbox on periwinkle blue letterhead: Winthrop, Stimson, Putnam & Roberts. Starting salary: $25,000. I shared a three-bedroom apartment with two college friends in Brooklyn; my rent was $1,000 a month, and I couldn't believe I'd have thirteen thousand whole dollars to spend as I pleased for the year. The week before my start date, I went to Century 21 with my roommates and tried on racks of single-button suits, feeling like Melanie Griffith in *Working Girl*.

I spent that year working ninety-hour weeks, sleeping under my desk, taking company-comped private cars home to my Brooklyn apartment, feeling rich from the overtime wages piling up in my bank account because I had no time to spend them. The legal assistant bullpen became my whole life—we worked together, ate together, cried in the bathroom together, went to bars after work together, vacationed together, slept together. The whole law firm was a complicated ecosystem of liaisons between legal assistants and other legal assistants, legal assistants and lawyers, junior lawyers and partners. One stormy night, when almost everyone else had gone home, David, one of the other legal assistants, led me to a dark conference room on the thirty-second floor with a perfect view of the Twin Towers. David's girlfriend worked as a legal assistant in a different department, and I was dating one of the lawyers at the time, but that night we cracked one of the windows and he told me jokes in his North Carolinian drawl as we smoked cigarettes and kissed, pausing to watch dramatic zigzags of brilliant white lightning strike the Twin Towers directly in front of us. The North Tower, crowned by a broadcast antenna, was 360 feet taller than the South Tower and was hit more often during storms, but they both acted as the city's de facto lightning rods, collecting the brunt of strikes from passing storms and keeping the rest of downtown safe, while delivering a reliable show from our conference room.

The party that night on the *Intrepid* was to celebrate the new crop of summer associates plucked from law school that year. My coworker Annette and I were excited to scope out the handsome ones. But despite the party lights and the wind coming off the river blowing up the women's skirts and pushing the men's ties over their shoulders, as I clanked up the rickety metal staircase in my roommate's strappy heels, I couldn't push away a feeling of gloom. The more we danced and drank, the sadder I became.

The *Intrepid* had survived five kamikaze attacks and a torpedo strike, and here I was, a twenty-something guzzling drinks with glow-in-the-dark swizzle sticks and just hoping to make out with someone in the cockpit of one of the helicopters perched on the ship's deck. I looked around at our bullpen group, most of whom would be leaving in the next few months. Annette was going to Tulane Law, David to Kellogg for an MBA. I hadn't understood that this job was meant to be a strategic stepping-stone for collecting experience and references to bolster law and business school applications. I'd missed the deadlines; I hadn't even taken the LSAT yet.

I wanted to go to law school, or I thought I did. I'd grown up in a blue-collar town on the south shore of Long Island, where a simplistic equation was engraved into my brain early on: job + suit = success. After a dozen interviews, this was the only place to offer me a job after college, so I went with it. The money was good and I didn't need to be in the office until 10am. Except for when I worked late nights and wound up sleeping an hour or so under my desk, of course; on those days I was technically the first to work after visiting the breakfast buffet in the corporate cafeteria and changing out my pantyhose.

I didn't mind the pace. But I was beginning to question some things. I noticed there were no female partners and very few female associates, for example. I cat-sat for one of them regularly, and mooned over her sprawling Tribeca loft. The apartment was on a cobblestoned corner straight out of *Life* magazine; from the building's front door the Odeon Restaurant hunkered low in the foreground, with the World Trade Center buildings rising impossibly high above everything else, like two stern teachers towering over a class of preschoolers. It felt like the Trade Center towered over the whole city in those days.

The lawyer's apartment was in a converted warehouse, the kind with a cage elevator that makes you feel like you're entering into a horror movie every time you pull the lever. I loved it. The kitchen consisted of an industrial sink and a microwave, and the toilet was in a closet all by itself. Along one whole wall stretched hundreds of books piled on chunky wooden bookshelves. Every other surface was covered in old *New Yorker* magazines and cat hair, the geometric faded shapes on the scattershot collection of Persian rugs clashing deliciously against the velour thrift store couches. Until then, I had not realized that one could show up to work in designer black crepe suits and a severe black bob with bangs and come home to a place that rejected every pin-straight hair and hem.

After my first few months at the firm, I'd been tapped for a case involving a group of Holocaust survivors who'd petitioned to recover valuables and cash that had been stolen by the Nazis during the war and secreted away in Swiss banks. In college I had studied collective memory in postwar Germany, and I had a working knowledge of German; I'd spent a summer in Munich researching my thesis on Holocaust memorials. The case would require extensive travel to Switzerland and Germany, and I couldn't believe my good fortune when I was offered the position. The only problem: my firm was representing the banks.

I asked for some time to think about it and was given until the end of the week. Some of the other legal assistants didn't understand my hesitation and argued that the travel opportunity was worth it; who cared about the case? Travel had become increasingly important to me; along with my summer in Munich and another school-funded research trip to Berlin, I'd traveled to Vietnam with the first group of American students allowed into the country on a History Department trip sophomore year, and during my junior year at the London School of Economics I used the breaks to backpack through much of northern and eastern Europe. But in the end, I couldn't stomach working for the banks. I politely declined and was shuffled off onto a Bangladeshi project finance deal, subjected to months of midnight conference calls due to the time difference, and constant headaches from losing files and packages to what seemed like ever-present floods and monsoons. I still felt guilty when I clicked swiftly past the placard-wielding protesters who stationed themselves outside our lobby after the Holocaust case hit the news, but I weakly rationalized that at least my paycheck wasn't coming directly from the Nazis' spoils, since I'd refused to work on that project.

After about six months of penance on the Bangladeshi case, I was given another chance to travel. The bank, our client, was in Tokyo; I flew there with my suitcase full of Century 21 suits and took a taxi to the most luxurious hotel I'd ever seen in my life. Pamela, the lawyer I was paired with, had been in Tokyo for a few weeks already. She had left her new baby at home for the gig, and now she kept apologizing for adjusting her swollen breasts under her blouse. We worked in the bank's office on a floor consisting entirely of men, except for a few female secretaries; everyone called us the "lady lawyers." The office was open-concept, which was not the custom yet in New York, and everyone smoked at their desks, as well as in the elevators. Even the bathroom stalls had ashtrays next to the complicated set of bidet buttons. Pamela and I took refuge in the smokeless privacy of a corner conference room, and the two of us fell into an easy rhythm during the day. We joined the team for dinner and drinks after work, but never socialized together beyond that. I spent most of my nights alone at the hotel bar drinking whiskey until I retired to my room to listen to American military radio just for the comfort of English, trying not to dial my college boyfriend's phone number before passing out staring at my own reflection in the mirrored headboard of the king-sized bed.

One afternoon, breaking news scrolled across the always-on television mounted in the corner of the conference room. Violence had marred an environmental protest; a group of people had chained themselves to trees and bulldozers in an attempt to stop a construction project in an ancient rainforest somewhere in the Philippines. The corporate security forces had shot into the crowd, wounding half a dozen and killing one man. I watched Pam's face go stony as she reached for the phone, uncharacteristically cursing under her breath. Within minutes, the quiet sanctuary of our conference room filled with chain-smoking bankers gesticulating and rubbing their furrowed brows, and I came to understand that the project we were helping the bank finance was the dam and power plant that was being protested on the screen. Thousands of villagers whose families had lived there for centuries and relied on fishing would be displaced. *Don't worry*, the bankers reassured me later at dinner. *We're paying them to learn new trades, like basket-weaving.*

I lasted another three weeks. The isolation of living in a country whose language I could not speak; the awful juxtaposition of reading paragraphs about profits and the average time it took fishermen to be retrained during the day and attending luxurious corporate dinners at night; the insulating distance between our conference room and those protesters chaining themselves to bulldozers; the amount of whiskey it began taking to get me to sleep: the effects were deadening.

On our last night, the bankers took the lady lawyers out to a hostess club—in the Tokyo of 1999, essentially a segregated strip club. The American girlfriend I was assigned for the night wore a high ponytail and a cheerleading uniform and said she was a college student from Texas, though she looked at least a few years older than me. We sat awkwardly together on the leather banquette; I bought her a $15 seltzer and excused myself to the bathroom. I was startled to open the door not to the staid upscale lavatory I was expecting, but a locker room of women in different states of undress. Half the stalls acted more as small offices rather than places to pee. Disoriented, it took me a while to realize that many of the hostesses were speaking English. I felt a flush of solidarity, but when the women saw me, they turned away. My suit betrayed me; I was not one of them.

On the cab ride back to the hotel that night, Pamela asked if I was still planning to go to law school after this trip. I told her I hadn't really thought about it.

"Well, you *should* think about it," she said ruefully, looking out the window as the flashing lights of Shinjuku blinked by like a pinball game. "You don't really want to do this for the rest of your life, do you?" I realized that as out of place as I may have felt that night, I hadn't stopped to imagine how Pamela felt, sitting between her hostess and the Japanese businessmen, her breasts an aching reminder of the thousands of miles between her and her baby.

Months later, on the grey heft of the *Intrepid*, wind from the Hudson River blowing my hair into my face, I wobbled in my borrowed heels on the slick deck and finally started to think about it. I worried I'd keep winding up on the wrong side of things if I continued on this track. The legal assistants who were moving on to law school seemed to tacitly acknowledge that the king-sized bed

and fine whiskey were worth it, but those things had left me hol-
lowed out. I wondered how on earth I'd get back down the stairs
in these heels, and wondered how on earth I'd gotten up here in
the first place.

I read recently about a study testing safety equipment that found
the majority of children slept through a blaring fire alarm. There is
something in a child's brain that hears a loud, obnoxious warning
bell in the night and says *don't worry, I'm sure you'll be fine, you can
ignore this warning bell and keep sleeping.* In a city like New York,
there are so many warning bells happening on a daily basis—
the oppressive heat or icy cold while waiting for the subway, not
enough money in the bank to cover the rent or a bag of groceries,
the man yelling at you because you took too long at the coffee cart,
the wallet lost in the yellow cab, the groping hand on a crowded
subway, the beginning twinge of a blister on your heel—that sometimes it is difficult to parse which ones need to be paid attention to
and which can be ignored.

Sometimes it feels like my brain takes a while to understand
that I am, in fact, in danger or discomfort. In my case, my therapist recently explained, I got the gene that once saved a caveman
from a saber-toothed tiger by standing so completely still the tiger
ignored him. *This can be helpful,* she cheered. But in the twenty-first
century, it doesn't feel helpful. It feels more like a stupidly delayed
reaction to fear and information. The warning bell is ringing, but
my body keeps sleeping. It feels like I wait for things to happen to
me, and then sit, still as a photograph, watching.

The morning of September 11, 2001, I'd woken up earlier than usual because I had a doctor's appointment before work. I'd quit the law firm by this time and was working as an assistant editor at a technology magazine in the Flatiron District; one of the top editors brought me along with him after the dot-com start-up we'd been working at imploded. I wasn't sure the magazine was for me, but at least I reported to a smart and funny female boss, and if I had to be stuck in a cubicle bullpen, I preferred this one full of writers and editors in jeans and t-shirts. I'd also switched from dating corporate-types to Williamsburg artist-types instead; I'd briefly dated a bassist, a rock 'n' roll karaoke host, a hairstylist, and a programmer, and now I was seeing a painter. I'd been dating my current boyfriend, R., for more than six months, my longest post-college relationship yet. We spent our weekends in bars, wandering the Metropolitan Museum of Art, looking at his paintings, and eating pierogies. He was eight years older, and there was a glimmer of serious possibility, but mostly I was more concerned with which party to go to on Thursday night and what color to dye my hair next. I had just turned twenty-five a few days earlier; I celebrated at a bowling alley and made treat bags for my friends filled with SweeTarts, paper cocktail umbrellas, and pink plastic flamingo drink stirrers.

I lived with my friend Jenny in a windowless two-bedroom on Spring Street, way west, just across from the Ear Inn. September 11, 2001, was a primary day, and after the abject disappointment of the 2000 presidential election, with its hanging chads and recounts,

I believed that my vote really did count, so I stopped to cast my ballot for the New York mayoral primary. The polling place was located in the coffeehouse on the corner of Varick and Spring Street. By the time I finished voting it was just past 8:40am, and I ran down the Spring Street station stairs and took the subway downtown to the World Trade Center stop.

Everyone knows what happened at 8:46am that morning, but on that day things did not become clear until much later.

When I worked as a legal assistant, I was always zipping over to the Morgan Stanley or Lehman Brothers offices in the WTC— that's what we all called it for shorthand, WTC—to drop off or pick up paperwork during deals. I knew that subway station in the buildings' cavernous basement well only because I'd gotten turned around there so many times. I also knew that if I had any hope of getting to my doctor's office on time, I needed to head up the stairs that opened directly into the WTC lobby so I could quickly get my bearings. When I stepped off the train, the subway platform was clogged with more people than usual, and I cursed along with the other commuters. The crush of complaining bodies forced me to a different exit than the one I needed, where I grumbled with the rest of the people around me until I hit the spot on the stairs where I could look up and see the towers outlined in the rectangle of the subway opening, a perfect portrait of fire.

The people behind me on the stairs, the people who couldn't yet see and didn't understand why everyone who hit this particular spot was stopping cold, pushed me up and out. I found an empty space on the sidewalk to the left of a fire hydrant. A woman in pearls and high heels and honey-colored freshly blown-out hair stood to the hydrant's right. We watched trails of computer paper reams, like comets, slowly spinning through the air, and flocks of white birds clustering at the mouth of the flames. There was no sound. All noise from above drifted away on the wind with the paper, floating out into the sky, kites of sound and fire.

The woman said or I said, "Was that—?" And we kept staring up to the top of the skyscraper, eyes forgiving, pretending we hadn't seen what we had seen. *No* we said, to each other, to ourselves. *No no no no.* Those are not people. They can't be.

But, of course, they were. We stood and watched the people, jumping from the windows so many hundreds of feet above, jumping down to us with arms stretched wide. We could see their ties, we could see their suit jackets, we could see their legs scrambling as if peddling imaginary bicycles.

We would have stared longer, our mouths a soundtrack of silent *no*s, if the policeman hadn't yelled at us, furiously, *Run!* The alarm on his face shook me out of my stupor and my mind slowly opened up to the possibilities of what the fire above my head meant. The woman and I both ran, though I quickly lost her in the crush. I slipped on the cobblestones in my flip-flops, the crowd's sharp heels and shiny wingtips biting into the soft flesh of my feet. I thought of Pamplona, and of the bull statue a few blocks away, and then I heard a crack so loud that I thought the top of the tower had broken off. It thundered through my head and body and I dove into a doorway, closing my eyes, waiting for the splinters of stone and glass and steel to rain down on the streets.

A man had ducked into the doorway with me and we both stood with our backs against the doorjamb, wordlessly facing each other while we waited for the top of the tower to crash down onto the cobblestones. But nothing happened. The man was older, maybe in his forties; he wore a tie, held his leather briefcase to his chest. The fear on his face, on such an adult face, shook me. I wanted him to look at me and see me and say, *Don't worry, I'll tell you what to do.* I wanted him to say, *Here, hold my hand.* Instead, he barely looked at me at all. The crowds kept running by us and after a few moments he slipped back in, too, like a fish into a school, leaving me alone. After another frozen moment, I took a deep breath and followed.

The top of the tower had not broken off; not yet. I learned later that the crack that had thundered through my chest was the second plane hitting the second tower. I only looked back when I was blocks away, at the foot of the Brooklyn Bridge. I was confused when I saw both towers in flames and simply assumed the fire had somehow jumped from one to the other building, finding its way across like Philippe Petit balancing between the twin buildings on his high wire. My cellphone, like everyone's cellphone, was dead. I stopped at a line for a pay phone to call in late to work, because I did not know what else to do.

I stood in line next to another freshly blown, honey-haired, high-heeled woman, this one in a crisp black crepe sheath dress. From the back, she reminded me of the lady lawyers I'd worked with at the firm, steady and not a hair out of place while I was sweating and panting from the dust in my throat. I stood behind her, moving slowly up the line, as people jogged past us, continuing north, some in small groups, everyone with the same wide-eyed confusion on their faces.

Only when the woman reached the front of the line and turned, receiver in hand, to ask me for a quarter, did I realize she was pregnant. Very pregnant. I stared at her belly as I handed her my silver coin, sweaty from my palm. She thanked me without expression and turned to make her call, and something strange surged through my body. *This woman is pregnant!* I wanted to scream. *Someone help her!* I wanted to lift her up in my arms, like a firefighter, or a groom, whisk her away from the soot and the sweat and the smoke. But I was just a girl in flip-flops with bloody feet.

It seemed so impossible, with all the bodies I'd just seen cascading through the sky, that a new life was nestled safely in the dark cavern of her stomach.

When it was my turn at the pay phone, I dialed my boss, Vicki. I spoke shakily into the receiver, apologizing to her voicemail, explaining that I would be late, that actually I didn't think I could come to work today, that I was downtown and now the 6 train wasn't working and neither was my cellphone and I was standing under the towers and there were people jumping and . . . my voice cracked. I think I just hung up then. We would never talk about that message. I don't know if she ever listened to it, that morning or days later.

When I stopped in a deli for a water, a little television set near the checkout was talking about terrorism. They mentioned other possible Manhattan targets, and it slowly dawned on me that the emergency might not yet be over. I kept walking north, away from the smoke and ash, trying to quench the burning in my throat with my bottle of water. Instead of walking home, which felt too close to the destruction, I caught the last L train out of Manhattan that morning before that line shut down, and walked to my boyfriend's building along the Williamsburg waterfront. The buzzer was broken; usually I called from my cellphone and he would run down to open the door. I waited until someone left the building and skirted inside, making my way up the stairs. Each floor of the old warehouse had a fire door that was locked. On the fifth floor, I banged on the heavy door in the stairwell, hoping someone might hear me. I dug through my bag and found a nail file and tried to pick the lock, but the file just broke in the door. I sank to the floor, defeated, letting the tears come for the first time that day. I stayed there sobbing until one of the other artists finally opened the door on his way to the roof.

By the time I got to my boyfriend's painting studio, I could barely speak; my throat was raw, and I didn't know what to say, anyway. We stood next to one another and stared out his wall of double-hung windows at the panoramic view of downtown Manhattan. Even through the scrim of smoke hanging between us and downtown Manhattan I could see that something looked different; he explained to me that one of the towers had fallen, but I couldn't comprehend it. I dialed my parents' home over and over from his landline, trying to get through. A moment after my mother finally picked up, the second tower crumbled, slowly and then all at once, sending another cloud of ash into the sky.

The towers, all the people inside them, the street corner I'd been standing on just over an hour earlier, were all gone.

Later, newscasters would follow the children who were in their first days of kindergarten down by the towers, kids who were just getting to school as the planes buzzed low before crashing into the buildings, sturdy bookends at the edge of the island. This generation would not have any memories before 9/11.

Later, these children would sit in a classroom in front of me, nearly the age I was when I stood cowering in the doorway, and I would stare at them from my side of the desk and they would stare back at me, a wholly different species.

In the days after the towers fell, it felt like the scaffolding of my own life had also collapsed; like so many others, I struggled to build it back into some recognizable form. I moved back to Brooklyn. I applied to graduate school. Watching those people in suits tumble down solidified what my time at the law firm had already taught me: a suit is not armor.

The city changed for everyone, of course. The people on the planes, the people in the towers, the emergency response teams who'd raced to help, all left a layer of loss behind that stretched across the still-smoking horizon. I hadn't realized how much I'd relied on those blinking twins to tell me where I was going. I had no sense of how to find south without looking to the sky and searching for their dependable spines in the distance. In the months after the towers fell, I consistently ended up walking the wrong direction, mistaking east for west and uptown for down

without those compass arrows anchoring me. Whole years after
9/11 were marked by the feeling of always being on the wrong
street corner.

In the economic instability that followed the attacks, the
magazine went through cuts; I was surprised to find I was disappointed when my position wasn't eliminated. I spent most of
my time in my cubicle on the sixteenth floor staring out the windows and imagining having to jump. When I'd thought I might
lose my job, I was surprised that such a dark reality came with a
sense of relief. I'd taken to digging my nails into my wrist each
morning to get myself to march down the subway stairs. Once at
work, I'd step into my office building's revolving door and want
to keep swirling until I emptied back outside instead of entering
the echoing lobby. Once at my desk, I fantasized about shoving
the carpeted cubicle walls around me until they fell down, col-
lapsing against one another in a cascading game of dominoes. I
began feeling the same drumbeat of daily despondence I'd felt in
Tokyo, staring out the conference room window into the parking
garage as Pamela shuffled papers and her swelling breasts across
the table.

I didn't know where I wanted to be, but I no longer wanted
to be here.

In his essay about leaving New York, E. B. White wrote that
although the city had one of the greatest seaports in the world,
he'd only ever noticed one small sloop in his time living there.
He goes on to say, "I heard the Queen Mary blow one midnight,

though, and the sound carried the whole history of departure and longing and loss."

I don't know if White ever got to see the USS *Intrepid*; the ship came to Pier 86 in 1982, decades after he decamped to Maine and just a couple of years before his death. But I imagine he would've been amused if he'd been among the crowds watching in November 2006 as a fleet of tugboats churned through the murky waters trying to free the *Intrepid* from its dock to bring it to New Jersey for much needed refurbishment. Cheers and hoots from the crowd that had gathered quickly silenced as the 36,000-ton mass of steel wobbled and stuck. The tugboats ground in place uselessly in the river, a pack of small dogs yanking impotently on their leashes. I watched the embarrassing gaff on NY1 on my boyfriend's twelve-by-twelve-inch television set.

Since that night of the party on the *Intrepid*, I'd quit the law firm, and then the magazine. I finally did go to graduate school, but for an MFA, not a law degree. As I watched the *Intrepid* strain in the water, I had a piece of paper from an Ivy League school, yet I was making less than I had in my first job at the law firm.

In the meantime, I moved in with the painter I had started dating just a few months before 9/11. The two felt directly linked, our bodies stationed at the old double-hung windows, in perfect view of the emergency engulfing the towers, their burning forms transposed perfectly over the ghostly reflections of our bodies in the window.

I had the strange sense that, like Lot's wife, I might disintegrate into salt if I turned away from this body left standing next me as the others collapsed impossibly in front of my eyes.

The United States Navy and the United States Army Corps of Engineers spent three weeks and three million dollars dredging the river floor and sending scuba divers down into the wintry waters to free the USS *Intrepid*'s propellers from more than two dozen years' worth of silt. In early December 2006, the tugboats hooked onto the ship for a second time. A crowd again gathered, and again fell silent when the great ship halted fifteen feet away from the shore. It took another hour, but they soon had the begrudging ship moving again.

When the boat finally broke free, I was surprised to find my cheeks wet with tears. There was something in the *Intrepid*'s leaving that felt final, like a pronouncement. I realized I'd been hoping the tugboats would fail again, that the *Intrepid* would remain like an anchor along the West Side Highway instead of drifting across those glittering waters, disappearing from the horizon the way the towers had five years earlier, disintegrating into a confetti of ash.

Sometimes, staying docked seems the safer option. But everything in New York moves on eventually. Until then, I'd spend years standing on the wrong street corner, that girl I once was still stuck on the deck of the *Intrepid*, a drink in her hand and the air blowing through her.

"His Wife Once Bit His Hand to the Bone"

IMAGINED HAVING ONE'S PORTRAIT PAINTED must feel like being truly seen. To allow someone to look at you for hours—to really look at you—and then create an image based on that looking, seemed like the bravest act of intimacy I could imagine. The result would be like a fortune cookie and an enneagram quiz result rolled up together, or one of those silvery daguerreotype ghost images, capturing something unseen by most people.

The only problem was, R. did not want to paint my portrait.

"I don't paint girlfriends," he said.

R. saw at least two naked women a week, not including me. His day planner was full of blocks of time carved out by long sweeping arrows and women's names: Aviva, Leslie, Francine, Elise, Maria, Eva. Sometimes they brought costumes: large peacock feathers, polka-dot baby doll dresses, leather corsets, fuzzy cow-print coats, vintage stockings and garters, flowers in their hair. But mostly they are naked.

He paid them twenty dollars an hour in cash and poured them Bustelo coffee from his old Bakelite and aluminum percolator. He smoked and squinted, dropping cigarettes from his lips and stamping them out. He stood on his pitcher's mound of crusted paint in front of his easel and gazed at their nakedness in his art studio.

The first time R. left me to go meet a model, I spent the three hours pacing my railroad apartment in South Park Slope, glaring at the phone each time I passed it, willing him to call and let me know the session was finished.

I imagined the two of them taking breaks, R. pulling one of his hard-backed chairs next to her plush rocker and discussing her tattoos or the birthmark on her stomach as she laughed and placed the hot coffee cup on the soft skin of her inner thigh until she felt the burn and removed it. I thought about the *shush-shush* sound his blue Staedtler pencil would make as he outlined her face in his sketchbook. On the chunky wood tabletop, paint tubes would be piled up, crinkled and deflated, nozzles caked and smeared with deep cadmium red, sharp phthalo blue, and muddy brown. I knew how, when he leaned close, his hair and neck would smell of a combination of the heavy musk of oil paint and the cloying, rich tang of linseed oil. I pictured the model close enough to him to smell these scents.

Although I couldn't get these girls out of my mind, I was too embarrassed to confess my anxieties to R. He was older than me, and I was always trying to seem more mature, cooler, more bohemian than I was. Once, during a writing workshop, another woman turned in a personal essay about the New York fantasy life she'd always dreamed about while she was a kid in suburban New

Jersey. The life included her affair with an artist, living in his painting studio in Brooklyn, smoking cigarettes and drinking whiskey
and having sex on the paint-splattered floor. In the hallway after
class, she said she felt embarrassed to turn that in because she
knew that was a version of my life. At the time, I thought she was
embarrassed because I was living her fantasy; today I wonder if she
meant she was embarrassed *for* me.

I was barely twenty-five years old. I hadn't realized yet that I
was living a trope.

I first met R. at a diner called Diner. I was dating a hairdresser who
moonlighted as a rock 'n' roll karaoke host, and we went to Diner
one night with a client whose hair he'd just cut in the living room
of his basement apartment. The client had called a few friends to
celebrate the inches she'd just had cut off, and invited us along. As
we stepped up the stairs to the converted railcar under the Williamsburg Bridge, the hairdresser's cellphone rang and he waved
me forward, saying he'd join in a minute, staying outside to take
the call. I walked into the diner with his client, who introduced me
to the group and sat me across from R.

The long table was tucked in a candlelit corner, all shadow
and amber light, straight out of a Vermeer. No one at the table had
any food yet, and as I sat, I first noticed R.'s large freckled hands
around the glass tumbler in front of him; his wide palms swallowed
the small glass, making it look like a child's cup. He wore a thick
black turtleneck that made his shoulders into a wide box and made
me think of a fisherman fresh off an Irish wharf. I imagined he

smelled like the sea. He was clean-shaven and his sideburns were red under his shaggy black curls. When he smiled, it was like an animal baring its teeth, one of his incisors a snaggle tooth in the corner of his mouth. He looked at me with an intensity that made me uncomfortable, in a good way. He said he was a painter, that his studio was nearby. We kept talking, but I didn't know what we were saying. Our words, the music, the other people at the table, me; everything was swallowed by his gaze.

A few minutes later, the hairdresser walked in, finished with his phone call. He stood at my shoulder, saw the way R. and I were looking at each other, and said we'd be going now.

There are plenty of movies glamorizing male artists: *Girl with a Pearl Earring, Frida, Pollock, Basquiat.* And there are the mythic flirts: Picasso, Toulouse-Lautrec, de Kooning. When R. and I first started dating, I wondered if this was what I was setting myself up for: a partner with a professional wandering eye. But when his gaze was set on me, all the other women disappeared from my head.

What remained lodged like a stone in my throat, however, was my insecurity about being completely shut out of his creative process, while all these other women played starring roles.

Each time I asked why he wouldn't let me model for him, he gave me his stock response: he didn't want to paint me because of the violent reactions of past girlfriends upon seeing their portraits. Years earlier, one had thrown her shoe at him, another smashed the canvas.

I understood. They were not necessarily flattering paintings.

He didn't add freckles or scars, wasn't even necessarily true to hair color or body shape. R. worked with a loaded brush, leaving a thick, almost sculptural layer of paint on the canvas. Up close, his paintings seemed abstract, slices and curls of unconnected color thick as toothpaste that snapped together a few feet away. In his paintings of tulips, the flowers sagged and buckled, and in his portraits many of the women's faces shared the same spent and forlorn look.

I'd met some of these women, and while I wouldn't say the paintings necessarily looked like them, I also couldn't say they didn't. Although the paintings themselves were beautiful, the women in them were not. He was adamant that he painted what he saw, though even when I knew the woman in front of him to be young and bright, she came out drawn and weighted down all the same.

But sometimes, we'd be at a bar or at a party with some of his models, and the longer I watched them, the more they began to look like their paintings. Not at first, and not straight on, but more in private moments, when they thought no one was looking, and the mask slipped. As the night wore on, I'd begin to see the image from the painting, as if it were there all along and the image I'd had in my head was the made-up one.

Portraits often take hours, he'd point out. A face at rest is naturally down-turned. No one can hold a smile for hours. He'd play music, and sometimes chat, but most of the time was spent in silence. He told me that some of the girls would meditate, some would just empty out, leave their body, go to whatever dark place one goes when alone with the sound of one's own thoughts.

I'd noticed that he didn't seem to have a type that he preferred to paint, or not a physical type, exactly. One could argue there is a self-selecting type of person who chooses to become an art model, who is willing to let strangers look at their body, clothed or unclothed, for money. I couldn't figure out, though, if the damage that showed up on the canvas was simply the way he saw these women, or if they somehow became this way under his gaze.

I didn't see R. again after that night at the diner until a few months later. After the hairdresser and I broke up, I mentioned R. to my roommate, who worked at *Rolling Stone* with the woman whose hair my boyfriend cut. *Oh, yeah, the painter,* she'd said. *He asked about you.*

She hadn't mentioned this detail to me while I still had a boyfriend, and she'd deemed the painter unsuitable. Apparently, he'd dated most of the women at the table that night at the diner, including the woman who had her hair cut. But I kept thinking about him, and so my roommate passed along a message.

I worked as an editor at AOL at the time. It turned out he'd dated the friend of a coworker there, too. I don't know why none of this gave me pause, why it didn't register as something of concern that so many women had decided they'd had enough, thank you, after a few dates. I just liked him. I knew he was different, but I wanted different. His obsessiveness, his certainty—about painting, about me—was alluring. I wanted to know what I wanted, the way he did.

I'd taken care to follow the rules and color inside the lines most of my life; seeing the way he delighted in smearing color everywhere charmed me. I'd tried convention and tradition, suits and

corporate boyfriends, safe bets. I was looking for the opposite and
he seemed to be it.

When he picked me up outside my office on 18th Street, he
wore jeans and a white t-shirt, what I'd come to know as his version of a uniform. I wasn't sure I'd remember what he looked like;
we'd only met for a few minutes the first time, and I'd only seen
him sitting down. But when I came out of the revolving door and
saw him standing next to a column and he looked at me, I knew
him. We walked for blocks and blocks of the city that day, almost
all of them with me facing forward and him walking nearly sideways, facing me. Looking at me.

So why did he not want to look at me now?

One night, at the opening of a group show, one of his models
showed up wearing the same black-and-white polka-dot dress she
was wearing in the painting hanging on the wall, and she stood
by the canvas all night. She'd brought her mother with her, and
the two drank plastic cup after plastic cup of warm white wine.
Late in the night, when everyone was smoking cigarettes on the
fire escape, the mother cornered R. and accused him of taking
advantage of her daughter, that he was going to make money off of
her beauty. He defended himself, saying he'd paid her, they'd had
a clear agreement, but the mother said it was her daughter who
was responsible for any brilliance in that painting. She was the one
who'd worn the polka-dot dress, she was the one who inspired
him. And now, after paying her less than a hundred bucks, he was
going to make twenty times as much. She got so heated that she

slapped him across the face, before her daughter hauled her away by the elbow.

I understood the contractual relationship R. had with his models. He had his favorites, those he thought were better than others, but he did not believe the work to be collaborative. I wasn't so sure. He often said he could only paint from life, which seemed to me to point to implicit need. Regardless, I wanted to be the one who inspired him. I didn't care if the outcome was less than glamorous. I wanted access to a space that I sensed was intimate in a way kindred to the space between lovers. In sex, you are working toward something together, too, but the closest artistic outcome you could point to and say *we made that* would be a child; I did not want a child. A painting, on the other hand, was static, and could be seen as evidence of consummated collaboration.

I suppose I thought that if the painting was strong, if it was something we could both look at with admiration, it would be evidence of the potential for our partnership. Not just evidence, but proof of the way we worked—or could work—as a couple. I imagined that the canvas would act like a tarot reading for our future together.

"We could be like Hopper and his wife," I said. After all, Hopper's wife had been his only model, and his career didn't exactly suffer for it. Didn't that count for something?

"Hopper wasn't a painter," R. shot back. "Hopper was an illustrator whose wife once bit his hand to the bone."

I tightened my mouth. I wasn't really talking about Hopper.

"I don't like painting girlfriends," he tried again. "It's too close."

But "close" was precisely what I wanted. "Close" was what

all these other women had, it seemed to me. Not only were they invited into R.'s most private and guarded creative space, they were also his inspiration. What could be wrong about that kind of closeness for us?

❧

And then, a few months later, there I was, naked in R.'s studio. He hadn't sold anything in weeks and didn't have money to pay for a real model, so he reluctantly asked me to sit for him.

The night before, I was so excited I couldn't sleep. In the morning, after holding a bag of frozen peas across my eyes, I showered and shaved, using shaving cream instead of my usual soap. I applied my makeup carefully, shadowing my eyes to hide their strain and wearing brighter than usual lipstick. I moisturized and remoisturized my hands, which I considered to be my best feature.

But now, only ten minutes into the session, my neck was sore, and the left side of my butt was falling asleep, as was my right foot. And I was freezing. I stared at R. staring at me.

"You're sinking into the chair," he said absently.

I straightened, pulling my back away from the comfort of the rocker and the warmth of the electric blanket. At the beginning of the session, he'd told me to pick a spot to look at somewhere just beyond his shoulder and to hold it, like I used to for pirouettes during dance class as a girl. But I found myself continually coming back to attention, realizing I'd been staring at his face or out a window instead. His studio was on the fifth floor of a warehouse on the East River, and two walls of windows offered a panoramic view of the city with its bridges, water towers and church spires.

The view might have been beautiful, but the winter wind was whipping through the studio's old double-hung windows, rattling the casings. As insulation to guard against a few cracked panes, R. had duct-taped sheets of plastic over them, and every few minutes the sheets puffed out like grey sails with the icy gusts. My legs were spotted with goosebumps; even sitting directly on the electric blanket couldn't reduce the prickles erupting on my skin.

R.'s eyebrows knitted and his mouth went slack. He looked at me and then looked at the canvas, back and forth, grimacing. He used both hands, pulling utensils from his paint table like a dentist.

His eyes were precise, working but blank. I was a still life, a bad one at that because of my fidgets, but a still life, no more and no less. I did not feel beautiful under his gaze, as I had imagined. I did not feel closer to him, but further away, and lonely.

I tried to catch his eye, to remind him who it was he was painting. But even though the canvas was turned away from me, I could tell he was already finished with my face and onto my calves and feet, which were dirty from the floor. So instead, I tried to see him the way he was seeing me, to become part of the process. I looked at the way the skin folded on the side of his neck when he held his head a certain way. I listened to the sound of the thick horsehair against canvas, like a scrub brush on bath tiles. I noticed how his freckled hands resembled curved paws, as if his four fingers were stitched together like a baseball mitt. Still, I did not feel closer to him.

Only after thirty minutes of staring did I see it: R.'s shirt was misbuttoned, one half hanging lower than the other below his stomach. Of course it was. I'd watched him misbutton his shirts plenty of times as he hurried out in the morning without looking down to make sure everything measured up. And it was in my knowledge of this habit—my intimate, every-morning knowledge of him and his ways—that I saw the real order of things. All this time I'd felt as if I were the one who was shut out of R.'s private world while this parade of naked women was let in. But now I saw what I hadn't before: I was already on the inside.

The girls would come for a few sessions, then move back home, or to Austin with their boyfriend, or quit modeling, or ask to borrow a few hundred bucks. I looked around the studio at all their faces along the walls, rendered in charcoal and paint, their dark eyes raccooned by the smudge of an eraser, their impasto flesh layered like cake. I noticed that R. was terrible at hands, at their proportions and detail, and I reset my hopes for my own. I thought about all the naked bodies that had sat where I was sitting, about their thighs and their breasts and their stomachs and their collarbones, about their skin and their scents and their poses, about the thoughts or stories or insecurities that inhabited their brains as they sat, still, separated from their own bodies, just a dreaming bowl of fruit.

I thought back to that night on the fire escape, when the mother of the girl in the polka-dot dress slapped R. across the face. And I knew she'd been very wrong. This painting had nothing to do with me. The finished product would sate my curiosity to some extent, in that it might be beautiful, but it would not be me. He was in a trance, completely removed—from me, from us—and I began to understand why his past girlfriend had thrown her shoe at him.

Many years later, when I was at an artist colony in the hills of Virginia, a painter there was working on a series of portraits. There were more than a dozen artists and writers there, and all the writers at the colony wanted to be chosen, wanted her to want to paint them. At dinner, we would furtively whisper together to see if anyone had been asked to sit, but none of us had. On one of her last evenings, the portrait painter opened her studio. The faces of nearly all the other artists were there on the wall in her ethereal purple and green brushstrokes. Later, after a few drinks, I asked a few of them how it felt to be chosen. They all looked at me strangely. They hadn't been chosen, they explained. They'd simply offered to sit for her.

For the artists, sitting for the painting was transactional, a gesture of goodwill toward a fellow artist, a kind of karmic altruism. The writers, meanwhile, waited for her gaze to alight on them, for her to be so captivated by the curve of their face that she'd need to imagine it translated into her sweeps of greens and blues. We were waiting for her to see something in us, something special that made her want to paint us in particular.

This is the trick and poison of exceptionalism. We wanted her to see us and then show us what she saw that was so captivating. We wanted her to help us see ourselves. The artists, meanwhile, sat without expectation, understanding this was not magic. This was just work.

After R. told me that Hopper's wife had bit his hand to the bone, I looked into their relationship. Her name was Josephine. Jo. She was a painter herself, yet is mostly referred to simply as "Hopper's wife." In a piece in *The Guardian* about a new exhibition of Hopper's work around the time I sat for my painting, the critic Gaby Wood considered the destructive relationship between the couple, writing, "In a telling caricature drawn in 1934, Hopper depicted Jo as an invisible woman, her earrings, collar, cuff and shoes dotted around a featureless blank space. Did he mean she was an empty canvas, to be built up out of fantasy? Or did he mean she was apt to disappear? Was Edward Hopper transforming his wife, or erasing her?"

In the studio that day, even when R. looked at me, it was with the eyes of a scientist looking at a slide. I did not feel transformed or erased; he was looking, but I was not being seen. This was the opposite of intimacy; it was intimacy withheld. I was simply a still life that he needed to paint, to the exclusion of our relationship. There was no place for us in his work. I stopped trying to catch his eye and instead, stared at him the way he was staring at me.

I spent the rest of the hour sitting up straight and watching R.'s jaw tighten and then hang loose with each brushstroke, his lips parted in concentration. I drew him in my mind from my perch, from his paint-crusted sneakers formless as slippers, to the finger smears of paint like feathers on his pant legs, to the nearly imperceptible tic of his head as he stared back and forth between his work and my body. I imagined him a stranger, erased what I knew of his smell, the softness of his hair. And I stared at his misbuttoned shirt when I got cold.

Cycling

DURING THE FIRST FEW YEARS R. and I were together, one of our favorite pastimes was to watch every motorcycle show on television. This was in the early 2000s, still the beginning of the reality television boom, and along with documentaries like *Motorcycle Mania* (1 and 2), we watched marathons of shows like *Monster Garage* and *American Chopper*, and, our favorite, the *Biker Build-Off* series.

We fell in love with some of the designs and trademark quirks of the different builders and fantasized about who we would commission to build our dream bikes. I liked Russell Mitchell's motorcycles because they reminded me of the movie *Quadrophenia*; Mitchell's choppers are never painted and have no chrome, so they look like they could have been constructed from a junkyard of old parts, simple and tough. R. loved Billy Lane's bikes, mostly because Lane fabricates each and every piece of the bike himself, bending metal against his thighs and twisting pieces with his bare hands until they fit. Both Mitchell and Lane came across like arrogant assholes on television, however, so we decided that we instead would fork over our hypothetical thousands to the sweetheart of the *Biker Build-Off* series, a man named Indian Larry. Larry's bikes were a combination of old-school fabrication—he also bent most of his pieces into shape with his hands—and whimsy, his signature question mark fashioned out of steel gracing the handlebars of every bike.

We looked Indian Larry up on the internet and discovered that his garage was only eight blocks from R.'s painting studio in Williamsburg. The metal rolling door of Larry's garage was usually closed, but sometimes there was an empty lawn chair propped out front, or the door was hiked up a touch so we could just see feet and the bottom halves of motorcycles being wheeled around. We took to walking slowly by the garage, necks craned, like tourists looking at celebrity houses in LA.

Around that time, R. received an email from his oldest brother. It was addressed to both R. and his other brother, and it read: *Come and join me, boys! It will be great—we'll take a long leisurely drive down the east coast on our hogs and send our women down to Florida on an airplane to meet us!* Attached to the note was a picture of his new motorcycle.

R. called me to the computer to read the email.

"Are you trying to tell me you want to get a bike?" I asked.

"No," he said, then shrugged. "I don't know. I thought you liked motorcycles?" He looked at me, reproach in his voice.

Now it was my turn to shrug. Of course I liked bikes.

Or at least I thought I did.

It was also around this time that R. started talking about getting married. He would ask me and I would deflect the question playfully; I'd never planned on getting married in general, or to him specifically. Ever since I was a child my father would often say, apropos of nothing, "You know you don't have to get married, right?" I'd laugh and roll my eyes. But his message stuck. Friends would fantasize about white dresses and floral arrangements, about two people sitting on a porch in rocking chairs, old and happy and holding hands. The only recurring fantasy I had was one in which I was very old with a long white braid and I lived alone in an adobe, which must have come from a period of obsession with Georgia O'Keefe. In this fantasy, I had a garden, and a dog, and space to write. That felt like abundance to me; I never needed or expected to want more.

Even without my father's subliminal messaging, I found the whole system suspect early on. The few couples I could identify as not unhappy, if not exactly happy, seemed more pulled apart from their relationships rather than built up. In my estimation, marriage was an eroding of the whole; $1 + 1$ didn't equal 2, it equaled $0.5 + 0.5$.

My parents loved each other, which is more than most of my friends could say about their parents. Their love seemed to be out of a kind of quiet relief. They'd both been married before, and both those marriages ended badly. They were married in a courthouse the day before Christmas Eve, and they have exactly one wedding photograph: a candid of my mother sitting on my father's lap at my grandparents' dining room table, Christmas decorations behind them. Neither is looking at the camera, but both are smiling real smiles. The only evidence that it is a wedding photo is on the back, in my grandmother's looping cursive.

They'd both lost so much already; they were good people, trying to be good to each other. Wasn't that enough? Unlike so many of the marriages I saw around me, theirs was a partnership absent of cruelty. But there was an unspoken something in their steadfast-ness, their calm love. Unlike parents of friends in my neighborhood, who raged at each other across the dining room table, or roped their children into taking sides, or loudly made love behind a locked door on Sunday mornings with their kids rolling their eyes at their car-toons in the living room, mine kept their marriage private.

I watched closely for clues, but their relationship remained a mystery. The harder I looked, the more elusive it became. It was like sitting on a porch at dusk and watching a field of fireflies. After catching a flash, you steady your eye, trying to anticipate the next blink. But the spark never lights where you think it will.

And now, here I was, with the same person for years. There was nothing traditional about our relationship, which was the main reason I liked it. He lived in his painting studio, and I lived in my apartment. He didn't have a 401(k) or a market portfolio; he barely had a bank account. He was singularly focused on painting; he had no hobbies, never went on vacation, and he didn't have a work schedule—Saturday at noon was just as good a time as Wednesday at 2am to crack a can of Coke and start a new canvas.

While at first R.'s painting sometimes felt like an obstacle, it grew to feel more like my shield. His emotional register was more intense than anyone I'd ever known. He felt everything harder—love, enthusiasm, excitement—but he raged harder, too. R.'s attention was like a stage light and made everything else dim in comparison; this could feel in turns invigorating or terrifying, but mostly exhausting. I took to simply waiting out my time in his light, knowing he would always turn it back to his painting eventually.

For these reasons, I liked the space between us. I kept my apartment the way I wanted, I stocked my fridge as I saw fit. I didn't have to share my closet or bookshelf or calendar. He could live in a warehouse and use the bathroom in the hallway, keep a kitchen consisting of a hot plate and a mini-fridge filled with half-and-half and film. Painting was his priority, writing was mine; we were on two different motorcycles, riding in the same direction. Neither of us was interested in domestication.

I did not understand why he felt the need to change anything.

When I was four years old, my father came sputtering home on an old rusty motorcycle. He worked at a golf course near our house in the Catskills, and he bought the bike from one of the greensmen. My father's car had died at the course that morning, so he just left it there, driving home on the bike instead.

My mother was not happy. She'd fallen off a motorcycle as a teenager. One minute she was riding with a boyfriend, her body curled around his, and the next she was on the ground. She has never offered any detail, except for the purple bloom of a few scars dimpled white from the gravel on the side of the road.

A week after he bought the bike, my father rumbled home with a sidecar attached to the motorcycle.

I can imagine him offering the practical reasons to my mother: *This way I can fit you, or you with Kelly on your lap, or even a bag of groceries!* I can also imagine my mother holding her silence the way she does, staring at my father's beaming face, keeping her hand on her hip so he knew she was still against the idea.

For the weeks my father kept it, I don't think my mother ever rode on the bike. Meanwhile, I looked forward to the days when he came home before dark and I could hop into the little seat and ride in slow circles around our dirt driveway. There wasn't much speed involved—my father may as well have been scooting me around on a golf cart—but it was exciting to feel every bump and pebble under the tires, the smell of oil and grease and metal in my nose. And looking up from my small egg of a seat, I loved seeing the crosshatch pattern on the denim of my father's worn jeans, and his shoulder and face just above that, his black curls flattened onto one side of his head as we circled slowly in the wind.

Once, as an adult, I mentioned this sidecar to my parents and they had no idea what I was talking about. They confirmed that my father did come home with a motorbike when I was four years old, but both swear the sidecar seat never existed. They said my father did ride in slow circles, as I remember, but that I was actually on the bike itself during these rides, my back snug against my father's chest, tiny hands clenching the handlebars beneath his loose grip.

I don't know why my memory placed me alongside my father, rather than curled together, navigating the road as one. I'm not sure why my brain prefers the separation, two entities moving in the same direction but on their own. I can still feel so vividly the safety of the aluminum egg cupping my body. It remains one of my happiest memories.

In those years, if you looked out the windows of R.'s painting studio, a long row of motorcycles was perpetually perched along the nearby strip of Wythe Avenue—dark, dusky birds on a line. An old rusty-voiced man named Slick presided over the bikes, usually from a nearby stoop. "It's not *if* you are going to be in a wreck, but *when*, and *how bad*," he used to tell us. This seemed like sage advice, if not the smartest sales technique.

When Slick said this, my mother came to mind, tumbling off her boyfriend's bike as a teenager. And there was Mike, once our high school's star quarterback, who was riding home from the beach one day when a car clipped him. His bike landed on his right wrist, crushing his throwing hand and, with it, his college scholarship. Pat, my boyfriend the summer between seventh and eighth grade, died a few years later when he crashed his motorcycle into the back of a parked UPS truck. And as a child, another friend liked to hang around her father when he fixed his motorcycle in their driveway. One day, her father wasn't paying attention to how close she was to the bike as he fired up the engine, and now the skin on the back of her hands is melted into molten, waxy ripples.

After the email from R.'s brother, my enthusiasm for the biker shows began to wane. I'd read a book instead of watching along with him, or surreptitiously find shows that were on at the same time that I suddenly just *had* to see.

R. continued to send me listings of old beat-up choppers he found on eBay, but I stopped acknowledging these as well. While

I enjoyed fantasizing about motorcycles, his brother's email had pushed that fantasy too close to reality—I never expected that he might actually consider buying a bike. I thought our interest in the bikes was centered on the build; we were watching fellow artists crafting their art. I respected the bikes the same way I respected R.'s paintings, for their form and fabrication. I never intended to ride one. And I certainly had no intention of being relegated to a shopping trip with his brothers' wives while the men rode cross-country.

Was this his idea of marriage?

R. had built a roster of art models over the years, many from the burgeoning burlesque scene that was surging in Brooklyn at the time. He had mentioned to one of these models, who went by Bob, how he loved *Biker Build-Off*, and Indian Larry's bikes specifically. Bob told R. that they knew Indian Larry, and had actually become close with him since he married a friend of theirs a few months earlier, another burlesque performance artist named Bambi the Mermaid.

The couple had met in the city in the mid-1990s, years after Larry was released from Sing Sing for robbery and Bellevue for addiction. They both worked at the Coney Island Sideshow; Bambi performed burlesque and Indian Larry would lie down on a bed of nails while a woman broke blocks of ice on his chest with a sledgehammer.

Bambi fell in love with Larry and his slow-breaking smile, scraggly hair, gaunt face, piercings, and neck and body tattoos.

He proposed to Bambi by tattooing her name over his heart in a circus font.

At home, I pored over their wedding pictures on her website. The nuptials took place on the Coney Island boardwalk; the bride wore a shiny white fishtail skirt with pearly white clamshells over her breasts, the groom a sleeveless white tuxedo shirt with jeans and motorcycle boots. Luna Park sparkled in the background and Bambi looked like a mix of Daryl Hannah in *Splash* and something from the pages of a Frederick's of Hollywood catalog.

It seemed a miracle to me that someone who dreams of wearing a mermaid outfit on her wedding day would actually find a partner who wants to get married to a woman wearing a mermaid outfit. I imagined them taking Sunday rides on the part of the Brooklyn-Queens Expressway that runs along the East River, Bambi sitting side-saddle with her tail flopped over one side of the bike, her arms wrapped tightly around Larry's chest.

Scrolling through the photos on her website, it occurred to me that marriage could be fun. I had thought marriage was about commitment and sacrifice, mortgages and drudgery, budgets and calculation, safe harbor and scars. I had never imagined a wedding that could double as an amusement park.

This kind of married didn't seem like the kind my father was warning me against.

Even if I didn't think I wanted R. to own a bike, I still liked the idea of meeting Indian Larry. I also liked the idea of becoming part of that world. The burlesque performers showed me a different planet

with a different set of rules, one in which you could call yourself
Bob, or have a job that required you to dress like a mermaid, or get
married under the Wonder Wheel. More than wanting to meet the
genius behind the bikes I admired so much, I wanted to watch the
way this couple interacted. R. had asked me to marry him again,
this time while watching television and lying on the couch in my
apartment. "Get a ring," I'd stammered. I told him I didn't care
what kind of ring, but I wanted him to be sure, and that required
carrying a token around in his pocket for more than twenty-four
hours, not just impulsively asking the question. But now I was
afraid he would.

A week before we were set to meet up with Indian Larry and
Bambi at R.'s painting studio, Larry was performing at the Liquid
Steel Classic and Custom Bikes Series bike show in North Carolina.
At one point, in front of the thousands of screaming fans, Larry
rode through a tunnel of flames on his Chain of Mystery bike, the
chopper he'd just finished building for the third Biker Build-Off
competition. Later in the show, Larry rode the bike across the field
preparing for his other signature motorcycle stunt—riding while
standing on the seat with his hands stretched out like Christ in
a pose called a "crucifix." The bike wobbled. Indian Larry came
crashing down with the bike on top of him. He wasn't wearing a
helmet; that was part of the stunt.

Bambi was in the crowd of onlookers. She was in jeans and a
t-shirt, and her long hair was pulled back in a ponytail, a mermaid in
hiding. She half-walked, half-ran alongside the stretcher to the ambulance parked in the field in the middle of the racetrack, climbing in
after her new husband. He died before they reached the hospital.

A few months after Indian Larry's death, R. and I were at a dive bar under the Williamsburg Bridge. Bob was throwing a fundraiser; their poodle, Movie Star, had broken its front legs in an ill-executed jump off the couch and they needed help with the vet bill. The place was packed with local burlesque performers in hot pants and feather boas, many of whom had sat for R.'s paintings. Movie Star's hair was hot pink, and the running joke of the night was that the dye had affected the dog's brain.

As I moved through the group in jeans and a black t-shirt, I felt serious and plain, a pedestrian sparrow among peacocks and flamingos. My one bit of sparkle, the small antique diamond ring R. had given to me a few weeks earlier, just exacerbated this feeling. R. had handed the ring to me on a beach while visiting his parents in Florida; after agreeing to marry him, I cried for three days straight. I had resigned myself to the halving I knew marriage required, but my body was still grieving it. In the corner of the bar that night, I twisted the ring around and around my finger, a red reminder string tied too tightly.

A few barstools away I spied a flash of Barbie-blond hair.

"Look," I pulled on R.'s sleeve. "Bambi is here."

We both peered down the bar, trying not to look like we were looking at her. Unlike most of the other burlesque performers around us that night, she was not in costume, just a sweatshirt and jeans.

When we read in the newspaper that Indian Larry had died and the story of his fall, we'd debated whether to leave flowers in front of Larry's garage, but finally decided against it after driving by and seeing some fans with Indian Larry t-shirts hanging around the street corner. The sidewalk was littered with burnt-down bodega candles and bouquets of rotting flowers, deli wrappings crinkling in the wind blowing off the East River. I wondered whether Bambi would be the one to clean up the mess.

But now, months later, Bambi was hunched over her drink, sipping clear liquid out of a highball through a small red straw. She stared at a spot on the lip of the bar and held her long hair back when she drank.

"Should we go over to her?" I asked.

R. shrugged. "What would you say?"

"I don't know. Just tell her how much we admired Larry, I guess. And that I'm sorry for her," I said, unsure.

"No," he decided. "You don't want to remind her about her dead husband in the middle of a bar."

R. crossed the room to talk to some other people. I stayed there, watching Bambi. She looked wooden, zombie-like. Her sadness created a halo around her. Bambi's friends were clustered nearby, gabbing, and every so often one of the brightly painted performers would snuggle in, or rub her back, or trail their fingers through her hair. But even if she smiled a bit, she didn't look away from the spot on the bar, and mostly, people left her alone and just talked to each other.

It seemed clear to me that we would not be reminding her about her dead husband; his absence was already heavy next to her.

She'd held his hand under the Wonder Wheel, and now he was gone.

Years later, after we finally got married, R. and I went to the Coney Island Freak Show. One of his models gave him free tickets, and as we sat in the bleachers in the dark, I imagined Bambi and Larry staring at each other across the stage, falling in love while the fire-eater swooped and swallowed his embers.

When it was time for the bed of nails act, the host invited members of the audience to come and stand on top of the man. The master of ceremonies chose us for the act. R. and I climbed onto the stage and the man lay down on his nail-studded board. The host invited us to stand on the man's chest and R., 200 pounds and about six feet tall, stepped up onto him, trying to find his balance. I held back, not wanting to hurt the man at my feet, until he smiled and nodded at me from the floor where he seemed to be holding his breath. I climbed up onto the board laid out across his tattooed chest and held on to R. in an awkward hug while the audience chanted a countdown. I forget how long we lasted. I imagine we looked like one of those gaudy plastic molds of a bride and groom atop a wedding cake.

At the end of the act, we climbed down and the performer stood with his back to us, his skin stippled red, thin tracks of blood pooling at his waist. But when he turned to receive his applause, his smile was wide. This was the trick, I realized. Lying on a bed of nails only hurts if you believe they're real.

I knew the solitude of the sidecar was safer, but I wanted to be a risk-taker, climb up on that bike even as Slick's refrain stuck in my ear: *It's not if, but when, and how bad.* I imagined marriage to be like stretching my body across a bed of nails and willing it not to hurt, grinning while the blood trickled down my back. *These nails are not real.*

Staring at Bambi sitting at the edge of that bar, I turned the tiny diamond in toward my palm, let the metal cut into my palm. I wanted to believe we'd never crash.

Still Life 1: The City

L ONG EVENINGS IN THE PAINTING STUDIO; I read and smoke cigarettes, drink coffee from a chipped brown cup. He smokes and paints or draws in the corner, raising his easel up or down with a metal crank like the old machines in beach towns that flatten out pennies. We stare out the rickety double-paned windows at the city blinking busily across the river, sometimes through the same square of window, sometimes different. The soundtrack is '70s rock from his stereo and airplanes and cement mixers.

The space is separated into two rooms, working and living, though he is careful to hide the living because this is a work-only building. The landlord is an abstract expressionist painter who was an art heavy in the 1980s, known for his encaustic paintings for which he heated vats of beeswax and pigment and solvents to create a waxy, sculptural look on the canvas. The process released toxic fumes and left him with permanent nerve damage in his feet and right hand, and now he shuffles through the building like an old man in slippers. When R. is low on cash, the landlord takes paintings as payment.

R. likes to collect things—an old industrial post office mailbag from the rocky edge of the East River a block over, the coffee cup left behind by an old roommate, a red garbage can from the corner in his building where people leave things they no longer want. He brought a stray dog home once, sweet but full of fleas. He sent the poor thing back out into the streets after the dog chewed a bunch of paint tubes all to hell.

From the windows we watch: the red-capped white layer cake of the Circle Line lazing by on the river; lightning storms; the mystery murmurations of birds swooping across the blue Brooklyn sky, tumbling together like snowflakes in an avalanche; roof parties; Fourth of July fireworks with our feet on the windowsill and Chinese food containers in our laps; the sad girl in the building across from us; the towers falling down like people buckling at the knees, first one and then the other until there is nothing but dust.

One time, from the window perch, we watch the concrete factory across the street explode into emergency lights and sirens. A worker had crawled into the hollow of a cement truck with a pressure-washer to clean the interior and somehow the hydraulic motor kicked on while he was inside, the drum turning and turning and turning. An hour went by, and then another, as the paramedics tried to extract him from the drum. Meanwhile, the sky was turning colors and the birds were coming out. The murmurations collapsed into one another in a dramatic ballet against the canvas of stark white contrails and pink clouds, a loose orchestrated dance above the human body entombed in sand and gravel below.

Hearts and Bones

WE WERE FOUR MONTHS INTO our marriage when R. and
I first stood in the long dirt driveway of the Pennsylvania
house that would become ours. It was the twenty-seventh place
we had seen, with the sixth broker we had used, and it was perfect: an 1860s eyebrow colonial on a generous ten-acre plot. There
was a sturdy dairy barn that we could transform into R.'s painting
studio, and not a neighbor in sight. The house's interior needed a
complete rehab: the wide plank floors were painted a gymnasium
grey, the walls were covered with buckling boards of knotty pine
or sheets of paneling, and the kitchen—well, there was no kitchen,
just three old appliances in an awkwardly shaped room. But that
was one of the reasons a writer and a painter could afford it at all.
Plus, the old fieldstone foundation was strong, and the hand-cut
support beams were solid, as were R.'s handyman skills. In the
morning light, the home that this could become—furniture from
local barn sales, space enough for a dog (or two), rooms stuffed
with books and paintings—shimmered in front of us like a mirage.
The old couple selling the house promised a new metal roof, and

accepted our offer within the week. Before we knew it, R. and I—both lifelong renters—were piling papers in multiple stacks across the living room floor in my small Brooklyn apartment in preparation for our closing the next day.

It was after five o'clock when the doctor telephoned. Just a few days before our May wedding, R. had suffered what the EMTs who answered my 911 call judged to be a panic attack. As a patient without insurance, they gave him two options: wait for hours in an emergency room, or rest and drink two gallons of water a day. ("You have to hold him to it," the EMT said, pointing in my face. "Otherwise, your honeymoon will be on the island of Notalottanookie.") Our honeymoon wouldn't be on any island, it turned out—we postponed our plan to stay at his friend's house on Bermuda a few months after the wedding when he still didn't feel well. Fit-looking and, at 37, relatively young, he had delayed for months the doctor's appointment that would confirm or refute that diagnosis. Now, insured thanks to my freelancer's union and our marriage certificate, he'd finally gone for a checkup and the doctor was calling.

My husband's eyes were far away while he listened. "Well, we're closing on a house tomorrow, so we won't be back in town for a few days—" The doctor cut him off. R. sat down, motioned for a pen. He scribbled a few notes and then hung up.

"They found something during the stress test," R. said. The doctor thought the results must be a mistake—a shadow from his rib or something—but wanted to be sure. He directed R. to see a cardiologist the next day, and offered to call the office himself to expedite the visit. I must have looked frightened.

"The doctor says that if it were a true read, I wouldn't be standing," R. said. "I'll just call tomorrow before the closing, try to get an appointment for early next week." And we went back to putting our papers in order.

The next morning, as we pulled into the driveway for the walk-through, the house looked different. We had last seen it in summer, and now the fruit and ash trees dotting the property looked gnarled and grey. The fascia board that trimmed the roof's edge was too short, like a skimpy miniskirt riding up on too much leg, and wasps were filing in and out of gaps in the corners. Inside, without posters and furniture to cloud the view, cracks that we had previously missed were suddenly visible. Why did the wooden floor of the bathroom have linoleum just around the toilet? What were those small circular stains on the ceiling? We realized that under each strangely placed plastic welcome mat—an oddity we had noticed but chalked up to the eccentricity of the owners—was a dip or a hole or a soft spot in the floor. The number of welcome mats was ominous.

That evening, we circled the empty rooms of what was now our new house, then settled shivering onto an AeroBed mattress in the corner of the living room. There was no moving van full of stuff; we had no furniture to move in. Our eyes blinked blindly in the dark, trying to find the source of strange scratching sounds and bumps. We would later discover a brood of rabbits living beneath one portion of the house, but in the depth of that night, their thumps sounded like the thudding footsteps of some dead farmer. We hardly slept.

There was a lot to do, and we wanted to get started right away. The next morning, as I jogged in the meager heat given off by our pellet stove, R. strode down the long driveway to the barn, the white trail of his breath chugging behind as if he were a locomotive. He returned an hour later with a table he had fashioned from two-by-fours and an old door. The door had a cloudy wash of white milk paint across most of it and a crimson red stripe down the middle—a readymade runner. I shuffled two white wicker chairs off the porch and through the door, spreading a couple of throw blankets across their seats. Our first renovation was a success: we had a kitchen table.

But when he began to sand our bedroom floor, R. could only work in ten-minute spurts. In between, he would lumber down the uneven stairs and sit on the creaky wicker, gulping down glass after glass of water. I primed the knotty yellow walls until my arms ached, moving my step stool around him in an arc. "The paint on the floor's too thick," he said. "It's just too difficult." His stamina didn't improve when he joined me in the kitchen to paint. "I must have really tired myself out," he said, pouring another glass of water.

Back in the city a few days later, the heart specialist's echocardiogram showed the same suspicious shadow that his doctor had seen.

"We should do an angiogram just in case," the cardiologist said. "You might be ten or twenty percent blocked, and this way we'll be able to see exactly what we're dealing with." But R. wasn't twenty percent, or even sixty percent, blocked. When the cardiologist inserted a tiny camera into an artery in R.'s groin, threading a long cord up into his heart, the doctor found a blockage of ninety-eight percent, with a large clot forming that threatened to close off the last two percent of space in his right coronary artery. "We have to push the clot out," the cardiologist said, circling a spot on the grainy photocopy he held out to me. The grey image looked like a baby in a sonogram. I stared at it, and the doctor stared at me, as if this hazy bloom and stem would explain everything.

So that day, the day before Thanksgiving, instead of preparing a turkey and cornbread stuffing for our new kitchen table, I was in an ambulance on the way from one hospital to another more equipped to handle the kind of surgery he needed. R.'s quiet head, black hair fuzzed and matted, was at my knee, the soft triangle of his chest pouring forth wires like a slump of twisted marionette strings. I balanced myself carefully over him, one hand gripping a steel box bolted to the wall beside my shoulder, the other hand splayed against the cool glass of the ambulance window as we glided over the Brooklyn Bridge. At the loading bay of the ER, one of the EMTs asked if I would walk ahead and hold the electronic doors open—they were always broken, he explained. I shifted the clear plastic bag I was carrying—full of the clothes R. had worn to his appointment that morning—and stepped ahead as the men rolled my husband out on his silver cart. I pushed open the heavy double doors and wondered whether it was a good idea to take my husband to a hospital that couldn't even keep its ER doors functioning. How could they make his heart work?

After doctors inserted a medicated stent into R.'s artery, they confirmed that he was in the middle of a heart attack—and that the episode before our wedding had likely been one, too. He had permanent damage, but with the right medication and lifestyle changes, they felt he would have a decent recovery. We still had a few months left on the lease of my Brooklyn apartment, so we planned for him to recuperate there. When R. was released, his leg was a constellation of purple, green and blue bruises from the multiple needle insertions and subsequent clamping of the artery, as if someone had spilled little pots of paint under his skin. He was not allowed to drive or lift anything, and the walk up the stairs to the second-floor apartment took a very long time.

We finally returned to our farmhouse a month or so later. We stopped every hour of the three-hour drive between Brooklyn and Pennsylvania so R. could stretch his legs to ward off any clots. We had left our thermostat at sixty-four degrees after some of the locals had warned us to keep our house warm, and arrived to find our propane tank empty and the pipes close to freezing (in the country, "warm" means fifty degrees, it turns out). We needed $2,500 to refill the 500-gallon tank. We still had no furniture and no kitchen, so we sat on the squeaky wicker chairs waiting for the tanker truck to lumber up the driveway. I charged the propane to my credit card and we stayed one uncomfortable night before returning to the city. R. seemed hollow and cold, like the house.

The rest of the winter was quiet. I extended the lease on my apartment, and friends came by with baskets of health food, cookbooks and bags of loose tea. Our real-estate agent sent R. a Pajama-Gram. I caught up on the bills for my apartment and R.'s studio, and then bills arrived for the house (snow plowing, insurance, more propane) and bills arrived from the hospital. I charged those to my card, too. We sent away our mortgage payments, detaching the squares from the little booklet one by one as months passed, but Pennsylvania seemed so far away, like a dream we'd once had. I couldn't bring myself to say out loud what must have crossed both our minds—that we had based our budget and mortgage load on the idea that R. would be able to do most of the renovations, and so should think about selling. That, I thought, would be like saying: *You are broken and can't be fixed.*

Instead, we went in the opposite direction. My life savings was sunk into the house and the bills were mounting, but with spring around the corner, we had hope. We ordered a real bed, our first, a queen-sized mattress with a split box spring so it could make the trip up the steep farmhouse stairs, and bought new sheets at Target. In the city, we usually lived a fairly siloed existence from one another. I lived in and paid for my apartment, while he lived in and paid for his painting studio. More often than not, he slept at my apartment, but sometimes he slept at his. There was a lot of space built into our relationship, and I'd looked forward to the idea of having a home where we could live the way I imagined normal married couples did. Not all the time, of course; I also wanted to preserve the autonomy and space we enjoyed in the city. But a shared bedroom felt like a start.

As the weeks ticked on and R. slowly recovered, I realized this plan had flipped. Suddenly we had a more traditional arrangement, except that instead of building our nest in the country, my apartment became homebase. Too weak to paint, R. stationed himself in the middle of my living room, feet propped up as directed by the doctor, sitting in the darkness, his face slack in the blue glow of the television, as he tried to absorb what had just happened to him. I worked from home some days instead of going into the office of the magazine where I was an editor, and started cooking all our meals to help lower his cholesterol. The doctor had said that stress was a contributing factor to heart disease, so each time the credit card bills came in, instead of asking him to contribute, I wordlessly paid the minimum. I took on whatever freelance assignments I could find, writing online curriculum for corporate clients and churning out bite-sized reviews for Zagat alongside my magazine work and the writing classes I was teaching to balance out the cords of firewood, new woodstove, home insurance, and the other bills that just kept mounting.

In the space of five months, I'd gone from single and completely independent, financially and otherwise, with my own space, to a full-time working spouse and nursemaid; my only time alone was during trips to the food store around the corner. Once the emergency abated, I realized I was spending more and more time checking food labels, taking my time going down each aisle twice. All I wanted was to be able to spread out on a blanket in the field next to our house and breathe in the silence. Instead, I scoured the internet for low-cholesterol recipes and bided my time until we could get back to our plan.

As soon as R.'s leg was healed and a stress test revealed that the stent had worked, we packed our trunk with pails of white paint and headed back. In the fresh air and sun, R.'s color improved, the grey pallor giving way to a healthy pink. Friends came to visit, making long weekends out of their trips, helping to tear out the living room ceiling and reveal a latticework of strong, beautiful beams and old cut nails. R. worked slowly at first, testing his limits and letting others take over when he needed to rest. He still had chest pains every so often, but the doctor assured him they were probably just muscle spasms, and every day he was able to work fifteen minutes longer than the day before.

The next month, we got a giant dumpster and moved on to the upstairs. As R. and I ripped out the walls, stores of nuts and bird-seed and cakes of tiny black turds spilled out. The source of those small circle stains became clear when we pulled down the low ceiling, and petrified mouse bodies rained down. As we unclogged the house, the structure seemed to breathe a sigh of relief. R.'s body, too, was reemerging: his energy returned, and, as extra weight melted off, his muscles surfaced like sandbars. That first summer, we removed a four-ton mountain of trash.

By Thanksgiving, the one-year anniversary of his heart attack and stent, our house had three beds, six kitchen chairs, a couch, a love-seat, two armchairs, a dresser and an armoire. We now had two woodstoves—R. had made the new hearth by dragging thin slabs of bluestone in from the property and piecing them together like plates on a turtle's back—and plenty of firewood to keep us warm. Our winter was much easier than the one before. We needed to stay in the city for work, but could no longer float all three places. I'd let go of my apartment in Brooklyn and moved into the painting studio; there was no shower, but showering at the gym two blocks away was much cheaper than the extra monthly rent. We celebrated New Year's with friends at the house, and as the last snow melted, the heads of hundreds of daffodils poked up across the fields.

We settled into a routine, although it was not a routine either of us had expected. My space in the city had shrunk to the clothes that could fit inside a duffel bag and the books that could fit at the end of a table in R.'s painting studio. R. was back to working at the easel, but painting sales had slowed; the markets were sliding into what would become the Great Recession, and most of his clients were bankers. I stopped mentioning the honeymoon trip to Bermuda that had been put on hold. One day I teasingly suggested R. carry me over the threshold of our farmhouse, like newlyweds in the movies. *Do you want my heart to burst?* he flashed.

I quietly tucked that fantasy away, too. Instead of looking back, I looked ahead. Each new season at the house revealed some new beauty and we tried to be patient. In the mornings over coffee he would swallow his pills and I would swallow my worries, the wicker creaking beneath our separate weights.

The Cow

D AVEY STARTS EVERY MORNING AT 4:30am with 100 sit-ups, 150 push-ups, half a hoagie from the local deli, a large coffee and an ibuprofen pill the size of a piece of chalk. His usual uniform is a pair of white-washed carpenter jeans and a ribbed tank top the glowy grey of white cotton that's been bleached many times. If it is below fifty-five degrees, he will pull a blue sweatshirt over the tank top. If it is below forty degrees, or if he has run out of propane and his single-wide trailer has no heat, he will layer a t-shirt, a long-sleeve thermal shirt, and a colorful wool sweater his daughter made for him. If he is working, an old pair of navy-blue Styrofoam pads will be attached to his pants at the knees with a flurry of duct tape. If he is not working, he will be drunk.

Two days after R. and I met Davey at the cow farm down the block from our Pennsylvania farmhouse, he chugged up our driveway in his shit-brown station wagon, the broken windshield catching the sun's glint like a crystal. "If we're going to be friends," he said, handing my husband a manila envelope smudged with grease, "this is what you need to know about me." He grinned, his top incisors straight and horse-like and false, his lower lip stretched like a tent across the empty space on the bottom. He shuffled back to his car, dragging his lame left foot along with him.

Inside the manila envelope were two items: a high school yearbook from 1976 and photocopies of Davey's medical records from 1978 through 2006. Inside his yearbook, on the hard cardstock flaps of the front and back covers and throughout the pages next to pictures of homely girls and hale and hearty boys were looping wishes for Davey to *Have a gr8 summer!* and *Lets get waisted at the lake!* As we flipped through the yearbook, R. and I recognized names from the local farms—there are Leonards and O'Neils and even Johanna McGarry, who grew up in the house we now lived in. Next to Davey's name, which was listed in the section for graduating seniors, was a line of recognition for Best Body and Best Athletics. In his picture, his blond hair curls around his face in waves. His skin is bronzed beneath his short sleeves, and he is smiling with all his teeth.

The yearbook tells what was. The medical records tell what is. In the summer of 1977, a year after he graduated high school, there was a car wreck. The pages don't talk about the other car, or blood alcohol levels, or the two boys who didn't make it. Instead, they report that an eighteen-year-old male presented with a broken jaw and nose, fractured skull, crushed torso and pelvis, and a possible broken back. The dates on the lined pages progress from summer to fall to winter as we flip, and Davey is still in the hospital. A metal rod has been placed through his head to hold his face together. He is suspended in traction to repair his back. Pain medication is increased and reduced and increased again. Reconstructive surgeries are listed. X-rays are discussed and described; progress, or lack thereof, is debated. As we shuffle through the pages, the distance between the dates grows longer, first by weeks, then by months, then by years. The pages themselves change from hospital stationery and lined report paper to notes about appointments scrawled on plain printer sheets, to reminders about addresses and phone numbers, the handwriting slanted and slow, lacking the urgent edges of the earlier annotations.

It was Davey who first told me about Little Kelly.

"Have you heard about your cow?" he asked. I was on the porch and he was halfway up the ladder leaning against the front of our house. He was helping R. install a pipe on the roof that would carry the exhaust from the new woodstove into the crisp blue sky.

"I haven't seen her yet this week," I said, suddenly suspicious. "Why?"

The farmers down the road, Pat and Tom Joe, had recently acquired a baby cow from another farm nearby. Pat and Tom Joe raised cattle but didn't slaughter or milk them—they were a feeder farm and raised the animals until they need money or someone needs a cow. They had seventy or eighty cows—no one knew, exactly—and this was the farm where we first met Davey. The three men had recently named the new cow Kelly, after me, because I had grown attached to her, a development whose wisdom they seemed to debate daily.

I'd asked them, one afternoon over a beer in the barn, to call me if a cow were ever ready to give birth, day or night; I wanted to watch what I'd imagined was like a scene from *Lassie*, cupping the cow's soft face as the vet and the farmer worked together to deliver the calf. They looked at me strangely until Pat cleared his throat and explained that birth didn't work that way on the farm. Usually, they just found a new calf in the field one morning, suckling its mother.

This calf had no mother to suckle, so I'd be her wet nurse; every day, I'd mix up her powdered formula and feed it to her from a bottle. Before they allowed me to feed her the first time, Pat warned me that many calves don't make it past the first few months. He only tolerated my attachment to the small, skittish animal because as a Holstein heifer she would be sold off to a farm for her milk, not for slaughter. If they had to sell her, I could imagine her on a nearby hill, happily munching bluegrass or clover. I swore that I understood that she might not make it and that I would be fine with that. But the first time I slid my fingers into her sandpaper mouth, she sucked with a desperation that stung deep in my belly, and I was lost.

"Uh-oh," Davey said. I grabbed the porch railing and waited. Without looking me in the eye, he started and stopped talking, mumbled something, and said maybe I should go down to the farm and talk to the brothers.

"Is she dead?" I pictured my cow's wet black eyes fringed with lashes long like string. She was white with black markings that shape-shifted across her body like clouds. I didn't breathe for a moment until he answered.

"No, no, she ain't dead! Kelly just, well, she ain't a she."

I climbed down from the porch and stood at the bottom of his ladder.

"What do you mean she isn't a she?"

"Well, your cow is an it." He pretended to be busy hammering at the pipe in the roof, but I remained standing by his ladder. His cheeks had turned pink.

"Wait a minute, Davey. I don't understand." When I'd feed her in the mornings, after unhooking the sack of powdered milk from the nail in the barn, scooping out an old faded plastic cup's worth of sweet candy-smelling silt and mixing it up in lukewarm water using a martini strainer, she always slurped hungrily. By the time I allowed Babe (a female pit bull) and Little Dude (a male mutt) to finish licking up the leftovers, a fountain of piss has usually erupted from between Kelly's legs. At the bottom of the ladder staring up at Davey, I imagined a cork plugging the fluid rushing out from her four stomachs. *Does* a female cow have a vagina and urethra like a human female? I'd never seen a penis between Kelly's legs, but I'd never exactly looked. I tried to figure out how I could get a straight answer from Davey without embarrassing him. Or me.

"Does she have neither, or does she have both?"

He struggled for a moment, during which I imagine he shuffled through his anatomical vocabulary. Then he shrugged and just came out with it.

"Your cow has no pussy."

❦

When we first moved to the farmhouse two years before Little Kelly came to the farm, the farmers were keeping a dozen or so chickens in one part of their barn. A small radio was perched on a beam and played all day and night, either to keep the chickens company or to keep the coyotes and weasels away, depending on which brother you asked. I used to stop by once a week to pick up a carton of fresh eggs from the old yellow refrigerator next to the chicken hutch, which was actually just an old cow stall stapled over with chicken wire. The hens would squawk and strut, protecting their nests whenever I visited.

Someone had scrawled a note on a piece of masking tape and stuck it on the old refrigerator: *$1.25 with a carton, $1 if you bring your own.* The idea was to place your empty carton in the freezer and trade it for a full carton from the fridge. One morning in late summer I pulled open the barn door and there were no chickens— the radio wasn't playing, and the refrigerator doors were flung open, inside dark. When I asked what happened to the chickens a few days later, Pat said they'd gotten rid of them because they were too much work for too little money. When we pressed him to elaborate on where exactly the chickens went, he shrugged and said simply, "We took care of them."

The barn was a sort of headquarters for the neighborhood. If Pat and Tom Joe weren't in the fields, they were usually in one of the two barns—the cow barn, where Kelly would live until it was safe for her to join the herd, and the "hang-out" barn, where they fixed machines and drank in the warmer months. The hang-out barn also had an upstairs, but this space was relegated to men only; they called it the barn bar, and I understood this to be a kind of special occasion bar, for birthdays and such. The houses in our area are far-flung and isolated, so it is a comfort to know that you can usually find someone at the barn. The neighborhood group is made up mostly of men. There are some women tucked into the hills, and a few of the men are married, but most of the men in the neighborhood are single.

Neither Pat nor Tom Joe nor Davey had wives. Davey was married shortly after his car accident, but his wife divorced him after a few years. They got back together and had three children, but they never remarried. She kicked him out for good a month before I first met him and he was living in a trailer on a hill near my farmhouse. The brothers lived in the farmhouse they grew up in with their eighty-six-year-old mother.

Pat, the younger brother, had recently retired from his job as a corrections officer on death row in a nearby prison. He had once been married, but wasn't anymore. He kept his white hair clipped close to his scalp, and had a tattoo of an eagle and a heart on his right bicep. Pat collected skeletons and skulls and hung them in the barn; the collection included a coyote, a deer, a raccoon, and the shriveled corpse of a weasel. He was dating Linda, a forty-something single mom who lived with her son down the dirt road. She had a yellow mullet and a deep smoker's voice, and Pat called her his "Linda Evans," from his favorite soap opera, *Dynasty*. We were usually the only women drinking beer in the barn.

After Davey finished his work on the roof and went home, I sent R. down to the farm to figure out what was really wrong with Kelly the cow. He came back two hours later, a little woozy from the plastic cups of Busch keg beer, and without a satisfying answer. "Pat told me, *she's got no lips*," R. reported. And then laughed.

I went down the road myself the next day. I lingered in the barn and had a few beers before broaching the subject. "So, how's Kelly?"

"She's fine, she's fine," Tom Joe said, not meeting my eyes.

Pat shifted in his seat on the picnic bench in the middle of the barn.

"Davey told me that she was having some problems." Both of the men were fidgeting now. "I don't quite understand what he means, though."

Pat cleared his throat and said he was going to kill the farmer that sold him the cow. "It's a freemartin. It happens. But he shoulda known it." He spat on the floor and lit another cigarette. "But she's gonna be fine. The vet came down last night and gave her a shot that he said should help."

I walked back into the dairy barn. Kelly lifted her head when she saw me and struggled to her feet. Sawdust pilings stuck to her body like confetti, and today the black markings on her right side looked like an old woman knitting in a rocking chair. I rubbed my fingers on her head between her little Spock ears, and she nudged my forearm with her wide mottled pink-and-black nose, gathering the cuff of my shirt and then my hand in her mouth. I could feel her teeth against my palm like the rim of a glass. I had heard about a baby cow who had suckled off the tail of a horse that had been kept in the same stall, and as I ran my thumb along her scratchy chin, I believed it. I made a move with my other hand to lift her spindly tail, in an effort to understand, but she refused to detach her mouth from my fingers. We circled for a few moments in an awkward dance, and then I gave up.

A website on the clinical examination of the cow lists a sloped tail head, small vulva, enlarged clitoris, or long vulvar hair as signs of a freemartin. An article at TheCattleSite.com called freemartinism "one of the most severe forms of sexual abnormality among cattle," marked by masculinized behavior and nonfunctioning ovaries. I learned that Kelly must have had a male twin, and when she was in the womb, hormones from her brother crossed over to her, and her hormones crossed to him. Usually, the males are stillborn or miscarried, and the female cow takes on traits of a male. Ninety-nine percent of freemartins are sterile. In *Brave New World*, Huxley used the word "freemartin" to describe a woman made sterile by the government policy of exposing her to hormones during fetal development; seventy percent of the female population in Huxley's futuristic novel is freemartin.

I casually mentioned some of these facts—the twinning, the hormones, the percentages, though not the Huxley—to Pat and Tom Joe the next time I visited the barn. R. earned his acceptance into the group through his carpentry, but I was a woman, from the city, and at thirty-two still had no children. I knew they were unsure what to think about me, and I often had a hard time understanding how exactly I fit in, too. But I wanted Pat and Tom Joe to know I was taking my part in raising Kelly the cow seriously.

Pat didn't seem to have ever heard about the causes of freemartinism. Nor did he seem to care much. "Well, all I know is a heifer is worth more money than a bull," Pat said. Heifers only begin to give milk after they birth their first calf, which they usually do once they reach two years old. Kelly would only have value if she could become a mother. I realized that if the hormone shots didn't jump-start her ovaries, Kelly would be sold as a bull, for her meat rather than her milk or her ability to reproduce. My picture of her future—happy on a nearby hillside, chewing cud and being milked by a man with soft hands who sat on a short three-legged blue stool—slowly dislodged and began to roll away down the hill, a small bundle of teeth and coarse hair.

The next day, I started making pies. I gave my third ever apple pie, made with apples from a nearby orchard, to the men at the barn. I knew it might be only weeks before we would be able to tell if the hormone shots were doing their job, and I was hoping they might spare Kelly even if the shots did not work. I understood that if they couldn't, they'd probably have to sell her for veal, or to another farmer to grow her into an adult cow for steaks and such, but I had to at least try to get them to give her a chance.

I drove in our red pickup truck down the road and parked in their long dirt driveway. Little Dude, the small black mutt they had found in a nearby ditch, ran up and tried to bite my tires. I balanced the pie as the small dog followed me into the hangout barn. I stood in front of the rickety picnic table and said hello to Davey, Pat, and Tom Joe. I put the pie on the table and told them I was new at baking and that suggestions were welcome.

"Thank you!" Tom Joe said, shaking his head so hard he rattled the table. "That'll be real good, real good." He smiled.

Davey kicked his lame foot out from under the table and stood up, lumbering over and giving me a hug. "That's so nice," he said. "Don't take it the wrong way if I tell you to put more or less cinnamon or nutmeg or whatever in it, okay?" He went back to the table, landing hard on the little wooden bench.

Pat simply raised his beer in salute.

"I'm going to check on my cow, okay?" I moved to the cow barn as the men absently dug into the pie.

It was early winter and had started to get cold. The barn door had been pulled shut. Inside Kelly rustled to her feet when she heard my voice. She was still very small but growing quickly; two weeks earlier she'd looked scrawny, shoulder and hip bones jutting out like a wet cat's, but today her belly was swollen.

The black mutt came near, trying to lick some milk caught on her chin, and Kelly stamped her hoof at him, hard. She was learning, I thought, smiling to myself as I slipped my hand in her mouth. Another thought crashed sharply against that one: or was she masculinizing? Was this the freemartin side showing through? She dipped her head, pulling on my hand as if trying to force milk out of my fingers. The skin on my hand pricked with pain as her teeth scraped my knuckles. I pulled away.

From behind the barn came a chorus of loud bellows—the sun was going down and the heifers were coming into the nearby field to feed. I looked at Little Kelly expectantly, searching her face for a shimmer of kinship as the female cows continued their raspy song. There was nothing. My fingers were raw and pink where her teeth had caught, and I wiped my hand on an old t-shirt hanging from a nearby nail. The heifers' cries slowed and gave way again to the quieter soundtrack of the barn swallows' soft murmurs and the rub of Kelly's chain against the wood stall. I returned the t-shirt to its nail, and as I turned to leave, a shock of laughter exploded from the picnic table, catapulting Pat and Tom Joe and Davey's voices through the barn as they shared some joke or gossip.

In the last light of the day, I saw my cow's white head whip quickly through the darkness in the men's direction, big black eyes shining. I didn't know what to think of my cow, or what to wish. I just wanted Little Kelly to survive.

The men at the table were all broken in their own different ways. If anybody could understand this cow's need for some extra time and patience to get sorted out, they would, I reasoned. Then again, the men in these hills all seemed like perpetual boys, falling down and breaking bones, getting into bar fight after bar fight, making mistakes over and over and over again. They had leeway. The women, though, were neatly divided into categories: (ex)wives, mothers, or other. If a woman deviated from those first two identities or couldn't at least pass for a version of them, the way I tried to most of the time in the barn, she became incomprehensible to them. I understood that in this barn, my value was measured in pies and babies. I'm not sure why I expected it would be different for Little Kelly.

I closed my eyes and breathed in one last time. I imagined the barn as empty as that broken-down refrigerator near the old chicken hutch, doors flung open and the inside dark, the warm and loamy smell of the small cow gone.

A few months later, the farmers granted little Kelly a stay of execution and moved her out of the barn and into the field. Her fate was postponed; if she could produce when she turned two, she'd be safe. If she could not become a mother, she'd be deemed worthless and carted off for her meat.

My visits to the barn were less frequent, since she didn't need me anymore, but I still swung by to share a beer or to talk. The year she was moved out of the barn and into the field, we were invited to a New Year's Eve party at the barn, the only time I'd ever been allowed into the barn's upstairs bar. R. and I had friends visiting from the city, a pair of actors, who came along with us. By the time we got to the party a bit after sundown, everyone was already blind drunk.

I was surprised to see that the men had built an actual bar out of unfinished plywood. Most of the men brought their own bottles of booze and kept them on a shelf behind the bar, names in Sharpie on masking tape stuck to plastic pints of liquor. There was a contractor bucket in the corner; this was their bathroom. When it was full, someone would pour it out the window, splashing down near the electric fence and a pile of broken posts.

That New Year's Eve, it seemed like the whole neighborhood was there, both men and women. Our group of four didn't stay long, maybe an hour—the smoke was so thick I could barely breathe. We drank whiskey without a mixer from red Solo cups and the evening had the air of the kinds of parties I hadn't attended since high school. Women had their arms slung around men's shoulders and the men laughed with their mouths wide open. Tom Joe was there, and Davey, of course. Linda sat on Pat's lap, his hands between her knees.

When we left, from the backseat of our pickup truck the warm

yellow stripes of light blazing through the slats of the white clap-
boards made the barn look like it was something out of a children's
book. At midnight, the hills exploded with gunfire instead of fireworks, a rural take on the holiday, the forest crackling blackly
around us.

In the morning, I woke up, looked out our bedroom window, and blinked. There was a mass of cows moving slowly up
our driveway toward the house. R. and the couple staying with us
went out onto the porch to stare at the herd. Our red F-150 and our
friends' small grey rental car were soon engulfed, just part of the
pack as the cows spread out nervously, eyes wide. I could tell that
these were the mature mamas from the field; they must have gotten loose in the night while the men were distracted, partying. The
fog was rolling up from the swamp and the animals were eerily
quiet, like apparitions in the mist, a ghost herd.

R. stepped carefully down the porch stairs but spooked the
cows closest to him. Like the flocks of birds we used to watch in
the Brooklyn sky from his painting studio window, the animals all
turned and swooped the other direction, lumbering back down the
driveway in a single, silent murmuration.

Upstairs, I opened the bedroom window, letting in the cold
and listening for signs of the cows, but it was as if they'd all disappeared into the fog. I hadn't spotted Kelly; every so often I could
recognize her shape-shifter markings from the side of the road,
though she no longer responded to my call.

I wondered what it would feel like to move among them,
warmed by their heavy bodies and breath. I thought about putting

on my winter boots and coat and trying to follow them. But when I went outside that morning, there was no sign of the herd. The only proof they hadn't been figments of our hungover imaginations were the torn-up hoof tracks along the driveway's dead grass and some piles of cowshit, still steaming in the morning silence.

The Ghosts in the Hills

Once a thing is set to happen, all you can do is hope it won't.
Or will—depending. As long as you live, there's always
something waiting, and even if it's bad, and
you know it's bad, what can you do?

—TRUMAN CAPOTE, *IN COLD BLOOD*

ROCK LAKE EXTENDS ACROSS THE sloping back of the Endless Mountains in northeast Pennsylvania, an area with more cows than people that locals like to call "God's Country." Curving along the Delaware River like a comma against the New York border, this area is about fifty miles northeast from Scranton, a place people born here refer to as "the city," even as weekenders take it to mean Manhattan. Tidy ranches and capes cluster along the main roads, house-proud with their military brush-cut lawns and American flags, interspersed every so often with a sagging single-wide trailer, belongings spilling out through the weeds like milk, stinking of abandonment except for the guy in the fishing vest off to the side tending a burn barrel blaze. The deeper into the country a traveler drives, the deeper the ruts along the sides of the road; the hay bales switch from tightly packed squares to giant cochlear curls, disembodied ears dotting the expansive fields, pressed to the soil, listening.

You can't find Rock Lake on a map. Kathy at the Lake Como Post Office will hold your mail if someone gets your address mixed up and hand it to you the next time you come in, whether that's a week from now or next winter. UPS and FedEx require a Pleasant Mount zip code; there are no mailboxes on our road. The main industry up here is summer camps. The estimated per capita income has hovered between $17,000 and $22,000 for the past twenty years. According to county data, the area is more than ninety-four percent white. The Wayne County website proffers plenty more statistics, but I learned most of the important things about living here at the dairy barn down the road.

The barn is where I went when I thought I was seeing ghosts.

Driving home one evening, at the curve just after St. Juliana's dramatic steeple jutted into the bright blue sky, before the road turned to dirt, I looked left out of habit. Sometimes at night, my headlights would flash across the old cemetery and catch sparks of light. Deer liked to bed down in front of the headstones, like grave blankets, and I liked the way their silvery eyes reflected my car's lights.

This night, though, I spied a handful of colorful orbs, blinking among the graves like fairy lights. These weren't eyes. They were more like little luminescent ghosts in the moonlight.

I reported my findings to the men at the barn later in the week.

"They ain't ghosts," Pat said, rubbing his big hands atop his grey-stubbled head. "They're lanterns." He explained that people left them on the graves as a kind of eternal light, a sign of remembering.

This started us on a tangent, though. Some of the other men said that there were plenty of ghosts around. The most famous one in the hills was Old Man McGarry, the man who built our farmhouse in the 1860s. Our road was originally named after him, they said, until the owner before us changed it when the county came through and put street signs in a few decades earlier.

Old Man McGarry died at the top of our hill, crushed by a giant sliding barn door one night during a storm while trying to guide a horse to safety. All that was left of the barn by the time we moved in was a collapsed and sagging nest of beams, the rest fallen and rotted years earlier. The men said that Old Man McGarry was a mean bastard, and that he still roamed the hills on stormy nights. He was buried in St. Juliana's, where most of the headstones were half a century old or more, the granite pitted and worn.

The next time I passed the cemetery at night I pulled over and stared into the darkness. The glowing orbs still looked eerie, but I could see Pat was right. The lights were only solar lanterns, just bits of plastic and battery, tamped into the cold ground.

According to Michel Foucault, a heterotopia is a real space, but one that exists outside of the society that produced it. When I first heard that word, I thought it meant a utopia for straight people. But the artist who explained the term to me said that it was the opposite of a utopia. Utopias are, by definition, unreal. A utopia is an imagined state; this was what rural Pennsylvania looked like to me from afar before I moved there full-time, a kind of dreamy pastoral, bucolic mirage shimmering in the distance. A heterotopia, on the other hand, is a real space, but not a mappable space; heterotopias exist all around us, though are often unquantifiable.

Foucault specifically meant places like cemeteries, prisons, or boarding schools. But in my mind, Rock Lake, the barn, and, increasingly, the farmhouse—Old Man McGarry's and our own— were all, in their own ways, examples of heterotopias, places where the normal rules of society did not apply.

There were plenty of rules, though. Everyone was welcome, for example, until they weren't. One of the men was barred after his teenaged son stole some tools from the barn one night; another neighbor, Jersey Joe, was no longer welcome after he rebuffed the barn too many times. I only saw him at the barn once and didn't understand why his decision to keep to himself was so egregious; he lived in Jersey, as his nickname intimated, and I figured he came out here for privacy. Choosing to spend time alone did not seem like a personal affront, but it was certainly the way the men took it.

R. and I wanted privacy, too, but found we could only take so much. When we were tired of each other, when our own ten-acre property was still too small to hold our discontent, the barn offered the respite of other people and their problems. Also, the barn was the closest place to get a beer, or the newest neighborhood gossip, or answers to questions you couldn't figure out with Google. Things like,

should you shoot a skunk
how do you repair a metal roof
what is the best way to cook venison patties

Sometimes, the internet seemed to provide an answer, only for us to later find out at the barn that there was a better way to do things. For example, regardless of how you cook them, you have to make sure your patties are "half-and-half" (half venison, half pork) or they will turn into hard pucks. If your metal roof needs repair, you wait until April when a band of roofers always drove up from the south and fixed roofs for cheap with leftover scraps, which is why so many of the metal roofs in the area looked like patchwork quilts, a crosshatch of red and blue and grey, whatever color the southern roofers had in their truck that year.

We learned about the skunk too late. One had been hanging around the little barn on our property, slinking through the fields. We were expecting weekend company, and didn't want the visiting kids to surprise the skunk and get sprayed while running through the paddocks. R. was not a practiced shot; his first one came just close enough to scare the skunk into its defensive position, turning its back on us and raising its tail high in the air like a flag before a drag race. The second bullet caught the animal right in its ass. It took a third to put it down, and the whole time the skunk just sprayed and sprayed. R. buried the carcass deep in the woods while I drove to the hardware store, returning with a remedy for skunked dogs. I spritzed the area closest to the house until the bottle ran out. I thought the remedy worked, but then the wind changed and our eyes began to sting all over again.

When we told the men at the barn, they just shook their heads. One said, "Canned tomatoes next time." Another recommended diluted Dawn dish soap. The blue kind.

❧

I never thought we would own a gun, never mind multiple guns. I never thought we would take such pleasure from shooting at our makeshift range at the top of the hill, candy-color paint can lids strung along two-by-fours like some modernist sculpture, bullet holes puncturing the pretty dots. I never thought we would shoot an animal from our front porch. But since moving to the country full-time, we both seemed to be transforming.

R. was a painter, had his favorite route in the Met, his bookcase full of monographs and back issues of *Modern Painters* magazine. But he was not part of the establishment, did not talk theory, did not write reviews, did not wear sunglasses indoors and make snide remarks to a bevy of skinny black-clad artists in the back corner of gallery shows. He looked more like a construction worker than a fine artist; when he told people he was a painter, often they responded with, "Like, a house painter?"

This ability to defy expectations was one of the things I appreciated most about him. Before marriage, our relationship seemed to thrive on the unconventional. But now, surrounded by the Pennsylvania woods instead of the tight belt of the city's skyscrapers, we kept running aground when it came to questions of family and providing and who was responsible for what. We'd never combined our finances, never really talked about budgets or planning aside from whether we'd be able to cover the mortgage that month. Up till then, I'd liked our separateness. It was a point of pride. I hadn't even considered changing my name. Convention? No, thank you. I felt fairly certain about what I did not want my marriage to look like, but I'd never stopped to really think about what I did want.

I think I just assumed that moving to the country would allow our relationship to inhale a different kind of oxygen, that we would find our new natural shape together outside the city in the same way an indoor plant might if transferred to an outdoor garden. Unfiltered sun, constant fresh air, and a garden full of green instead of table legs and couches, dust-covered bookcases and kitchen smells: couldn't this only be healthy?

Some plants are simply not meant to be put outside, of course. Some plants need the structure of the pot, require the stability of a constant temperature, can only flourish with a floor and ceiling and walls as guideposts. When I look through my books about gardening now, I recognize the limp leaves and sagging frames of the plants on certain pages. This is called Transplant Shock. It usually begins as a kind of stasis, where the plant fails to thrive.

For a period, the plant looks just fine. But in reality, it is already dead.

❧

One person's secluded paradise is another person's isolated nightmare. So I learned each time friends visited from the city. They'd steer their rental up our long driveway, unfold out of the car after the long trip, look around in a daze. *Isn't it peaceful?* I'd ask. In response, some would whisper back: *Aren't you afraid?* I would look around, surprised, and realize that where I saw the homes of frogs and deer and birds, they saw nothing. No other house was visible from our property; for a few weeks in the dead of winter, you could stand at our front door and see one small cabin on the opposite hill, but it was deserted, a tree growing through its porch, towering over the squat cabin itself, waving in the breeze when we looked at it through binoculars.

Shortly after buying the farmhouse, we decided to install an alarm system. This afforded some kind of psychological balm, a totem to prove we were not completely cut off from the rest of the world. Along with the on/off button, there were three plastic square nubs on the pad: police, fire, and medical. I was comforted by the idea that with one quick push a bell would ring in a far-off place and help would be on its way. Never mind that the nearest precinct or hospital was forty minutes from us.

"Besides," the teenage son of a neighbor reasoned one day when he was over to help with some odd jobs, "If someone really wants to get in, they're getting in." He nodded at the window next to the front door as he said this. There was no menace or threat in his voice, but I found his calm calculation terrifying.

The ADT truck arrived to complete the install when I was home alone. The technician and I stood in the sunshine outside while we discussed my "needs." He wore a wrinkled short-sleeve button-down work shirt and baggy jeans cinched with a belt, held a clipboard in his hand.

"It's really more for protection when we are away," I said, explaining we often spent time in Manhattan for work. "I always have this feeling that the house won't be standing here when we come rolling up the driveway. This way we can keep an eye on it when we aren't here."

He nodded sagely. "I guess you won't be needing an external alarm," he said.

"An external alarm?" I asked.

"Yeah, one that makes a noise outside the house if something is wrong." He turned in a full circle, taking in the acres and acres of trees, pasture, emptiness. "No one to hear it anyway."

He cupped his hands to his mouth and let out a sharp yelp. He sounded a bit like a hawk, or the coyotes that screamed at night in the swamp down the hill.

We looked at each other for a moment in the quiet after the echo of his call evaporated into the trees.

"No," I agreed, taking a step away, suddenly wishing him to be finished with his work, wishing to see his van leaving the driveway. "I guess that won't be necessary."

One spring, I noticed a giant metal contraption on the lawn of Pat's girlfriend Linda. She liked to decorate for the season; along with whatever holiday baubles she stapled to her garage, bouquets of tropical-colored plastic flowers lined the driveway all year round. She was smoker-thin and her skin seemed draped over her bones, but she was tough; when I first met her, one of my favorite Janisse Ray lines, from *The Ecology of a Cracker Childhood*, rustled up: "She was so strong a ship could have been hewn from her body."

I asked her about the big metal bin the next time I saw her at the barn. I thought it might be some kind of barbeque; I'd seen a similarly shaped portable pig roaster at the Wayne County 4-H Fair the summer before, though this was much larger.

It turned out, the old lady who lived next door to Linda had taken to handing out marshmallows to bears through her kitchen window. One morning, when a bear grew impatient, a giant paw tore straight through her window screen. Linda was afraid to let her son play in the yard, annoyed at the bears ambling across her driveway to get to the old lady's. Linda had asked her to stop feeding them marshmallows, but the old lady lived by herself and said she was lonely. She refused to stop, even after they ripped apart her screen.

So, the game warden hitched up a bear barrel and trailered it to Linda's front yard, where the bear-sized beer can sat until one of the animals wandered in and the contraption snapped shut, sealing it until the game warden could trailer the bear to the other side of the state forest.

"She'll just keep feeding them," Linda said, shaking her head, taking a drag off her Parliament. Sure enough, the old woman was soon luring the beasts to her kitchen window later that same season, and the process started all over.

There are things one can do to ward against Transplant Shock. When you move a plant from one place to another, the manuals caution, the more roots that come with the plant, the more likely the plant will settle into its new location.

One gardener suggests sugar water. If a plant has been moved and looks to be suffering from shock, mix some conventional granulated sugar into water and feed it to the plant for a week.

Simple sweetness, in other words, is what the gardener is suggesting. Like the old woman's marshmallow routine. Of course, sugar water is also widely used as a placebo, a control or a measure to calm. Any effect requires a patient's belief in the treatment in the first place. Belonging is subjective; one's belief in the heterotopia does not guarantee one's welcome.

Most of the men who came to the barn lived in old family homes or dilapidated rentals, single-wide trailers often overrun by animals and heated by jimmied propane tanks stolen from summer people's BBQs. Tom Joe and Pat still lived at their childhood home, smoking at the kitchen table they'd always eaten around, sleeping in their childhood bedrooms.

Few had jobs, or regular work, and most were usually drunk by noon, regardless of the day of the week. This was before the age of smartphones, and few had computers. They liked their television, but most only had basic cable. If they had a vehicle, it was usually a pickup truck dented from nights when they drove half in the bag. If they couldn't afford a car, or if they'd had too many DWIs, they caught rides when they could and rode bikes when they needed to. When I first moved to rural Pennsylvania, the number of grown men riding around the roads on bikes perplexed me, until someone kindly explained the reason.

These men were also some of the most inventive I've ever met. I've watched them raise a pole barn on a hill by hand and splint a cow's leg with a branch. I've watched them dismantle a toolshed on one property, drag it on what can only be described as roller skates for a house to another property, and rebuild it again. There is not a machine they cannot fix. They share their food and boats and beer and smokes. When Tom Joe and Pat's mother's need for a wheelchair became permanent, the barn boys built an elaborate set of ramps for their farmhouse. Their gardens are lush and wild, bursting with giant pumpkins and broccoli. I've been given gifts of freshly butchered venison wrapped in plastic CVS bags and bouquets of freshly picked wild ramps folded gently into wet paper towels.

The men mostly wore Carter's work pants or jeans, t-shirts from family picnics or store giveaways, and lots of camouflage. They wore heavy boots, regardless of season. Their hands were spatulate and rough, dusky white with callus. Few had wedding rings. The barn was lined with tools, and there was usually a tractor or vehicle or some other mechanical project in the center, splayed open. The dirt floor was littered with cigarette butts and dirty rags and dark clouds of oil. A contractor bag full of dried marijuana leaves from this year's small harvest stood in one corner, and black garbage bags full of empties stood in another, ready to be returned when they ran out of beer money. The cheapest place for a case of beer is the CVS in Hancock, twenty miles away. There were a few bars nearby, but many of the men, most of whom had grown up in the area, had been thrown out for fighting too many times and weren't welcome back. The barn bar was home and headquarters.

Tom Joe took care of the cows on the farm and knew all of them by name. Pat presided over the barn. They lived in their mother's house and their sister lived in a single-wide across the

street, with petunias growing out of planters made from old bar-
rels and farm equipment.

When we first moved in, Pat took my husband under his wing.
He let him paint landscapes in the pasture, allowed R. to tote his
French easel and paint box in among the cows until he found the
right view. Pat showed him more views that he thought would
make good paintings, taking him for slow meandering drives
around the hills, off road and through private property, a pitcher of
beer by their feet, stubbed-out cigarettes overflowing in the cupholder between them. Pat was a caretaker—he watched over the
neighborhood, his brother, his dogs, his farm. He was the de facto
leader of the barn, and his opinion was the one that counted the
most during conversations. He rarely spoke, but when he did, it
was decisive, and everyone listened.

When someone killed a bobcat with their car on the road, Pat
strung it up in a tree at the top of one of his pastures, just to look at
it. I went to visit the cat, whose body was hoisted high enough that
predators couldn't get to it. Pat had bound each leg so the carcass
was spread-eagle. The cat was covered in black flies, but I could see
there was something beautiful in the loll of its head.

Foucault writes that the history of spaces would "at the same time
be a history of power." A heterotopia cannot, by definition, be a
strictly public place. One of the principles of heterotopias is that
they "always presuppose a system of opening and closing that
both isolates them and makes them penetrable." Anyone could
drive through Rock Lake, or even enter the barn—there were

no locks on the doors. But not anyone could enter the barn and see the same interactions that those who were of the barn would see. "Either the entry is compulsory . . . or else the individual has to submit to rites and purifications," Foucault says. "To get in one must have a certain permission and make certain gestures." Think driving a pickup truck. Think hunting. Think rolling your own joints and making your own bullets. Think offerings of beer, or venison, or gas cards.

In the barn, the powerless became the powerful. The broken became the brokers. The rules in that barn were unspoken and required learning, practicing, just as the rules of living in the country did. And that fantasy life—the utopian country life that many weekenders experienced—was only possible with this heterotopia. Adam Sills, author of *Against Maps*, likes to use sweatshops as an example of heterotopias; he asks his students if they think about where their sneakers are made. Sweatshops are real places, of course, but are relegated to a state of alterity, being required for normal life and yet excluded from normal life at the same time. "You can't type *sweatshops* into Google Maps," Sills points out.

Rock Lake's isolation also enforced its experience as a liminal space. In a rather poetic essay called "Of Other Spaces," Foucault declares ships to be "the heterotopia *par excellence*." He writes, "the boat is a floating piece of space, a place without a place. That exists by itself, that is closed in on itself and at the same time is given over the infinity of the sea. . . ." Rock Lake was like a boat in this way. The isolation of a boat on the sea was certainly familiar; we were thirty minutes from a carton of milk, forty-five minutes from a doctor or the law, so the men became one another's doctors and providers of sustenance, became the law themselves. The place also seemed to fold in on itself in the way Foucault describes; Rock Lake did not exist on a map, and time stood still between the old farm equipment, the eternal forms of the men standing around the barn, and Old Man McGarry himself roaming the farmhouse he built, which was now our farmhouse, and yet never would be, not fully. "In civilizations without boats," Foucault cautions, "dreams dry up."

When heterotopias and fantasies collide, there is inherent conflict. The heterotopia becomes superimposed over the everyday, waking world. And sometimes the heterotopia displaces it.

With the help of the barn, we'd made it through our first seasons as part-timers and then full-timers. R. still borrowed the brothers' wood splitter, feeding logs into the terrifying slamming gas-powered pump, but he no longer needed their help to work it. I supplemented my adjunct teaching in Manhattan, zipping back and forth on the Shortline bus, with a part-time magazine job in the nearby town, editing the Jokes and Riddles section of the kids' magazine *Highlights for Children*. One of Pat's dogs, the squirmy black mutt named Little Dude, liked to nip affectionately at our tires when we drove up until I got out and gave him a scratch. He took to running the five miles between our houses, hanging out on our hill drinking water from a green bowl we bought just for him. He would sun himself for an afternoon here and there before returning to the farm to abuse the cows. We were slowly becoming regulars in this life.

One year, a new face showed up at the bar. Travis had shaggy dark hair and the lanky stride of a surfer. He was a reader, had road-tripped his way across the country after getting kicked out of his father's house in California. He planned to stay with his mother in town for the summer, find some work and save some money before moving to New York City. His stepfather initiated him into the barn bar group.

After the first few weeks, Travis traded his board shorts for carpenter pants. He went on odd jobs with whoever needed an extra hand, got a girlfriend. By his second summer in the hills, he'd cut off all his hair, started smoking. Pat and Tom Joe's sister hired Travis to refinish her front deck. When he completed that job, he took it upon himself to scrape and repaint the entire barn as a thank you to the brothers. The paint on the side of the barn had been peeling for years.

As I drove by that season, zipping to and from my job at *Highlights*, I'd wave to Travis scrape-scrape-scraping, Little Dude running circles around the bottom of his ladder. He got nearly three-quarters of the way across the giant barn. After a while, he'd stumble out of one or another person's truck and into the open bay, forearms thicker from the manual labor, middle thicker from the beer, and take up a spot among the other men instead of heading up the ladder. Sometimes, one of us would rib him about not finishing the job.

"I'll get to it," he'd say, his watery pinked eyes matching the rest of the men's.

If Travis was an example of how easily someone could slide into this strange world and be consumed, Jersey Joe was the opposite. His complete rejection of the barn community irked the other men. For me, the country was an escape, a jolt of color after years of concrete grey, and I assumed it was the same for Joe, could understand not wanting to participate, to just hide out instead. I didn't understand not wanting to make use of the resources the barn had to offer—Joe lived just one property over, much closer than us, and even if he didn't want the company, everyone needed help sometimes.

One of the men from the barn, Paulie the Fireman, retired from the FDNY, was a one-man neighborhood watch all on his own. He carried a Swiss Army knife at all times. He would check on us, and all the other neighbors, after winter storms, summer power outages, and floods. He knew who was on vacation, the status of Ned's marriage, of Tom Joe and Pat's mother's health. He would inevitably turn up just as we were trying to drag a giant tree out of the road or get the tractor wheel out of a ditch, and he would magically produce what we needed out of his green Subaru Outback—a thick rope, plywood, a chainsaw. He retained his Boy Scout disposition, even as his mind began slipping slowly into dementia, and he took to adding Joe to his surveillance rounds, even when it was made clear Joe preferred to be left alone. Mostly he just noted how quiet the property seemed to be, but every so often he would report footsteps in the direction of the red barn that seemed to disappear into nothing or the way the blinds were never open. Paulie was the first to raise suspicions about something strange happening at Jersey Joe's property.

Helicopters buzzing low over the nearby fields was not so out of the ordinary in those days. Sometimes, they hovered low enough to bring us out on the porch. We'd crane our necks, and, seeing the sheriff's badge plainly visible on the belly of the helicopter, wave. They were searching for pot farms, Paulie reported to us when we mentioned this passing on the road one day. They must have had a tip, he surmised.

The pot farm they must have been looking for was not on our hill, nor was it one of the many small plots the barn boys had woven throughout the acres. It was at Joe's, tucked in the barn behind the red house.

One morning, when she hadn't heard from him in a few weeks, Joe's girlfriend in Jersey called the local police. She asked them to go check on Joe. The cops headed over to the home later that morning and knocked on the front door. A man answered, identified himself as Joe's roommate, and said he hadn't seen him in a while, either. The cops took down his name and went back to the barracks, but when they ran the name the roommate gave them, the faces did not match. They soon figured out that they had been talking to a man named Gaston.

Whether the cops had been watching the house for a while or they'd previously identified Gaston as a person of interest is unclear. After they realized Gaston had given them a false name, a slew of cops returned to the house with a search warrant. When the cops knocked on the door this time, Gaston did not answer. They called the cellphone number he'd given them earlier. He answered, directed them to the barn out back, the barn where Paulie had noticed the footsteps going in and not coming back out. Then Gaston hung up, and shot himself in the head with a pistol.

When the police entered the barn, they found hundreds of pot plants, clearly a commercial growing operation. They also found a burn barrel smoking from a recent fire. The cops kicked the barrel over, likely thinking Gaston was trying to get rid of some kind of evidence. When the barrel tipped over a clatter of bones spilled out.

Inside the house, the police found Gaston's body. They also found a freezer chest full of body parts wrapped in black contractor bags. That afternoon, the Pennsylvania Wildlife and Game Commission determined the bones were not animal bones, that they were likely human. It would take a few weeks, but the coroner would determine that the bones from the burn barrel and the body parts in the freezer were, in fact, Joe.

The murder-suicide made the local news but didn't garner much attention beyond that. The property was roped off in yellow police tape and the grass was left to grow long. For some, living apart from the rest of the world clearly pushed the boundaries beyond uncultivated and into something else.

One afternoon, Pat's pit bull Babe came into the barn pawing at her face. She'd caught up with a porcupine and had a muzzle full of quills. She went straight to Pat, who wordlessly hoisted her onto the picnic table in the middle of the barn and proceeded to pick them out of her face with a pair of needle-nose pliers, whispering and hushing to the dog for more than an hour until it was done.

Stoned or sober, Pat loved the natural world. He spoke once of hunting deer, and how after hunting his whole life, a few years back he stopped when he killed a buck so regal it made him cry. He said both those words: *regal* and *cry*. He collected carcasses and skins, and the barn was dotted with small dead bats and weasels. One season, some paper wasps made a gorgeous globe nest on a tree branch that grew and grew until it hung over the road like a bunch of heavy grapes on a vine. Pat kept his eye on it all summer, and when the wasps vacated the nest he climbed on top of his pickup truck and cut it free from the branch. He hung it in the barn, where it soared above us like a Lindsey Adelman chandelier.

I'd probably spent hundreds of hours in the barn with these men, who were as likely to comment on the shape of a cloud as they were to curse their ex-wives, or the government. One day, looking up into the cavernous bays of the barn above me, staring at the wasp's nest and a withered bat body in mid-flight hanging by a string, I saw the unmistakable blocky black arms of a swastika. The red on the flag was faded and was almost the same soft brown as the slatted roof of the barn, which may be why I'd never noticed it before, even though it was about the size of a small tractor.

Once I saw it, I couldn't unsee it. I stared, gawking, unable to speak, until my husband caught my line of sight. *Look!* I said with my eyes, gaze darting from him to the flag. He looked up, unfazed. A short time later in the truck on the way home, cans of warm Yuengling nestled between our legs, he tried to calm me down after listening to me sputter about how we could never go back in that barn again.

I can't believe you haven't seen it before, he shrugged calmly. *I just thought you didn't want to talk about it. You've been standing under that flag for years.*

"Spaces that accumulate time, such as museums and libraries, are a reservoir of imagination," Foucault wrote in *Different Spaces*. The barn was a kind of museum, cataloging a taxonomy of Rock Lake, in its layering of the natural world, the tools of work, the blood and oil and piss matted into the dirt floor. In "Heterotopia—Art, Pornography, and Cemeteries," the Norwegian artist Knut Åsdam says a heterotopia is a place that "reveals all the 'real' spaces as built on illusion," and that it is this liminal space that is the most real. In Rock Lake—far away from the watchful porch lights of the suburbs or street lamps of the cities—the thousands of empty acres and the depth of darkness at night gave us permission to luxuriate in our own ferality.

When we enter into a place that is outside of our usual experience, it is our position as an outsider that often allows us to see things differently. It also magnifies those things about ourselves that remain constant, no matter what world we enter.

When Truman Capote traveled to the rural farm community of Holcomb, Kansas, to report on the murder of the Clutter family, he became obsessed instead with the murderer, Perry. In the 2005 movie *Capote*, based on the writer's reporting experience, Philip Seymour Hoffman, who plays Truman, explains the obsession in this way: "It's as if Perry and I grew up in the same house. And one day he stood up and went out the back door, while I went out the front."

Sometimes it takes a while to know which doorframe you are standing under. The relationship between savagery and beauty can be both intoxicating and ephemeral. The curve of a murderer's smile, the loll of the head of a cat strung up in the woods; often, the things we are drawn to surprise even ourselves.

I think of Foucault and the thin membrane of imagination that insulates us. I think of Capote, standing on those wholesome Holcomb street corners. "It is easy to ignore the rain if you have a raincoat," he wrote in *In Cold Blood*.

If the Clutters had had an alarm, no one would have heard it ringing.

Even if I never went into that barn again, that wouldn't change the fact that I stood under that flag with those men, season after season.

By the time we gave up our place in the city and moved to the country full-time, I rarely went near the barn bar anymore. I'd wave as I drove by, but couldn't stand the cigarette smoke, didn't have afternoons to waste shooting the shit between my two jobs. And I couldn't stomach standing beneath that damn flag.

The longer we stayed away from the city, the farther away the world of salad forks and museums and sidewalks full of people felt. The country began feeling more real than the city. And the people we were in the country became more real than the people we had been in the city.

Every few years, tent caterpillars moved through the hills, squirming in their white web nests in the crooked arms of our apple trees. I delighted in lighting these nests on fire with a butane torch, watching the small writhing bodies char and sizzle. I could spend whole afternoons burning these cottony webs down to ash. R., having learned his lesson with the skunk, borrowed iron-sized bear traps from the barn and set them out when a groundhog started burrowing too close to our foundation. He pried the rusty teeth open with a walking stick, pushing until he heard the click, setting the trap next to the hole, a gaping mouth of spikes. One morning, he checked the trap to find the teeth shut on a bloody, brown leg. The groundhog must have torn himself apart to get free, limping to the woods to die.

We were surrounded by so much beauty, all the time, it was almost as though we decided to sharpen our knives inside the house to cut against it. The sprawl of so many rooms, so many acres, became a distance we weren't able to cross to find each other anymore. And when we did, we were no longer gentle with one another. We spent our days wrapped in gauze, like those tent caterpillars. And we began to delight too much in the hiss of the butane torch and the gleam of the mouth of spikes.

Out there in the middle of Rock Lake, we lost perspective. When the neighbors were stringing animals up in the trees, stuffing each other's body parts in the burn barrel, our own small savageries became normalized. Heterotopias inherently activate the people within them in a contradictory or transformative way. I like to pretend that the person I was at times in Rock Lake is separate from the person I know myself to be out in the rest of the world.

But which one was more real? Utopias are perfect, dystopias terrifying, while heterotopias are mirrors, but these mirrors show us more than our own faces, our own hearts.

Have you ever stared at your own face in the bathroom mirror? Really stared at it? Until you couldn't anymore?

🙤

This was all a long time ago. The last time I drove down the road, a bit of yellow plastic police tape was still tied around a tree in front of Joe's red house, like a shredded party ribbon. Down by the barn, pumpkins were rotting into themselves along the garden's edges, and the fields were fallow. In one short season, Tom Joe and Pat's mother died, and then Pat was diagnosed with a brain tumor. Once Pat went into hospice, the barn bar fell off. It was too hard for the men to get together and feel Pat's absence. It took him about six months to die.

After Pat's death, Tom Joe sold off most of his cows. He also died a couple years later.

I wondered if the cows had been sold off alone or together, if they were on some other hill, guarding some other barn filled with some other men, their shapes ghostly white in the moonlight. But I had no one to ask.

The barn was still only half-painted; Travis had started working at a coffee shop in town, got an apartment of his own, was going to be a father. When I ordered a coffee from him one day, even after having spent all those hours together, we barely recognized each other. We squinted and pointed, unable to place where we knew each other from as we stood across the gleaming counter, basking in the buzzing brightness of the overhead fluorescent tubes and the civilizing scent of roasted beans from Costa Rica.

The road looks a bit more lackluster these days. Buckshot still stipples most of the street signs, and Linda's fake flowers still line her driveway, though the plastic petals are faded from the sun. Out of habit, I still slow my car as I roll past the farm, expecting one of Pat's crazy dogs to come out and bite my tires. But then I remember that Little Dude and Babe are both dead, too.

The last time I passed St. Juliana's cemetery, I could easily pick out Old Man McGarry's gravestone from the car, spotted Tom Joe and Pat's mother in the back left corner. Next to her, Pat's grave was only marked by a plaque because the family hadn't had the headstone made yet, though someone already stuck a lantern there. In the daytime, the red plastic looks a little cheap, not ethereal like a ghost at all. But everything looks different in the night; the lanterns ring the graveyard like the solar lights Pat once used in his garden, small points of brightness lighting the way through the darkness, a chorus of *I remember, I remember.*

Lessons from a Starry Night

A FEW MONTHS AFTER my first son was born, I read Rachel Carson's essay, "The Sense of Wonder." Written in 1956 and published in *Woman's Home Companion* magazine in July of that year, the essay offered suggestions for fostering connections between children and nature, something I hoped to do with my son, and I looked forward to hearing more from a woman and writer I so admired. Carson never had any children of her own, but in "The Sense of Wonder" she shares memories of time spent with her young nephew: a nighttime visit to the ocean, a rainy walk in the woods, listening to soft whispers of wind and insects. She designed the work to be a kind of instruction manual for parents, assuring them that even if they didn't know the difference between a sandpiper and a plover, they could work to instill an appreciation for nature in their child. As with most of her writing, a discomfort lingers just beneath the surface, a warning. I hadn't expected a sunny children's story, but the darkness was unsettling.

According to Carson's essay, "A child's world is fresh and new and beautiful, full of wonder and excitement. It is our misfortune that for most of us that clear-eyed vision, that true instinct for what is beautiful and awe-inspiring, is dimmer and even lost before we reach adulthood." At the time I read these words, I'd felt the natural instinct and awareness Carson talks about slowly returning to me. Our small farmhouse was in the middle of hundreds of undeveloped acres full of soft hemlock forests and ferns, rambling rock walls and thorny wild roses, nut-brown grouse and barn swallows. During the ten years I'd lived in the city full-time, my life was all dark angles, hard surfaces, sharp shadows. But after a few days in the country, it was as though my brain snapped open and color flooded in—the shock of the shimmering gold heads of skinny poplars in the pasture out back, the soft, salmon newts with their purple, diamond-studded backs darting through the leaves, the electric lime of the new grass under the last of the melting snow— all arriving in a magnificent sensory rush.

Late in the season the winter I was pregnant, I marched on April's last snow around our front field in my boots and heavy coat while my husband puttered in the barn, the large sliding door cinched open, the floorboards dusted white. I was just big enough for my stomach to get in the way of things, grazing the steering wheel, or the edge of the washing machine as I bent to pull out a load of clothes. I missed my body, or rather, I missed being certain of my body, of where it began and ended. It no longer moved as quickly as I commanded. I tromped around, feeling fidgety, and finally flung myself onto my back into the snow.

I felt the cold on my neck and thighs and watched the grey sky, clouds moving fast. From my spot in front of the barn I stared into the branches of a cherry tree arching over me, the frozen buds enclosed in ice. I shut my eyes and let the hard metallic smell of the snow into my lungs. When the wind blew, a sound like pencils snapping echoed through the air, the tree cracking its thin frozen shell.

After a while, I could hear R. tamping ice, then smelled the sawdust as he spread handfuls of the curled yellow shavings out near my car so I wouldn't slip. I placed my hand on my stomach and imagined I could feel the heat of my belly through my thick coat, a small furnace working hard. I thought of things I hadn't thought of for a very long time, like igloos and hot chocolate, mittens linked together with a string, the magic of snowflakes and icicles. For so long, winter had just been something to shovel out of or drive through. Sinking down into the hillside, I remembered how, as a child, those hours playing in the snow felt unwavering and enchanted, as if winter would last forever, time suspended and caught in a snow globe. I looked forward to returning to this time through my own child's eyes.

In her essay, Carson suggests, "Exploring nature with your child is largely a matter of becoming receptive to what lies all around you. It is learning again to use your eyes, ears, nostrils and finger tips, opening up the disused channels of sensory impression." Pregnancy is a good exercise for this state of hyper-awareness. When a craving was satisfied—the tart squirt of a wedge of grapefruit or a mouthful of bitter arugula—I felt as if I'd doused a fire. I could smell everything: a student's coffee from across the classroom, the spit of beer left in the bottom of a can in the recycling bucket, the first flowering of milkweed on the hill. I felt as though I had both my son's and my own senses coursing through my body.

The morning of his birth, I sat in the bathtub and traced the knob of his elbow beneath my stretched skin. Understanding that today would be the day I'd get to see that elbow, I began to mourn his absence within me. Never again would we be so close, so safe. And yet, even after our cord was cut, we'd remain tethered. What Carson felt between her own fingertips and nature, the opening of that disused channel of sensory impression, was the same: a connectedness that exists whether we want it to or not, even if we've lost our ability to see it.

When my son was five months old, my car hit a patch of ice not far from our house. This was the first time I had been in the car without my son, one of the first times I'd even driven since his birth. It was early January and the first day that snow wasn't falling after a long stretch of storms. The sun was bright and the sky blue, but as I rounded a corner between a pasture and bog, I came upon a section of road where snow had drifted over, hiding a slick scrim of ice on the blacktop. I felt the back tires go out first. I turned the steering wheel, thought I'd come out of it. But then the car spun and I was backwards until the driver's side hit the bank of snow on the edge of the road and I felt the car go over. I thought to myself, "So, *this* is happening." I gripped the steering wheel hard and closed my eyes as the car rolled and rolled and rolled.

The first thing I heard was silence. The first thing I smelled was the woods. I opened my eyes and slowly understood that I was hanging upside down by the strap of my seat belt. My arms were still locked straight out in front of me, hands still gripping the steering wheel. The sharp trunk of an evergreen had broken through the windshield and nearly impaled the passenger seat beside me. The loamy smell of sap was thick in the air, and I heard the crack of thin ice breaking, like the sound of a winter walk through the woods, boots crunching through the frozen mud of a trail, except this was impossible because I was still in the car. I looked above (below?) my head and saw the moon roof, still shattering, spidery breaks crisscrossing the glass, opening to the darkness of the ground.

When I finally released my belt and crawled out the back of the car, pushing aside my son's empty car seat dangling limply upside down, I stumbled out into the snow. Minutes had passed—maybe five? fifteen?—and no one had arrived. No other cars were on the road when I careened off, and no other cars had gone by since. I took a few steps through the deep snow, my legs heavy, my head cloudy and off-balance, and fell into a drift. I stayed there for a moment and went through a checklist: legs? arms? I seemed fuzzy, but fine. My glasses were still on my nose—not even a scratch. The top of my head ached where I'd smashed into the metal roof again and again as I rolled, my body bouncing up and down, but when I reached up I was surprised to feel no blood there, only the soft tassel of my hat. The wind blew over me, and I watched the top of a nearby pine push slowly to the side. The silence, the smell of the pines and the snow, the deep dark green against the bright white; everything seemed amplified, preternatural.

I reflexively placed my hands on my stomach, but the flatness there was quiet as the wind through the pasture. My son was home, a few miles away; I'd left his father with a kit to make a mold of the baby's feet and hands, a craft project while I spent the afternoon with a local library book club. I finally flagged down a passing pickup truck and, once I was finally able to recall my home phone number, I called the house. R. and the baby arrived before the ambulance and we caravanned to the hospital, them in the truck and me feeling so small, swaddled in the stretcher in the back of the ambulance.

Later, at the hospital, I lay on a bed for hours until the MRI machine was free so the doctor could check on my concussion. My husband and son were in the waiting room. Mind swimming, breasts swelling with milk, I wondered how much time had passed, and worried about the baby who must be so hungry, just a few hundred feet away.

But R. had thought quickly, swiping a bottle and two packs of emergency breast milk from the freezer, stuffing them into the baby bag along with the extra outfit and diapers I'd folded in that morning.

They were fine in the waiting room without me.

I wasn't able drive for the rest of winter, would simply freeze anytime I climbed into the driver's seat. We passed the scene of the accident whenever we went to town; over time, the cracked tree sank into the snow, its needles turning from green to brown and finally falling from the limbs until the pine resembled some broken carcass, a pile of bones on the side of the road.

We continued to go back and forth between the city and our home in the country, traveling on off days as my teaching schedule at the university allowed. In Pennsylvania, I found myself staring out at the stretch of white, the frozen landscape reflecting my own fear while I waited for both to thaw. I found comfort in Carson's words: "There is something so infinitely healing in the repeated refrains of nature—the assurance that dawn comes after night, and spring after the winter." But only when early-morning birdsong returned to the dark woods did I truly believe spring would come again.

By April, the snow finally melted in Pennsylvania. We started returning to the country more often, and I assumed I'd start driving soon, and planned to bury my old car keys—the only part left of the totaled black Subaru—next to the skeleton of the fallen tree once the ground thawed. Then one day the tree disappeared. All that remained was a crooked stump. I tried to drive, but just wound up sitting in our pickup truck in the dirt driveway, saying, *After the next song, I'll go. Okay, after the next song.* In July, I noticed from the passenger seat that some daisies had pushed up alongside the stump, a small ring of white. The scar on the ground left by the car was nearly healed. The wooden marker, the simple flowers, the mounded earth all reminded me of what I'd narrowly escaped. My breath caught in my throat each time we drove past.

Returning to our farmhouse late one night, having tried not to look at the broken space in the pines as we passed the accident site, I lifted my son out of his car seat while R. took our bags inside. I pulled his small body out into the deep darkness and let his head droop against my collarbone like a folded flower. He was not afraid of the night, but in the space between the darkened porch and the blue silhouette of the barn I tried not to guess how many pairs of eyes stared at us from the forest or to think about the coyotes calling from the swamp. I forced myself not to calculate how many steps it would take to get to the front door, how much time I would need to fish the keys from my pocket. I worked hard to not let him feel my fear.

I thought of Carson's essay instead and cupped the back of his head in my palms so we could both look up. The sight of the stars washed across his face. I listened to his breathing, felt his heartbeat through his back. We looked quietly into the night sky, the kind you get only when far from the blaze of cities and towns, more stars than sky nearly, like a spray of flour on a cutting board. I whispered to him about the ghost swirl of the Milky Way, the blinking satellites, a planet glowing pink above the barn. My face close to his, I watched him watch the stars until he saw them, really saw them. Finally, he lifted his small arm and pointed to the sky, turning his amazed face to mine, as if to say, "Have you seen this, Mama?"

Near the end of "The Sense of Wonder," Carson writes, "Those who contemplate the beauty of the earth find reserves of strength that will endure as long as life lasts." But whose life did she mean? In 1957, the year after she wrote the essay, Carson's young nephew Roger, who is the center of her story, became her charge when his mother died. And one year after that her own mother, with whom Carson had lived for most of her adult life, also died. Cancer would take Carson herself in 1964. I imagine Carson and her nephew in Maine before this, though, newly motherless daughter and newly motherless son, standing on the rocks between her cottage and the ocean, breathing in the salt and sea, staring into the bright night

sky, speaking to each other the names of the shells and birds dotting the shoreline, feeling less alone than we might assume.

In the fall, I finally drove for the first time. Not far, but far enough.
We had planned to move to the country full-time by then, but for
a while continued to go back and forth, and I realized that a year
would come and go and then it would be winter and I'd just have
to try to drive again in spring. The three weeks preceding the
crash, including my son's first Christmas, had been wiped out of
my brain from the concussion I'd suffered when my skull cracked
against the car roof over and over, and I was slowly accepting that
the memories would likely never return to me.

Instead, I used Carson's essay as a blueprint to create more
memories, to help with the heartbreak that lingered when I
thought about how nearly not just my memories could have disappeared because of that crash. I clearly could have died. I thought
of my husband and son sitting in the hospital waiting room, wondered how long my cache of frozen breast milk would have lasted,
what my son would have remembered about me, if anything at
all. My family was safe now, but I knew we would never really be
as safe as on that faraway morning in the bathtub, my son's small
body curled inside me, R. asleep upstairs.

In October, as R. and I tucked small ear-shaped cloves of garlic into the ground, the season's first snowflakes began to fall. We
celebrated, relieved to get the garlic covered just in time, and then
turned to the baby, who had been sitting contentedly at the edge
of the rows, dwarfed by the tall fence circling the remnants of our

summer vegetable garden. He was looking up, smiling, mouth open. The flakes were huge and movie-white: snow-globe snow. I squatted next to him and held out my hand, and his eyes followed one of the large flecks of snow as it landed on my dirt-covered palm and disappeared, melting into my skin. He stared at my hand, then looked into my face. *Do it again, Mama.* And we sat there, the two of us, snow swirling in the small circle space enclosed by our garden fence, R. humming as he covered the mounds of dirt with leaves so the crows wouldn't tease out the garlic; our son staring at us both, working hard to understand, to remember; and me with my hand out, trying my best to hold on to the idea of wonder as I caught flake after flake in my open palm.

The Leaving Season

THERE IS ALWAYS SOMETHING to hunt in northeast Pennsylvania.

There is squirrel season and beaver season; grouse and bobwhite quail season; mink and muskrat trapping season; bobcat and buck and bear season. There is both a fall and a spring season for wild turkey. And you can shoot crow from July 4th through April 5th, but only Friday through Sunday. Starlings and English sparrows are fair game all year round, except during spring gobbler season, when these small birds can only be shot before noon. But, according to the state's 1843 Songbird Protection Law, you can never kill an Eastern bluebird, or you'll face a two-dollar fine.

Since moving here from Manhattan, these are the rhythms to which I grew attuned. Who is hunting what, who is harvesting what, and which chores need to be done. The old man down the road starts splitting logs for next winter on Memorial Day. St. Juliana's, the creaky wooden 150-year-old Catholic church around the corner, begins selling homemade pierogies midwinter; the stooped and withered church ladies huddle together in the steamy warmth of the church kitchen a few evenings a week to make them. The camp traffic starts in June, shiny BMWs and Lexus SUVs speeding like dusty comets down the dirt roads, leaving an entire summer economy in their wake. During all of this, no matter the time of year, gunshot cracks break across the backs of the hills that surround our small farmhouse, echoing through the sky like an old-fashioned call and response.

They are the music to which I shake out autumn's last load of laundry to be hung on the line out back, and the beat I keep to as I thrust my thumb into the ground over and over and plug the holes with bulbs of garlic. Most of the men shoot bolt-action rifles, and the gunfire chirps in staccato pops throughout the day. My head spins in the direction of the shots automatically; left, right, left, right, over the hill beyond the summer camps, across the way near McGarry's swamp. The short bursts shake me out of naps and force my eyes to blink. Jerry, a neighbor who as a kid used to work the farm on which we now live, comes over and trudges deep into one of the old fields out back with R. to test out his .44 Magnum on our makeshift practice range of old tin cans. Jerry shows off his home-made bullets, melted and molded silvery nubs. R. is a good shot. I can barely lift the cold dark metal to my shoulder.

When we first moved to the country full-time, it felt as though we were let in on a secret. Instead of cracked sidewalks or manicured lawn, my bare feet sank into soft patches of clover and alfalfa. Instead of daily trips to the corner bodega for small bites in plastic packages and containers, I found food on my own land: sandy-webbed puffball mushrooms, strawberries the size of my fingernail, tart stalks of rhubarb, handfuls of delicately haired raspberries which bled the same color as the scratches the thorns gave me on my arms. Instead of grocery store bouquets wrapped in clear plastic, the table bloomed with wild daisies whose stringy stems had fought to stay in the ground; tall curled clutches of garlic scapes, elegant and stinking; and, just once, bulbous heads of purple milkweed, teeming with black ants.

Late summer nights, instead of sirens and city sounds, the frogs were so loud we had to close the windows. In the morning, sharp bursting chirps from chipmunks or high-pitched gobbles from roving packs of wild turkeys woke us. During walks, we collected bits of our new landscape, placing them on our bookshelves like evidence: soft spotted feathers, sweet wild roses, driftwood-like curves of spring-shed antlers. Our water came out cold and clear from an underground spring.

A vacation house is like an affair, I suppose. A weekend or summer house offers excitement, possibility, and contrast from the everyday. When you choose to be with a person other than your partner, and usually for small bits of time, part of the allure is the freedom to be a different person yourself. The same happens when you are with a different house. Sometimes that fantasy feels so real and so much better than what you've already got going on, you leave your partner for the affair. But ultimately, you still have to figure out how to pay bills and who is going to make sure the propane tank is full and who is going to change the toilet paper rolls. Suddenly, the person you imagined you could be is eclipsed by all the same small mundane worries.

Marriage is also a kind of fantasy; in my mind, I imagined that in our farmhouse we would write and paint and raise our children with intention and integrity, surrounded by the beauty of the natural world. I imagined our new home to be like a dollhouse, moving from one room to another and another, a tiny galaxy held within our creaking walls.

But the longer we lived full-time in the farmhouse, the further away from one another R. and I drifted. By our second summer there, neither of us were finding the work we'd hoped and the aging house required more funds to keep it running than we'd planned; our mortgage was an unspoken weight yoked between us. Our baby became a toddler, and now I had another son on the way. I took on more part-time and contract jobs—private editorial work, freelance writing, working for a magazine in town—but nothing resulted in the sea change we needed. R. spent more and more time away from the house, taking the truck we shared and visiting the woodshop or barn where the local men spent their days, downing cans of watery beer and talking about spring fishing or ice fishing, their horseshoe league, their dilapidated cars, their pole barn project, hunting. He bought his first gun. Then another.

When we moved to the country, R. fit in so well that I stopped recognizing him. He has a feral quality that always made the city a bit difficult for him—he couldn't hold a normal job because he couldn't (or wouldn't) bear to show up at the same place day after day or be told what to do. He spent his days painting. He couldn't read menus, couldn't keep track of bills, and his phone was always getting disconnected. He slept on the floor of his painting studio, bathed in his sink, traded paintings when he was short on rent, boiled hotdogs for dinner in his percolator one night and went to a five-star restaurant with his art collectors the next. He allowed other people to buy him shoes and winter coats, stole toilet paper from public restrooms, threw space heaters across the room when angry. There was a wildness to him, and this was one of the reasons I was so attracted to him when we first met; he was like a tiger prowling the city streets, beautiful, untamed, out of place, and different from anyone I'd met before.

In the country, the other men—mostly a band of similarly feral men living alone and scraping by in rented, rusted single-wide trailers tucked away in the hills—recognized him as their own, accepted him, brought him into their fold. Being an artist was something they tolerated (read: lots of gay jokes), whereas in the city it was the reason people put up with his moods and eccentricities. His wildness became compounded, and although he still painted, it didn't define him as much. His studio in our old dairy barn was as full of power tools and chop saws and two-by-fours as it was paint and canvas. Not having a traditional job or regular income, patching things on the house himself, day-drinking, shooting guns, burning garbage, punching holes into the wall and then smoothing spackle over them with a putty knife gripped in the same tight fist, wearing the same outfit five days in a row—this was all status quo in the hills. After a while, I stopped recognizing him.

❧

Many of our friends who lived in the city and had weekend or summer houses in the country had warned us about making the move full-time. As I looked around, I realized there were many other couples who'd tried the same thing. Nina and Erik had moved up to their country house after the birth of their second child so she could write full-time. Erik planned to work as a carpenter, but quickly realized what felt like "experience" in the city just held him on par with everyone else, since the locals here grow up fixing everything themselves. They stuck it out for a year and even started their son in the local public school, but returned to living mostly in Manhattan in less than a year. "Thank God we kept our lease in New York," Nina told me over paella in her Washington Heights apartment. "Otherwise, I guarantee we'd be divorced right now."

There were our friends Paul and Bill, whose gorgeous house I'd written about for a magazine and whose home decor shop was one of the most successful stores in town. But they hadn't quite moved completely either; like Nina and Erik, they also still kept a small apartment in the city and they both returned to the city periodically for consulting jobs for weeks at a time. Micki and Graham had two kids and a rambling old Victorian, but Graham drove the daily three-hour commute to Manhattan to work as a lighting designer on Broadway most of the year, staying over at his mother-in-law's apartment when it was too late or snowy to make the drive home.

There were many artists in the hills, but most of them were women, and most had corporate partners. One such couple, an artist and an advertising executive, also split their time between rural Pennsylvania and Manhattan, like us, though the wife had moved up to the house full-time and only the husband went back regularly to the city for work. She painted large canvases full of birds and lizards, and, from what I knew of her, she chose the peace of isolation and the opportunity to live within the natural world over the city and constant presence of her husband. I was hoping to see how she was faring.

They are both tall and spindly, and in their very small car they look folded up, like a sheet of ticket stubs, when they drive around town. They were standing outside of their small A-frame house tending to the barbeque when we pulled up in our truck. They left the chicken and steak and sausages on the grill and took us up the rickety front steps and into their home, which was like a little blue birdhouse perched on a cliff. Bits of ribbon and feathers were tucked into wooden slats that made up the kitchen ceiling. The four of us stood out on a small deck overlooking their pond and watched hummingbirds dart around some flowering bushes.

"Once, I came home and a hummingbird was stuck in the screen door," the wife said. She was from South Africa and her c's came out like g's, her r's nonexistent. "His beak was like a little dart through the netting. I plucked him out and he just shoomed away." She fluttered her long fingers in the direction of the pond.

We sat on the deck picking apart a cluster of delicate, tart table grapes and grazing on a cheese plate while the meat smoked on the grill. The wife identified different flowers in her garden for us, and when we turned one way we noticed a doe close by, munching on a bush. Her tawny down looked soft and shiny in the light, and she stared up at us for a moment with her dark black eyes.

"Uch. I hate them! They are teak boxes!" The wife cursed at the deer, with a vehemence that surprised me.

"Teak boxes?" R. asked.

"Tick boxes," her husband translated.

"They're the one animal I could imagine shooting," she said.

Her certainty surprised me. I imagined this woman standing on her porch, lining up the shot, pulling the trigger. The deer looked placidly in our direction, jaw moving mechanically. The wife stomped her foot, feigning a lunge toward the animal, and she took off running, tail lifted in a white flag salute.

There is a brutality to the country, and to part-time country houses turned full-time residences. There is so much that you miss when you click on your alarm and drive down the road back to your real life elsewhere. You can choose to miss the piles of snow, the icy roads, the constant blackouts from electric lines down from wind or trees, the smells when something dies in your wall, the scorching summer days where the heat makes little waves dance on the metal roof. You have somewhere else to go. But when the place where you hide from the real world *becomes* your real world, you suddenly realize you have nowhere else to go.

Then there is the way the paint blisters on the house in the sun, the sudden stink of a septic system revolting under the strain of regular use, the unrelenting smell of dank earth emanating from the dirt basement. There are the swarms of ladybugs coating the walls in masses too thick to be sucked up by the vacuum; the heavy orbs of carpenter bees at work on the front porch; fleets of angry sleek-bodied wasps hiding in the folds of the unopened patio umbrella and the soffits of the poorly executed metal roof, buzzing behind the thin drywall inside the house. A dairy farmer from down the road stands in our three-bay English barn and pokes at the piles of sawdust created by the powder post beetles boring holes into the beams and says, "Everything's gotta have a place to live, I guess." Yes, but if this place belongs to them, what belongs to me?

Then, of course, there are the myriad varmints that are tolerable on the outside, but demand to come inside the house: the mice and the rats, the snakes and the bats, the blind felt-soft opossum babies stuck to the glue traps in the kitchen with their small searching snouts quivering. And there is the jewel-blue Eastern bluebird I scoop out of the cinders in the belly of the wood-burning stove one summer morning, who got trapped in the stovepipe trying to start a nest and couldn't get back out. Not everyone can make it out here in the wild, not even those who are wild to begin with.

In the middle of my second pregnancy, early contractions sentenced me to bedrest. A joke to any mother with a toddler, this prescription felt particularly laughable since a caving-in floor required major kitchen construction at the same time. Even boiling a simple pot of water meant going outside and sparking up the grill. The carpenter we'd hired had disappeared after a few days, stopped answering calls. He showed up a week later, chagrined, still reeking of alcohol, the tailgate smashed off the back of his pickup truck. A few days later he was gone again on another bender, most of the kitchen still an empty hull, tarped in blue.

One particularly hot summer afternoon during this period, R. and I started to snipe at one another. I was cranky, didn't feel well, was anxious about the pregnancy and the kitchen, itchy from being forced to stick close to home. R. was annoyed: at the carpenter, at his bank account, at me. We fought first in fierce whispers so as not to wake our son napping upstairs, but the fight soon began to boil over.

I thought about putting on my tall blue rain boots and walking out the door, the way I used to when I needed to escape these swells during my first pregnancy, just walk the hills or dirt roads until night fell. If I stayed out long enough, by the time I got home he'd be in front of the easel or patching the hole he'd made in the wall or making dinner, the storm finished. But my child was sleeping upstairs, and R. was blocking the door, and by the time I saw the darkness move across his brow and realized what this argument was turning into it was too late.

At one point during the fight, he retrieved his gun and stood in front of me, holding it. In that moment, I didn't know his intention: Shoot up the damn blue tarp? Find the missing handyman? If he told me, I could no longer hear anything anyway; as soon as I saw the hard black metal wave in the air, all sound was swallowed up in a vacuum of terror. Electric tethers shot out from my chest, pulsing out to my son sleeping above us and the small body tucked inside my stomach. I froze like a spider on a web. I calculated the thinness of the floorboards above my head, the membrane of flesh that acted as a screen between my new baby and the entire hard, ugly world.

I became still. I am a stone, I told myself. When he saw I had no fight left in me, he walked out, tearing down the driveway in our only vehicle.

I was kneeling now, and it took a while to remember how to

breathe. My belly had tightened into a compact ball against my ribs, the contraction holding me in its grip, and I started counting out of habit. *One Mississippi. Two Mississippi.* As the cloud of dust from the dirt driveway settled over the grass like low fog, sound slowly returned, first birds, then crickets.

I scanned the room for my blue rain boots, but then I heard my toddler shift in his bed upstairs, the tether between us no longer urgently electric but the pull just as strong. I knew his little legs couldn't walk as far as we needed, for as long as we needed. And so instead of walking out the door that day, I collected all the bullets I could find in the house and tucked them high up on a far shelf behind our beach towels in the laundry room and then climbed the stairs slowly, one hand cupping my belly. I slid into bed next to my still-sleeping son. We cradled each other and I matched my breathing to his as I watched the shadows shift across the room, until all that was left of the fight was birdsong and brown dust.

In her poem "Once the World Was Perfect," Joy Harjo writes:

> *And once Doubt ruptured the web,*
> *All manner of demon thoughts*
> *Jumped through—*
> *We destroyed the world we had been given.*

I didn't leave that day. Or the next. Or the day after that one. But something had ruptured. And though I could still rely on bird-

song, on poetry, on the softness of the skin behind my son's buttercup ear, the rest of the world had been permanently knocked
off its axis.

❧

In northeast Pennsylvania, schoolchildren get the first day of deer
hunting season off instead of Martin Luther King Jr.'s birthday.
The men who grew up in these hills tell stories about bringing
their guns on the school bus, for ROTC and rifle club. The opening
of hunting season is treated like a holiday, and weekenders aren't
included. For the first few years, the closest I came to a hunting
party was an open bed of a pickup truck full of ten or twelve men
decked out in full camouflage, large black guns slung against their
shoulders. They usually head out in the early morning, when even
lovely days are still cold and wet, and many wear black or orange
ski masks pulled down on their faces. Only their voices or a familiar wave will reveal them as neighbors. Once we moved here full-
time, it wasn't long before the men knocked on the door and asked
R. to join the push.

A deer push is exactly what it sounds like; at the end of the
season, the men fan out in a line across a swath of forest and, with
whoops and claps and the clear tang of their own musk, they drive
the remaining deer toward another group of men waiting with
guns. Within the surrounding 600 acres or so, there are only a
handful of homes, including two single-wide trailers, two ranch
homes, and one other farmhouse like ours dating back to the
1860s. Our property looks out onto craggy shelves of bluestone,
dark and dense hemlock forests, and stands of tall, skinny poplar

trees whose round golden leaves shimmer in the wind. Our hill is a thruway for animals heading toward the swamp for a drink. Which means our house is also a great place to shoot animals heading toward the swamp for a drink and a perfect place for a push.

Although we posted No Hunting signs when we bought the house, the locals continued to stroll up our long dirt driveway during deer season, carrying wooden sawhorse-like contraptions, small seats that they pound into trees, front-row balcony seats from which they scan the forest. For years, when the house sat abandoned in the 1970s and 1980s, men would sit in rocking chairs and lawn chairs on the porch, or prop themselves up on the wooden banister, one leg on the beer cooler, and pick off the deer as they crashed through the tangle of rose hips and thorny crabapple trees that mark the edge of our property.

One morning, as I mashed banana for our new baby's breakfast, our friend James showed up on the porch before the coffee finished brewing. His day-glo orange hat and vest were visible through the blinds, and when R. opened the door I could see his camouflage jumpsuit and the strap of his rifle slung over his shoulder like a purse. It was the last Saturday of deer season, and they always ran the push on this morning—everyone who'd already bagged an animal would form a line and spread out, slowly creeping through the woods for miles to flush any deer left out of the swamp and over to a line of men who hadn't shot their catch yet that season.

R. pulled his orange hat and gloves on and grabbed his rifle, following James to the line of trees just beyond the garden. I watched them fade into the forest.

Not long after, I stood in the kitchen as sounds from a horror movie track echoed across the landscape: sharp whoops and high-pitched shrieks, catcalls and curses. The men were invisible in the forest and swamp, but their sound surrounded us. Every so often I would spy a flash of orange or yellow. Every time I passed a window, I looked out into the emptiness. The children piled blocks, we read and we slept. We stayed inside. Then a gun would crack close by, and the whoops would grow louder, like coyotes after a kill.

Hours passed. I kept looking out into the woods, searching for human forms. I felt blind and on show at the same time, like being on stage for a concert and knowing the audience is there but not being able to see past the glare of the stagelights. I stood at the window, feeling unmoored, unsure of my place within this landscape; the property belonged to the hunters, the house belonged to wasps, the powder post beetles, the mice and snakes and voles. All of it belonged to the bank. In the process of trying to fit into this new life, in order to survive in this place, a part of me floated off over the hills, just another bit of loose summer hay on the wind. I wasn't sure how to get it back, but I cupped my baby's soft-socked foot in my palm like a talisman.

After a while I drew the blinds, sealing the kids and myself inside. Alone, just the three of us, closed off from the men and the landscape outside, we could have been in any living room, anywhere.

Still Life 2: The Country

THERE IS THE FATHER at the easel. There is the mother at the kitchen sink. There are the children in the field, in the tire swing, in the raspberry tangles, hands full of mud, of baking flour, of wildflowers.

The outside never shuts off. Soundtrack: The frog opera. Hysterical turkeys. The hard huffs of deer in the woods, the original pranayama. The bobcats yowling, coyotes crying, the barn swallows chattering overhead. The clomp of boots on the porch, the plaintive yawn of a screen door's springs. The desperate blinks of fireflies, *lookatmelookatmelookatme!*

The sheer quantity of green is like an assault. Spring explodes in new green and sap green and leaf green, *terre verte*. Summer is parched and the greens are sucked dry, crumbling into ochres and golds. Autumn is swamp green, heavy, viridian and verona. Winter goes slick with glassy jadeite, a mix of cobalt and underwater grey, rare green earth. Through it all, buzzards and hawks make mars-black swirls in the sky, terrifying in their slowness.

We are careless. We kill deer with our vehicles, grass with our urine, bees with insecticide. We break lawn mowers and tractors and dryers, sump pumps and generators and swings. We break water pipes, windows, walls with fists. We break promises, confidences, each other's hearts. The day after a surprise storm I come upon a contractor bucket filled with a few inches of rainwater. There is a bird floating perfectly at the top, flat, with a wing extended, chromatic black like a Kerry James Marshall painting, no eyes, no features, just silhouette. When I look into the water I am startled; for a moment, the bucket is a wishing well, the dead bird my reflection, my prophecy.

The hills are filled mostly with men, but there are a few women. Red-headed Peg hails from Jersey, tends her donkeys and horses with day-glo, rhinestoned nails on the property next to ours. She calls her ex-husband "My Asshole." When she spurns the affections of a neighbor who tries wooing her with a litter of blocky-headed English Labradors and country rides in a fumy four-by-four Gator, he sets up an AR-15 on his front porch and squeezes off shots in her direction, staccato valentines. The rat-tat-tat becomes part of our soundtrack; when the shots puncture the night, waking us in our bed, we jolt, then relax. "John's just shooting at Peg again," one or the other would say, before rolling over and returning to sleep.

The slow dance of tall trees in the wind. The black lace of leaves against a moon-bright night sky. The pulsating *yesyesyes, nonono* of the nighttime katydid mating call, wings rubbing in desperate stridulations. The cold slap of the first raindrops of a summer storm. The sky airless and grey, like a weathered padlock.

This is love in the country.

The Bookshop: A Love Story

I think here I will leave you. It has come to seem
there is no perfect ending. Indeed, there are
infinite endings. Or perhaps, once one begins,
there are only endings.

—LOUISE GLÜCK, "FAITHFUL AND VIRTUOUS NIGHT"

HONESDALE, PA, WAS ORIGINALLY BUILT as an old railroad town in the 1830s. The proud birthplace of the Delaware and Hudson Gravity Railroad, Honesdale had declined into a run-down rural has-been by the early 2000s. The town continued to cling to its railroad past; the dormant tracks still cut behind Main Street and there was a small museum dedicated to the Stourbridge Lion, the first steam locomotive to operate in the United States. Toy trains tooted and circled on a track above the heads of customers at the Townhouse Diner and the owner of the Whistlestop Café outfitted his staff and himself in blue-and-white conductor's stripes under their aprons. He even wore the little cap.

The town's two commercial anchors stood only a few doors away from one another, though they serviced a polar-opposite clientele. Northeast Firearms (motto: The 2nd Amendment Starts

Here!) boasted a heavy black fire door with gold hand-painted lettering above, while Nature's Grace deli served alfalfa and homemade hummus pitas to the crunchy hippie holdovers left scattered in the countryside after a local yoga cult went bust in the 1970s. The rest of Main Street had the usual insurance companies, pubs, and banks, but mostly the commercial picture was bleak. Half the storefronts were empty, and many were home to transient shops, opened by people with no experience and little money—instead of purchasing signs for their storefronts, new business owners often wrote their shop name in soap on the windows. When they went out of business, the next shop owner simply washed and repeated.

The town had been named after Philip Hone, a one-term mayor of New York City and president of the Delaware and Hudson Canal Company, though he was said to have only visited his namesake town once. One of the century's most prolific diarists, Hone said surprisingly little about the town named after him in his daily musings. His life mostly centered around Manhattan, where he was known as a cultural ambassador who held salons, inviting artists and writers and astronomers to join him for dinner in his downtown home at 1 Great Jones Street, just a few doors from the painting studio we lived in after our Brooklyn days until we moved to Pennsylvania full-time. I enjoyed standing in front of his opulent building on the corner of Broadway, now a GNC, his diaries (both volumes) tucked into my tote bag, amused at the wildness of sharing a Manhattan block address with the namesake of our rural town.

In truth, although it is three hours away, much of the area surrounding Honesdale remains rooted in New York City to this day. While the area still turned on full-timers, when the farms died out in the 1970s the old homesteads were divided up into subdivisions or sold as bucolic second-home spots, like ours. This second-home market kept what was left of Main Street afloat for the summer months.

Our friends Bill and Paul had spent years as part-timers, splitting their time between Manhattan and northeast Pennsylvania, and knew what that market could sustain. When they moved to the area full-time, they bought two buildings on Main Street and created a kind of luxury oasis in the desert of the town's dried-up commercial strip. Instead of painting their shop's name on the window in soap, they worked on the properties for nearly a full year before opening.

I'd initially met Paul when my editor at a design magazine assigned me a story about a passive solar house just fifteen minutes from my own farmhouse. Paul is woodsy and strong, at home in bib overalls with sawdust shavings in his dark hair. He could be seen most mornings that year carrying a ladder in primer-encrusted hands or groping for the rectangular pencil tucked behind his ear. Inside, Bill was the shop's main proprietor. Bill is the light to Paul's dark; the first time I visited their home for the magazine article, Bill rounded the corner in cargo shorts and a tee. He was tall and lithe and tan, sunshine making a luminescent halo of blond curls out of his hair. I mistook him for the pool boy.

Turns out, my pool boy was a Yale-trained graphic designer. He'd worked as a creative director at his own agency in the city and continued to design coffee table books for museums and other high-profile clients after moving out to the country. Paul and Bill named the store Milkweed, after the ever-present pods that laced our hills.

Where others saw certain death, Bill and Paul saw opportunity. After a successful opening season, the couple bought the building next door. Three additional storefronts were carved out and rented: a clothing shop, a bakery, and a garden shop. But after the second summer, there was turnover. The baker became a grandmother and wanted to spend more time at home, the gardener had a second child, one of the young clothing store co-owners was diagnosed with cancer. Winter was bleak for Main Street shops in the best of times, and when all three decided to call it quits, Bill took over the largest space and extended his shop into women's clothing. That left two more spaces.

We talked about these open spaces with Bill and Paul at a dinner party one autumn night. Our hosts, Jim and Laura, were artists hiding out in the woods nearby, living in a family-owned cottage and planning their next move. Jim painted bright Caribbean scenes, often collaged with words or photographs, while Laura's paintings were like stained glass set to jazz. They looked a bit like their work; Jim was serious and methodical, an engineer's precision in his movement and dress. Laura was all warmth and laughter, flowing blond hair and bright blue eyes, always humming or fussing or fixing.

Their stone cottage sat on a lake, and they'd already taped their windows with plastic against the gusts of wind that sluiced across the water and through their tiny living room. I joggled the baby and sipped some wine while my older son sat on the couch, watching a Thomas the Train video and chewing his sock. R. was relaxed and expansive next to me, warmed by the wine and excited to be surrounded by real artists and real art talk.

We'd hit that point in our marriage where the chilled distance we often cultivated in the isolation of our home thawed in public. In front of others, we slipped into a version of our former selves, pouring wine for one another, actually listening if the other was addressing the group. Maybe even smiling for real at something the other said. These two couples were older than us, childless, were partners in ways we could no longer imagine. But for the night, it felt good to be reminded of what was once between us, what might be again, if we could only peel back the layers of resentment that clogged our mouths and cottoned our days together in the privacy of our home.

As we munched on Laura's homemade spring rolls, talking about the new Jiro Ono documentary and the next submission date for art portfolios at White Columns, Bill and Paul subtly tried to convince our hosts to open a restaurant at the shops. They'd run a restaurant in the islands, wouldn't they like to do so again? But Jim deflected, posing the question to the table instead: If you could open any kind of shop, what would it be?

I'd been only half-participating in the conversation up till this point, trying to steal bites of food without dropping them on the baby's head and coaxing my older son to eat something other than bread. But my response was instantaneous. A bookshop, I blurted out, not even aware that I'd had the answer so close to the surface.

"Could you make any money with that?" asked someone at the table, someone who clearly had more business acumen than me (that is to say, any). I didn't know. I'd grown up in a blue-collar town with no Main Street, and the library had been like my second home. I couldn't imagine what a bookstore in town would've been like for me. Since we'd given up our foothold in the city my kids would be growing up in a town without a bookshop, too, since the closest independent was Woodstock's lovely Golden Notebook, ninety-nine back-road miles away (or 121 miles by highway; faster, but with a toll). As the baby pinched my shoulder and yowled for more milk, mostly I fantasized about how quiet a bookshop would be, and how wonderful it would feel to be alone in a room of books of my choosing. I settled into my daydream and let the conversation pass by me.

R. began brainstorming about making an artist's print shop or a kind of print collective, connecting both of the available spaces and moving his giant etching press out of our barn and into the shop for classes and studio use. He had been thinking about a series of woodcut prints based on the flora and fauna surrounding the farmhouse, and this seemed like an opportunity to exhibit the work. We could host art shows, he said. Maybe put a few books along one wall. This was an eternal fight in our house: he argued that walls were for paintings, while my perfect home would be filled floor to ceiling with bookshelves.

In the city, his painting studio was often a place where our creative lives converged. For years, I hosted the KGB Nonfiction Reading Series on Tuesday nights, and some evenings I'd lead the writers and friends the few blocks back to the studio on Great Jones Street for more drinks, sitting among the paintings, talking and drinking with R. into the early morning. I like to think Philip

Hone would have approved. The idea of recreating something like that in the country intrigued me.

I was surprised at his suggestion of a print collective, though. We'd lost a number of friends after another dinner party years earlier when, surrounded by the leaders of the Wayne County Arts Alliance who were kindly trying to invite R. into the organization, he declared *I've always believed the group diminishes the individual.* Maybe living out here full-time made him reevaluate the value of an artist community? I imagined a lively working space, with classes and workshops and book clubs, just like the old days in the Great Jones studio, a mix of writing and art, creatives and conversation. Perhaps it could be a joint venture, I suggested to the table. A celebration of works on paper: books *and* prints? But then the main course was set out and I returned to observing and listening, enjoying the warmth of the baby on my chest, the wine in my cheeks.

The talk was fun, but that was it. We had no money, a new baby, and a falling-down farmhouse that had warped walls, a bathroom floor that threatened to cave in at any moment, and a hundred unfinished projects littering the rambling rooms, from bare bulbs poking out of the ceiling in the baby's room to half-built cupboards above the laundry machines. We relied on my freelancing and adjunct salary and R.'s painting sales to pay our mortgage and bills. And we still owed his parents the money for the new roof on the painting studio and mine for a loan to rebuild the kitchen. We were in no position to start a business.

Also, neither of us was any good at business. Anything to do with finances sent R. into a frenzy—we couldn't talk about a monthly home budget, so how would we organize an LLC? He'd always been what we politely called moody. Even the first year we dated, I'd taken to marking my wall calendar with little red marks for "rage." I'd try to chart these shifts like a menstrual cycle, diagnose their cause: low blood sugar? drinking? his bank account? There were some things that were certain to set him off, like driving or bills or forms, but mostly the lows were baffling, something I'd taken to riding out, whether that meant leaving the room when he started to fume or demanding to be let out of the car under the Williamsburg Bridge one night so I could walk home alone. Then, just as quickly as it began, the anger would depart, in twenty minutes or twenty hours, and he'd be his other self, the one at the dinner table this evening, charming and gregarious. His moods had returned to a kind of numb normalcy since our second son's birth, but lately, I could feel the darkness creeping back in along the edges.

I stared into his face over dinner, his wide-breaking smile so easy and open with the other guests. His black hair shone in the candlelight and I noticed how he crossed his ankles beneath his chair in his way, his body leaning forward over his plate. In company, we'd taken to performing, moving in a careful dance around one another, laughing as loudly as everyone else. But if someone watched closely, they would notice that we never looked at one another, never touched outside what might be required to pass along a coat or a child's toy.

Perhaps, I considered, if we partnered in a shop it would remind us of how good we used to be together. It might be like riding a bike, putting our feet on the pedals and remembering what it was like to be in sync, trick us into a momentum that might take us up and over what looked like a dark storm threatening on the horizon. We'd been married for six years at that point, together for ten. What had been between us must be stored in muscle memory. Maybe we could start pedaling and simply ride straight into a new land entirely, where we might remember how to love one another again.

By the end of the night as we drove home, I was repeating numbers in my mind: *250 dollars a month, 250 square feet*. The boys fell asleep in their car seats after only a few moments on the washboard roads, and one of them was snoring softly. As I stared out the window, I imagined greeting the boys from behind a counter piled with books as they walked into the shop after school, slinging their bookbags off their backs as they sat down in a reading corner to tell me about their day. *250 dollars a month, 250 square feet*. I imagined R. at work pulling prints from his press in the corner, giving classes and finding community and purpose in a local artist collective. *250 dollars a month, 250 square feet*. I repeated these numbers to myself like a question, as though I were just turning them around in my mind, as though I hadn't already made a decision. We were still miles from home, just a small firefly of light bouncing along the dark dirt roads between the stone cottage and our farmhouse, but I could already smell the acrid scent of new-book pulp, hear the satisfying crack of a paperback cover.

Six weeks later, the bookshop opened its doors.

The first time I sliced open a box of books in my new bookshop, I breathed in deeply. The pulpy starch of the paper caught in the back of my throat, while the faint chemical sting of the new ink burned high in my nostrils. I imagined a world where this smell was a constant in my life and smiled to myself.

When you live in the countryside, "new book" smell is scarce. In rural Pennsylvania, used books abound in antique and thrift shops, library and church sales. Our house reeked of them; my bookshelves were full of old books soaked with the funk of other people's sweat and smoke, speckled with grey mold, full of crumbs and marginalia. New books are an expensive novelty; Amazon and e-readers are the closest you can get. In the city, I took for granted that in most places I lived I had a neighborhood bookstore, and I never had to walk more than a few blocks to get my fix.

At various times I'd been a regular at Housing Works, the Strand, McNally Jackson (when it was McNally Robinson), Book Culture (when it was Labyrinth), BookCourt (before it closed). I traveled to get to other favorites like 192 Books and Greenlight, but never more than one or two chapter-lengths on a subway train. Years out from living in the city, I hadn't realized how much I missed that smell. I didn't understand how much I'd taken bookshops for granted. And suddenly, now, I was standing in my own.

My younger son, almost a year old, shifted on the green chaise lounge in the corner. He was napping while I set up the store, a few days before opening. I'd kangarooed him in the baby carrier as I readied the room until he fell asleep, and then I laid him out to rest on the chaise, unhooking the carrier from my waist and shrugging my shoulders out without waking him. He lay there now, brow furrowed, lips pursing as he nursed from a phantom breast in his dream, chin jutting out in defiant pleasure. I calculated the length of his typical nap and held this against the work that still needed to be done, mentally building a list of things I would be able to do while holding him and things I needed to do while untethered.

As I calculated, the winter light filtered in softly through the old window panes. The shelves stood empty, waiting to be filled. Folded paper trees lined one table, waiting to be hung, an offering from R., homemade holiday decorations. Aside from the tall counter borrowed from the shop's landlords, the furniture was mostly pulled from our barn: two display tables, a high stool behind the counter, the weird green velvet chaise we'd bought years ago from a friend in Williamsburg who'd lost her job as a fashion publicist and was selling some things to make rent. It astounded me that all we needed to make a bookshop was some furniture, some books, and a room in which to put them.

In the year before we opened the shop, I'd stopped wearing makeup or coloring my hair, allowed R. to cut it instead of going all the way to town to the hairdresser. I wore only clothes that had elastic at the waist and shirts that could be easily pulled down or lifted for nursing. I stopped reading.

I hadn't made many friends yet and wasn't certain how to go about fostering relationships out here. I tried to make plans with the wife of our real estate lawyer; she was a kindergarten teacher with two children similar ages to mine and she'd seemed friendly enough when we chatted at the farmer's market on the weekends. I dialed her number and asked if she might want to get together for a coffee one day and I felt her voice tighten before she even spoke. "I take a twenty-minute walk with the double carriage every morning at seven o'clock sharp," she snipped. "You're welcome to join me any day of the week." I thanked her and told her I'd get back to her, knowing I'd never be able to ready myself and my children early enough to make the forty-minute drive to her house just outside town—not that she really wanted me to, anyway.

I didn't miss the city, but I missed who I'd been there on those bright streets, bag heavy with books slung over my shoulder, sure-footed and full of direction and purpose. My days had become a blur of softness; blending soft bananas and avocados into baby food, folding soft cotton burp towels over my shoulder, hands kneading soft toddler thighs or running through soft baby hair, my own body plump and unrecognizable without its intention and tautness.

Even my movements became a slow churn, repeated each day. Baby's room, toddler's room, kitchen. Bathroom, living room, kitchen. Baby's room, toddler's room, bathroom. Kitchen, living room, porch. I lived in three-hour spurts, marked by naps and feeding schedules. I took long walks down the driveway with my older son as he practiced walking. We threw rocks into the little stream, went mushroom hunting after rain, all with the baby strapped to my chest, nursing, sleeping, nursing, sleeping. That whole year felt like one very long day. We sang songs, held hands, held buttercups under one another's chins. But still there was an unquantifiable ache that ran beneath even the sweetest moments.

It had only recently occurred to me that our ecosystem was only made up of three when there should have been four. Every so often, from our perches in the kitchen or snuggled on the couch, we would hear the painting studio's screen door strain open and then slam, followed a few moments later by a clomp of boots coming up the steps of the porch. Our heads would swing to the front door, like dogs. Tense. Waiting.

I hadn't grown up wanting children, hadn't dreamed of being a mother or a wife or having a family. When my children were born, a love flamed inside me that I hadn't known was possible. Still, I would never be a natural caretaker. An only child, I was not comfortable in the company of small children, but now they were my only companions. We became a secret constellation, moving together as one. I was not a cook, but I cooked. I was not a mother, but I mothered. I was not a wife, but I wifed. I felt like a broken compass needle, spinning and searching for purchase.

Meanwhile, R. had turned away from us. It was natural after children, some friends told me. But if I were honest, it wasn't that he turned away, really. He just hadn't turned toward us. In pregnancy and then with motherhood, my life was uprooted, unrecognizable. R.'s stayed mostly the same. He was frustrated that I had less time to spend on him, but he still spent most of his time painting, and his body remained his own, as did his clothes, his sleep schedule. When he worked, I watched the children. When I had to work, he reasoned that I should get a babysitter.

I made my own baby food, taught our toddler sign language, read up on preschool options and vaccinations. When I would talk about these things, or about my students, or about the way my writing was starting to feel like something I used to do, his eyes would find the clock or his feet would move restlessly under the table. Mostly, it felt like he was passing the time until he could get back to his easel. This wasn't a new feeling, but I'd never needed his partnership the way I needed it now.

In the weeks before we opened the bookshop, I could feel R.'s interest spark. He paid attention during our conversations, stayed at the dinner table longer. He was not very interested in learning how to build an e-commerce site or keep accounting records, but he liked the idea of selling prints, of hosting art openings. He had no interest in building a gallery or showing anyone else's work— just his. But he had the energy he's always gotten right before a big opening, the energy of possibility, of hope.

Of course, I knew too well that the elation of opening night was always followed by a cliff dive of emotion. No matter the crowd or sales, it never measured up to his hopes, or what he thought his work deserved. These were simple equations; even my toddler grasped that what went up must come down. Still, I ignored that portion of the pattern, even though part of me must have known it would come; it had been so long since I'd seen that kind of fire in him, and I wanted to help sustain it.

It was clear to me through my midnight calculations and YouTube-trained business plan drafting that this venture would not make us much, if any, money. We wouldn't be able to take salaries for at least three years, every dollar pouring back into the store. But, like Bill and Paul, and Jim and Laura, and so many of our friends in the country, we'd become masters of improvisation, juggling multiple side hustles that we would continue while we shared the shop hours, chose the books together, hung the prints together, maintained the website together. There would be sacrifices, but we would make them as a team.

At each step of our relationship, we'd seemed to get thrown off-course. We'd been in New York the day of the World Trade Center attacks and that morning had grafted us to one another. Early in our relationship, he'd had two heart attacks, one shortly before our wedding and another a few months after, just as we bought the farmhouse. We'd had to adjust our expectations and plans. We put off the honeymoon, the house renovations, travel. Then the kids came. The past ten years seemed to just happen *to* us. But this shop—this was a fresh start, something we could plan and build together, with intention.

Even though every atom in my body told me opening a shop would be an economic failure, I'd hoped it would save us. I could stand a failed business; I didn't think I'd survive a failed marriage. And so, I kept pumping the bellows, trying to keep the fire between us burning.

We opened in winter, just before the holiday rush. When I first walked into the 250-square-foot room, I was disappointed. But where I saw one too-small window, not enough shelving, and some floorboards that needed a good scrub, he saw a giant blue vase in the corner with an apple blossom branch, a corner nook that would make a perfect checkout desk. As an opening gift, he cut out strings of red paper birds to hang from the shop's ceiling in a Valentine homage to Chaucer's "The Parliament of Fowls."

The first few weeks running the bookshop were hectic and

exciting. Some days, R. would sit at the counter, with a sketchbook and charcoal to keep him entertained. On most days, though, I'd drop my older son at preschool in the church basement and bring my younger with me to the shop, nursing in a corner between customers. On a few blissful days, I'd leave him with a sitter.

I was amazed at what a few hours away from my children could do for my desire to be nearer to them. I found enjoyment and color spilling back into the many hours I spent together with the children, especially when it meant I was coming home to them after being at the bookshop, a place where I was able to remember who I had been, who I might still be. The stillness of the shop was a gift. It felt like years since I was able to sit and read, much less write. Feeling a sudden burst of ambition, I pitched a monthly column to *The Paris Review* about running a rural bookshop, and they accepted. Armed with a deadline and paycheck, I felt more forthright in claiming my time.

All the same, within that first month I could feel R.'s interest in the shop waning. He'd determined the space was too small to hold his printing press; his idea for a collective with classes dwindled into a single wall showcasing his framed prints. Although we'd initially planned to split the hours behind the counter, R. quickly decided his time was better spent in the studio. In those cold months, the bookshop had fifteen customers on a very busy day. Most of the time, the only person in the room was simply the person behind the desk.

I pushed R. to stick with the plan at first. But I soon noticed inaccuracies in our handwritten receipt book. Sometimes the Pennsylvania sales tax would be rounded down to five, or up to ten percent. Sometimes it wouldn't be there at all. When I asked him about it, he waved with annoyance. *What's the big deal?* I explained to him that as an LLC we had to keep careful accounting of our sales, that we would owe that money to the state, so if we didn't collect it, that cash would have to come out of our profits. I could see him stop listening halfway through my lecture.

When he'd first arrived in New York, he'd tried to hold down jobs working as a set designer or art handler, but inevitably, he wouldn't pay attention to a start time, or would paint into the night and forget to set his alarm. With a pang, I realized the bookshop would be no different. I eventually agreed it might be best for everyone if I just sat the shop most days.

In our marriage, R.'s role was always to tend to the beauty, to dream up ideas; it was only after he conjured the possibility of what a bookshop in this space could look and feel like that I could imagine it, too. In the house, he covered the walls with grids of paintings, the tables with bouquets of wildflowers in jelly jars, always knew how to sniff out and refinish the best side table or old chair from the barns of antiques in the hills. As an artist, he created masterful still lifes everywhere he went, little narratives of hopeful beginnings. He wasn't as good with the follow-through, however.

Back in the city, when we first started dreaming about owning a house, we'd bought a little blue spiral notebook, the kind that fits in a pocket. We decided we'd start a bank account and put ten percent of every painting sale and every article we sold into that account. We called it our ten percent fund. His paintings went for more money than my articles, but I sold mine more often. The little notebook now sat on my bookshelf at the farmhouse. At home, after work one day, I flipped through it. The first entry was in R.'s hand, for $120. The next few were mine, at varying amounts between $25 and $50. There is another one of R.'s, for $75, but then the next twelve entries are all mine. The rest of the notebook is empty. It wasn't that he hadn't sold more paintings; the upkeep of the ten percent fund just wasn't as alluring as the idea itself. Back then, it took me about six months before I got the message. This time, it only took a few weeks.

Winter began to wane, and one day, after packing up to leave and reaching for the light switch behind the desk, I looked in the corner below the little window and was stunned—a few weeks earlier, my friend Katharine, who used to run the gardening shop in this space, had given me a cutting from a curly willow tree on her farm to brighten the place up and now, impossibly, the branches had bent toward the window and at the tip of each slender stalk was a burst of green. There wasn't even any water in the vase. And yet, the cutting found the light and was trying to bloom.

Maybe, if we could make it through winter, we had hope.

I began cultivating a group of regulars. The small size of the shop quickly colored interactions with a surprising intimacy. The space took the air of a confessional, with people pulling up a chair and sharing things across the desk they never would have otherwise. The woman at a neighboring shop told me about her son's heart ailment, the time her boyfriend wrapped his hands around her throat so hard he left bruises. An artist talked about his debilitating depression, the woman he loved long ago who'd left him, how it still gutted him every morning when he realized she was gone.

One woman with long wispy grey hair and unsteady legs would visit every week. She used to run writing workshops, was a writer herself, and loved to debate psychology and literature. She would come in and ask for my seat behind the desk so she could rest, and then, usually, stay an hour or more. Sometimes I resented her taking up part of my day, especially if the shop was quiet and I was trying to write. *This is the only time I have when I don't have to take care of other people*, I wanted to shout. But then a week would go by without her and I would worry—did she have a fall? Was she stuck in her house, driveway unplowed? She brought in a meticulously hand-drawn map of my astrology chart one afternoon, told me her daughter and grandchildren wanted her to move in with them in Pittsburgh, but that she would hold out as long as she could before becoming a glorified nanny. "Besides, they don't know anything about books," she said. "I'd rather stay here and talk with you." I don't think she ever bought a single book, but she probably clocked more hours in the shop than any other customer.

Another woman from town came in on a Friday afternoon on her lunch break, shoulders slumped, fingers trailing the spines of the books while she told me that she needed a good cry this weekend. "Can you recommend a book that will just destroy me and let me weep?" I sent her home with *Never Let Me Go* by Kazuo Ishiguro. She came the following week, renewed, and bought *Remains of the Day*.

Sometimes the shop offered a new perspective on people I already knew. We'd been friends with the local framer, Peter, for years. I'd recently had some of my children's drawings framed as a Father's Day gift for R., and when my credit card was declined for insufficient funds, Peter gently suggested I pay him in a few weeks, in installments if I had to, and continued wrapping the small framed work with care. He was a brilliant framer, but a terrible businessman. He ran his shop alone, and slowly, and closed down on weekends. We'd had some conversations, but mostly in social situations I chatted with his wife, about kids, about leaving the city, about what we missed.

Main Street business was slow during the week, though, and Peter would wander in every few days. We'd both recently read and become obsessed with Hilary Mantel's *Wolf Hall*, and I was the only other person he knew who'd read it. One afternoon, he came in to drop off some flyers for his frame shop and picked up the paperback of *Wolf Hall* from my display table, holding it like it was a treasure. "I wish I could go back to before I'd read it just so I could read it again for the first time," he said wistfully. He missed the story so much he'd taken to searching online for more about the history of Thomas Cromwell and that time period. We listened to an NPR show together one afternoon featuring Mantel, and Peter confessed to having Wolf Hall–inspired dreams, losing himself inside Mantel's landscapes. The only thing I'd seen him more animated about was his own family.

Peter had visited our farmhouse to talk about framing thirty-seven pieces for a drawing show of R.'s and he'd brought his wife and children along for the afternoon. Peter, tall and gentle, his wife, Cathy, striking and even taller than him, and their two children, elf-like and beautiful, all moved in a unit, fluid, always touching. During his bookshop visits, he explained he didn't open his shop on the weekends because he wanted to spend as much time as possible with his children while they were young; he'd become a father late in life, hadn't thought it would happen, and he regarded his luck in finding and falling in love with his wife and having children as something of a miracle. He was always so concerned about squandering time with them. He was worried about them growing up and leaving him too quickly, but it was Peter who left. He died in his sleep one February night, three days before his forty-ninth birthday.

After Peter's death, I listened to the Mantel interview again. In it, she explained why she loved writing about the past. In her family, "the dead were discussed along with the living, and the difference didn't really seem to matter. . . . Instead of thinking there was a wall between the living and the dead, I thought there was a very thin veil. It was almost as if they'd just gone into the next room." I had the same feeling at Peter's wake, which fell on his birthday. Peter wore a kilt; a string of rosaries wound through his fingers. The room was full of local poets and painters, photographers and printmakers, the same people who were always in his frame shop. After his death, I couldn't bring myself to remove the flyers for his shop from my counter. Friends came in and held them to their chests, the same way he'd held *Wolf Hall* that day.

By late spring, the bookshop had become like air to me. For the first time in years, I felt like I was expanding instead of shrinking, at least in one part of my life. I'd started writing again, publishing again. I felt renewed, in both my career and my life at home with my kids. I enlisted a friend's teenage son as an intern at the bookshop, brainstormed with a local young-adult writer to build a writing workshop for teens. I became friends with some of the women in the hills, other mothers who were flower farmers, writers, artists, actors, nurses, furniture makers. We met for happy hours and birthday parties for our kids, held women's meetings where we taught each other things, whatever we could offer. On my night, I led them through writing exercises in a friend's towering Victorian house in town. One mother, who always seemed so put together and confident, wrote about a childhood memory she had of being in the middle of a lake, alone in a canoe, afraid she'd never make it back to shore, no matter how hard she paddled; the women at the table all confessed they felt the same way now, in their adult lives. On my birthday, another woman guided us through fabricating Hula-Hoops out of parts we bought from Home Depot, using a blowtorch to bend the pipes while eating homemade carrot cupcakes. I was finally finding a community, belonging beyond our hill.

My children and my shop were growing, blooming. Both of my sons were tucked into the church basement at the Montessori preschool most days now, making friends of their own. When we were home together, we took our walks, read, made chalk drawings on the bluestone patio. The three of us laughed easily, working on baking projects or dance parties or building extravagant Lincoln Log settlements. But then their father would come home and we would all tense, waiting to see which version of him we would get.

Others started to notice. One morning, some friends came over to collect their half of a lamb we'd split. My younger son was in his high chair and my toddler was at the table, too. I was busy splitting the lamb at the kitchen counter, separating out ribs and shanks between two bags, and one or the other child spilled something across the table and onto the floor. R. became agitated, and I automatically stopped separating the lamb and crouched on all fours to clean up the spill. He towered above me, continuing to chide me about clumsiness and mess, while I scurried below him with a towel. I have only a vague memory of this, but these are the words my friend later used, *towered* and *scurried*. The fact that the moment had not even registered on me as out of the ordinary, much less something to be embarrassed about in front of guests, concerned me more than his behavior.

I could not recognize that person crouched under the table to clean up the spill, under her husband, apologizing. When did she get here? Where had I gone?

In the country, we were so isolated that most of our fights were acted out on the private stage of our secluded hill. But now, his anger seeped out across the fields and into town, reared its head in public. I hated the way friends had begun turning to comfort me in his wake.

I started taking longer to pack up at the end of the day at the bookshop. Sometimes, I'd pull over to the side of the road on my way home, just to watch the sky.

My good friend Lauren came from the city for a weekend visit and injected some much-needed magic into the way I was thinking about the bookshop. She took the Shortline up from Port Authority, walked from the bus stop into the shop as if just coming from the next room, looked around nodding, and then gave me a once-over. *You're looking very elementary-school-art-teacher*, she cheekily pronounced.

We hadn't seen each other in quite a while, not since I'd moved full-time to the country. I'd felt like I'd managed to push a little closer to the person I once was in the city, wearing pants without elastic and actually paying for haircuts again. But, I realized, she was right. I was still far from who I'd once been.

In short order, she had Tegan and Sara piping through the speakers and launched the bookshop's Twitter account. Her first day there, we talked over my ideas for the reading series, and by the end of the day she'd watched over my shoulder as I drew out a calendar for the series in my notebook and invited writer after writer at her suggestion, some authors I knew and others I'd only read or read about, authors who quickly responded positively simply because Lauren told me to tell them she'd sent me.

That first night we closed up the bookshop together and crossed the street to the old Hotel Wayne, a proud yellow brick building from 1827. We had a bite and a pint at the bar as we continued to discuss the reading series. *Most of the writers you are inviting are from the city,* Lauren pointed out. *You need a place for people to stay.* She waved the bartender over. *Are you the manager?*

Within the hour, Lauren had convinced the manager to allow the writers invited for the reading series to stay the night at the hotel for free in exchange for bringing the guests over from the bookshop for drinks at the hotel bar after each reading. I sat next to her as she brokered the exchange, watching in dumb amazement as she spoke in hushed tones so the manager had to lean closer and closer to her over his bar. She glowed in the low yellow lighting, her confidence like a halo around her.

We walked across the Main Street bridge for a fundraising event hosted by the local artist cooperative after finishing up at the hotel bar. As we crossed the town bridge, I stared at her silhouette in the moonlight. Her hair flowed like a mane, her fur coat wrapped luxuriously around her, jeweled brooch shining, heels clicking. I'd seen her last at the Rona Jaffe Awards at a tony private club on the Upper East Side more than a year earlier; I'd worn a dress I hadn't taken out of my closet since. She looked unchanged, effortlessly glamorous. I tried to view myself from her eyes, my shlumpy Mom-swap clothes and my bushy country haircut.

Within a few hours, working together with Lauren, I had a reading series up and running and booked with amazing authors from the late spring to the end of summer. The shop's Twitter account already had dozens of followers. She asked to see my business cards, clucking when I said I didn't have any, and quickly sketched out a design on a napkin, highlighting the *Paris Review* column and reading series, naming me "proprietor" because she liked the way it sounded. I kept mumbling *thank you*, feeling chagrined that I hadn't thought of these things, wouldn't know how to make them happen even if I had thought of them. She was kind, but also slightly annoyed, as if she wanted to shake me, or slap me like Cher in *Moonstruck* (*Snap out of it!*). By the end of the night, I wanted to slap myself.

At the fundraiser, we looked around at the crafty wares and everyone stared at Lauren. I spotted a necklace I liked, a chunky piece with black beads and geometric brass baubles. I put my name down, the amount of $25 next to it, the fifth bid of the night. Lauren snorted. "Do you want it?" she asked me.

I looked at the necklace. I hadn't bought anything frivolous for myself in a very long time. "Yes," I said.

"Then bid like it!" She elbowed me in the side. I crossed out $25 and wrote down $30.

We made the rounds one more time before sitting to watch the performance. At the end of the evening, the names of the winners of the auctions were read off. When it was time for the necklace to be announced, they called Lauren's name. She collected her prize from the stage like it was a Golden Globe and handed it to me upon returning to the table.

"Lauren! How much did you bid? I will pay you back when we get to the house tonight." I was already doing the math in my head, worried she'd bid more than a hundred bucks.

She shushed me. "You need this necklace," she said sternly. "You need to remember what it feels like to want something, and then to get it."

A few times during her stay that weekend, Lauren pulled a book off the shelves, either in the bookshop or at my home, shuffled the pages under her thumb, and stuck a finger on a line like an arrow hitting a bull's-eye. Then she'd read the single line aloud, a kind of party trick.

This would typically happen in the middle of a conversation, talking about some big questions that were churning at the time, the should-I-or-shouldn't-I, will-this-work-or-not, should-I-take-this-chance kind of conversations that tend to occur after some Southern Comfort on a patio. She used whatever book was in her hand as a literary tarot and believed the line would tell us all we needed to know. Bizarrely, it usually worked.

I tried this on my own, but it fell flat. After the house was asleep, I would pose a question in my head and stalk a book, pull it from the stack before it could resist, flip open its pages and point hungrily at it, waiting for its answer. Each time, the result was tinny, hard-pressed, wanting. It reminded me of late nights with my Ouija board as a kid, waiting desperately for something to speak to me when I was really just waiting for my own voice. *You have to believe in it*, Lauren had counseled.

Lauren left after the weekend, returning to the city. A month later, as the reading series was about to kick off, R. left, too, for a two-week fishing trip. I was alone, fielding the shop and the children and farmhouse on my own. I worried I would not be able to handle it, but I made it through. His absence hit me in ways I hadn't expected, that I didn't really want to think about too deeply. Instead of being more difficult, the load felt lighter, the house brighter. I felt my shoulders relax.

Summer exploded, and so did the foot traffic. Writers like Leigh Newman and Mason Currey and Domenica Ruta took the bus up from the city, read from their work in the bookstore's garden, stayed the night at the Hotel Wayne. The reading series buoyed the shop's sales, pushing us ahead of my three-year plan prognostications. But the summer season was short. I continued to hold on to my adjunct position in the city, traveling to Columbia once a week by bus. I also taught online classes through Mediabistro, as I'd done for years. The autumn and then winter yawned ahead of me like a giant dark mouth. My stomach was perpetually unsettled. The bookshop was in good shape, but I wasn't sure I would make it through till next summer at this pace, trying to keep up between childcare and the bookshop and my other paying jobs.

I thought about the next book I should read, flicking through the pile of galleys on my desk, but nothing grabbed me. I needed story, I needed depth. I was on edge, and I needed a book to anchor me.

Back at home, I found my old copy of *White Noise*, a book that had seen me through another restless time, and decided to try Lauren's literary tarot card trick again. I flipped it open, finger landing:

"I'm right here," I said. *"If there's anything you want or need, only say the word."*

That summer, I went to my fifteenth college reunion a short drive away in the Hudson Valley. I felt guilty closing the bookshop on a Saturday, but Bill could open the doors if a customer really wanted to buy something. And I told myself this was also a marketing trip: there was a reading for book authors from the various classes attending the reunion, and I could write off the rental car and other costs. My two closest friends couldn't make it, and so I found myself meeting and greeting familiar faces from long ago, explaining my situation.

"Oh, I left the city a few years ago for rural Pennsylvania. I wrote a book, had two kids, and my husband is a painter. Now I run a small bookshop and teach writing at Columbia once a week." I heard myself as if from a distance. I knew this was my voice, and I knew I was talking about me, but everything was layered in a faraway haze. It was all true. And it was not exactly the truth.

Which is why the uniform response had me clawing my fingernails into the flesh of my thigh through the new black linen dress I'd bought from Bill's shop for the occasion. *Wow!* the person I was talking to would undoubtedly begin with some kind of affirming exclamation. *You are living my dream life!* I smiled and nodded politely the first few times this happened, then as the day wore on and I'd had some wine I started getting rude. "No, I'm not," I'd say, rolling my eyes.

"Why are you being such a grouch?" my friend John finally asked, jabbing me in the ribs. "People are just being nice to you and you are throwing it in their face, kid." We hadn't seen much of each other since school, but we'd been close friends in college, and found ourselves quickly falling back into our old rhythms of real talk.

I argued a bit, but realized he was right. I excused myself and took a walk, circling the flowering trees on campus, little sparks of memory shooting out of the leaves and blades of grass. Why *was* I being so rude?

I walked down Sunset Hill and sat in the same spot where I'd rested after turning in my thesis all those years ago, sitting in the sunshine and watching clouds roll by, trying to create a memory of that moment. I stepped back into that twenty-one-year-old self, zipping into her skin surprisingly easily. It felt good to be back with her again, to feel her hopes and beliefs and ambitions course through my veins, an intravenous rush. I let the flood wash over me and then felt it begin to drain, until she slipped out of my fingertips and back into the green grass on that hill.

I'd let her down. She hadn't even recognized me.

I spent my days happily in my bookshop on a rural Main Street, where old farmers clunked in with mud and cowshit on their boots to ask if I had any David Foster Wallace. I lived in a farmhouse on a former dairy farm with craggy rock walls, forests of cherry and beech trees, and a garden with a hundred heads of garlic expected to come up in the next few months. I'd left a fourteen-year stretch of city life for the quiet of the Endless Mountains, and with a new baby and young son on my hip, I thought I was finally at home. But there was a darkness in my marriage I couldn't tame, no matter how many books I sold or pies I baked or wild raspberries I plucked.

The petulance I felt, I realized, was akin to the feeling after being shaken awake from a lovely dream. I wanted to stay inside that 250-square-foot room of books with its blue door forever, just keep walking those trails behind our house with my sons' hands laced in mine as we circled, circled, circled. But in order to stay, I needed to break with the girl on that hill forever. I had to choose now; I could stay asleep and try to hold on to the dream, or I could wake up.

❧

We edged into autumn, and customers took on a harried, back-to-school, back-to-work, back-to-whatever look about them. I felt like I was watching summer—and the hopes that came with it—slowly disappear, a small island swallowed back into the ocean.

The bookshop closed in on its one-year anniversary, and the familiar shiver of desperation crept up my spine as I toggled between the shop's bank account and the calendar, anticipating the holiday season, still so far away. I'd begun to feel like one of those stuntmen stretched between two unhitched train cars, feet on one platform and fingertips clawing at the other.

Over the past year, the bookshop had become a lens through which I was able to see my partnership with R. more clearly. Like a magnifying glass catching the glint of the sun, this lens burned a hole into the fabric of our home together, making it impossible for me to ignore the truth any longer.

In couples therapy, we talked about the division of labor at the shop, how when we'd started this venture, we'd promised fifty-fifty. I asked him what he thought the division looked like now. I expected him to hedge; he hated looking bad in front of our therapist. Instead, he shrugged. *Probably eighty-twenty*, he said unapologetically. I was caught off-guard. I'd assumed he just wasn't aware how much more I was doing. But he was, he just didn't care to change it.

I told him he was being unreasonable, that he was putting himself and his art above everyone else in the house.

You knew who I was when you married me, he leveled, one of his favorite defenses. *I'm the same person.*

Yes, I thought. You are.

The evenings home after therapy were the worst. Anger, as I'd always understood it, was a response to something. But his anger seemed to wax and wane according to, well, I didn't know what. It would just suddenly appear, like another body in the room. Sometimes I saw it in his face first, a shadow passing over, a stitch at the brow, a smile I realized too late was a snarl. At the beginning I would engage, push, question, but I soon stopped. Engaging never ended very well.

And then, as quickly as the shadow appeared, after an hour, or a day, or a week, the sun would burst through. When he shined on me, it still felt as glorious as it had during our first date, when he walked for dozens of blocks sideways just to look at me. Somehow, against the darkness of his anger, that sun felt even brighter. It reminded me of that Ray Bradbury story, "All Summer in a Day," when the little girl moves to Venus from Earth. The other children there were mostly born on Venus, or left Earth so long ago they have no memory of the sun, which hasn't shone for seven years. Margot, on the other hand, misses it dearly. Moments before the sun emerges, the children cruelly lock poor Margot in the closet and she does not get to see its rays. I'd felt this story so acutely when I first read it as a child. The unfairness, and Margot's desire, stung in the pit of my stomach. I remember curling up under the desk in my bedroom and writing an analogous story, one in which Margot does see the sun, gets to feel it on her face. It was the first time I understood I could change the direction of someone else's narrative.

There were some reliable things that would cajole R. into shining brightly: Painting. Money. Parties. Parties where people said complimentary things about his paintings and bought them. I realized too late that there were fewer of all of these things here in the country. There was just me, the children, and the house.

One evening, I sat on the porch listening to the frogs in the swamp as the children played in the yard, and reread the Bradbury story to see if it still held me as an adult. This time, it wasn't the scene of Margot getting locked in the closet that did me in. It was these lines instead: *It had been raining for seven years*, the story went. *A thousand forests had been crushed under the rain and grown up a thousand times to be crushed again.*

I stared out to the swamp and let the frog song wash over me as the children clamored for dessert, little saplings at my feet.

October turned cold. Snow started blowing in over the hills. I'd been dreading the turn of the season, the trees shaking loose their final leaves. The garden looked dead and dank, no more soft edges along the forest, sounds from the road not so muffled. Everything was stark. There was nowhere to hide.

I'd taken to slowing down on my way to work at a corner in Bethany, a small pass-through hamlet between our house and town. There was a pretty grey house across the street from the library there, near the kids' Montessori preschool. A *For Rent* sign had gone up in the front yard. Unlike many of the rentals in town, the property looked tended to; there were window boxes and a porch swing. I imagined a version of my life where I pulled into that driveway after work, made dinner in that kitchen, listened to the radio and drank coffee on Sunday mornings while watching the kids play in a sandbox on that porch. A version of my life where I did not watch the front door, listen for steps, tense at the crunch of car wheels on the gravel driveway. I took the number down after dropping the kids off at school one morning, folding the page over in the back of my journal, like a secret.

I'd started looking for teaching jobs, too. Full-time positions, the kind that came with benefits. I used the quiet time in the shop to work on my Philosophy of Teaching statement, my CV, my cover letter. I sent applications to Iowa, upstate New York, Ohio, without really thinking about what it would mean for the shop if I got one of these jobs, what it might mean for our home. I was crafting a fiction, an alternate plot, like a choose-your-own-adventure novel, exploring what would happen in the Bradbury story if Margot escaped from that closet. As I hit *send* on application after application, I looked around at my empty shop, the slice of sunlight from the window a minute hand moving across the books.

Those books became the background and staging space for first-round interviews for visiting and tenure-track assistant professor positions. The interviewers always wanted to talk more about the bookshop than my work; *but what will happen to the bookshop if you move here for the job?* I didn't have the heart to say that either way, I didn't think we'd last much past the holiday season this year. R. never asked what would happen if I got the jobs. He knew I was applying; earlier in the year, we'd had to put the kids on CHIP, the state's medical assistance program for low-income households. I hated those canary yellow cards tucked into the darkness of my wallet, saw them as a signal flare that something needed to change.

When I said so to R., he shrugged. R. told me that if I wanted any-thing to change, I should get a full-time job; I started looking the next day. I don't think he thought I had a chance at actually land-ing a position, or that I would actually take a position. I also didn't think much past the interviews, what a successful one would mean.

I weighed the stone in my hand, but I didn't really think I would throw it.

For a while, I thought that if I could keep the bookshop open, we'd still have a chance. That R. might turn back to us, turn back to the fantasy he'd conjured, the fantasy he'd made me fall in love with and believe in, too. But the bookshop dream he created was just another still life. He painted it, and then once the paint dried, he tucked it into the painting racks and started on another canvas.

It wasn't intentional. It was just his way.

Still, I felt like a failure once I realized the bookshop would need to close. It was such a public act, and I hated that we were just another in the long line of shops to try and fail, part of the Main Street machinery of shop owners who couldn't hack it. We were nearly on track with the three-year plan I'd drawn up before open-ing, but we were still just breaking even. Closing the bookshop wouldn't save us money. Outside of the shop, we were drowning. Credit card bills, student debt, the mortgage, those damn yellow Medicaid cards I had to show every time I took my children to the doctor; I didn't know how to fix this yawning hole we'd somehow fallen into. I didn't understand; I owned a bookshop, plus I was

holding down three part-time jobs, and still there was not enough.
I could not make the math work.

One afternoon, a friend came into the empty store near closing.
She stood in front of the desk where I sat, impatient to close up,
though not impatient to get home. She wanted to talk to me, to ask
me something, and she hoped I wouldn't mind. So many customers and friends confessed things in this small space; it was almost
like the bookshop was more a church for some people. Of course,
I told her. Go ahead.

"You know," she began, "that you can leave, right?"

I looked at her dumbly. She clarified.

"Your marriage, I mean."

Until that moment, I hadn't truly known it. The water
whooshed in the pipes behind her, the only sound in the place. I
don't remember what I said next, or what she said, or when I began
to cry. But I will never forget the feeling of a lock giving way and
a door opening.

It only took two weeks to dismantle the shop. On one of the last
days, I sweated puddles into my shirt as I loaded half a dozen boxes
of books into my trunk. These books were going back to the dis-
tributor, an attempt to bring our balance sheet closer to zero. The
nearest FedEx was over an hour away, and I drove down the highway with the windows open.

The woman behind the FedEx counter loaned me her hand truck and I rolled the boxes from my car in the parking lot back to her scale. I watched as she printed out labels and slapped them on the last remaining bit of the shelves of my dreams. I thanked the boxes silently, afraid of what would come out if I opened my mouth.

I got back in the car and drove with the windows down again, letting my sweat and tears dry. Halfway through the drive, my phone beeped with a message. Cellphone reception is spotty in the hills, and I figured that someone must have called while I was out of range. I clicked the button and listened over the wind. When I realized it was the college in Lancaster, Pennsylvania, where I'd interviewed for a teaching gig the previous month, I pulled over and listened.

They offered me the job.

I sat there on the side of the road, windows down, trunk empty, radio quiet. I stared at my reflection in the rearview mirror as I listened to the message again to be sure I'd heard correctly. My eyes flipped to the empty car seats behind me. I took a deep breath.

I returned that final afternoon to the empty room with the blue door, this time not as an unemployed bookseller, but as a Visiting Assistant Professor. I thought about the job offer, how when I'd last closed this door behind me a few hours before I'd had nothing—no bookshop, no security. It was still months away, but now I had a job, with a steady paycheck and benefits for my kids—just for a year, but a year is long enough when you are driven so far down into the ground that even a temporary glimpse of sky feels like freedom.

R. had been right—I did know who he was, and he hadn't changed. But we had changed. We were no longer two kids smoking cigarettes and drinking coffee in a painting studio; now we *had* two kids, plus a mortgage and a failed business. And I needed more from him. It wasn't the bookshop that hadn't worked, I finally realized. It was us.

I thought back to the first days in the shop, when we strung up red paper birds in honor of Valentine's Day. The flush of excitement we'd had when opening the bookshop was exactly like falling in love—reckless and full of hope. The empty room sounded so different now, tinny and full of echoes, and I imagined one of those old science movies where you watch the life cycle of a flower as it grows from a seed, blooms, and then crumples and dies, returning to the same empty square of dirt.

That's how falling out of love feels. That's how closing a bookshop feels.

I turned off the light. I was crying and I didn't want anyone who might be passing by to see. The walls were lined with empty shelves, waiting to be filled. But not by me. I had two boxes left to tape up—these were the books that would come with me, books I planned to keep.

I thought of my friend Lauren's parlor trick and reached for the book on top to play one last game of literary tarot: *A Farewell to Arms.* Of course it was Hemingway, that asshole. I stared out the little square window that sat above my head for the many months this room belonged to me and I flipped through the book, pointing to a space on the page before looking.

The world breaks everyone and afterward many are stronger in the broken places. But those that will not break it kills.

I closed the book, placed it back in the box and dragged the tape along the top to close the seam.

Our Castle Year

OUR NEW HOME IN LANCASTER is made of stone. The renovated carriage house sits at the edge of the Lancaster County Historical Society, and I tell the children the museum's expansive leafy grounds are our backyard. The carriage house is carved up into four apartments, and ours is on the ground floor with a lovely porch and sliding glass door. Our apartment, we will discover, has very little heat, but novel luxuries like a dishwasher and a converted silo we turn into the playroom make the place feel magical. At the conical tip of the silo's cylinder is a small iron flag; we've never been, but it reminds the children of pictures they've seen of Disneyland, and my youngest calls this home *our castle*.

Their new school is two blocks in one direction, located in the old clock factory at the end of a lush tumble of gardens and stately homes. The college where I teach is five blocks in the other direction. The first time I see my name on the office door, I enter the small room and weep for my good fortune. I don't even realize the office has no windows until another junior professor points this out. The room has wraparound bookcases and a giant old-fashioned desk under which my children curl with blankets and snacks when they are home sick from school and I need to bring them to work with me.

The place is perfectly manageable for a single mother pretending not to be a single mother.

The boys learn chess in their aftercare program. They come home with a paper board, lay it out on our table and proudly name the pieces, telling me how each one moves, their special powers. Usually, the game devolves into a fight between the horses. *They are called knights, Mama*, they admonish. I am learning, too, I remind them.

I don't like the way the sets of kings and the queens sit so primly across the board from one another, the way each piece has its defined place. I enjoy the moment when the game turns silly and the squares become a great lawn or forest, instead of a regimented blueprint for the required structure, a married couple and their spawn. *Pawn, Mama*, they correct. *Not spawn.*

In *New Ways to Kill Your Mother: Writers and Their Families*, Colm Tóibín says that in creative writing, "mothers get in the way." He argues their connection to their children renders mothers too difficult for juicy plot. "They take up the space that is better filled by indecision, by hope, by the slow growth of personality."

In Lancaster, I cannot afford to bother with indecision, or with hope. Instead, I keep the shades of our stone house drawn and sit in the middle of the round playroom while the children circle around me. I keep them close, and I keep smiling. We tape their paintings on the walls, blow bubbles indoors. They are so small that time is still elastic, so I can mold our world without attending to logic, or truth. We will see their father "later," we will be staying in this new place "for now." It sometimes feels cruel to distract them with ice cream or a drive to see the baby animals at the Amish farm-stand down the road.

On the days the children stay late so I can teach, they emerge from their clock factory school chattering happily. We walk the short distance home, taking care over the section of broken sidewalk we call the roller coaster because of the way the tree roots have forced the concrete up and out. We stare into the houses, pick out our favorite future homes. We decide to live right next to each other in a row, to always be near.

The chess vocabulary spills out of them on these walks. There are *King's leaps* and *captures* and *home squares*. When I hear the word *castle*, I think they are talking about our apartment. But no, the youngest tells me. The move is named this because the rook looks like a castle.

When a player castles, they move their rook from the outside of the board into the middle, trading places with the king. The king then gets tucked nearer to the corner. I ask them why they would put their little rook out there in the middle like that.

They shake their heads impatiently. *Castling is the best protection,* they say matter-of-factly. It sounds more to me like sacrifice, but I keep my thoughts to myself.

When we walk up the driveway to our apartment complex, we look at the stone silo with new eyes. The three of us see it at the same time. Our new home looks like a rook.

Much of motherhood is deciding how to mete out the world's cruelty. Some days, I feel like The Giver in Lois Lowry's seminal young adult novel of the same name. The dystopian coming-of-age tale weaves the story of a society in which emotions are regulated so that there is no sadness or pain; all memories are held by a single person, and the main character, Jonas, is chosen at the age of twelve to take on these memories, to be that single person for the community. The Giver transmits these memories to Jonas in daily sessions that quickly verge on torture, though these memories are simply truths about our world that most of us already know. I find myself making similar calculations as I decide what and how to share with my children: How much pain do I inject into them today and how much can I stave off for another week, or month, or years?

The college students I teach adore *The Giver,* seem to wish they could be tested in the way Jonas was, as the old man puts his hands on the child's back and transmits the world's memories to him. For so many of them, it is *the* book, the book that set them on a course to my creative writing classroom. But when I read it, I am horrified. I chalk this up to my coming to the book as an adult, rather than as a child—*The Giver* was published in 1994, the year I graduated high school, so by the time I check it out of the library I am far from its intended audience.

The idea of forcing memory onto a child turns my stomach. I do not want to transpose my memories onto my children, even the ones for which they were present. In our stone castle, I instead work on making new memories. We play soccer in our parking lot, search for turtles in the Historical Society pond, build gingerbread houses for the very first time. Our Christmas tree that year is a potted shrub, though still taller than my sons, its decorations made of construction paper rings we loop around our wrists in the playroom.

Mostly, the children are fine. But I am vigilant in searching for signs of distress. My oldest comes home from school each day with a square of fabric and a button sewn into the middle. He chooses to do this work, as they say in Montessori, and I am alarmed, worried that he is using the solitude and repetition to quell anxiety. It will not be the last time I project my own behavior onto him. When I observe his classroom one afternoon, I see him go to the sewing corner, where he sits alone like an old woman, so expert now that he doesn't even have to look at his fingers as they swiftly handle the needle and thread. Instead, he watches the groups of children and his teachers, listening to their chatter and recording their movements in his head. He is not isolating at all; this is his way of being with people, I consider. He knows who had a bad day and who loves math and who got a new baby brother. I'd thought he was learning these details because he was engaging the other children, talking while playing or at circle time. Instead, he is like a spy, and when he returns home each day he tells me all the things he learns and I fish out the new button-work from his backpack. We hang his squares of fabric on a clothesline that soon stretches the length of the living room wall.

In *The Giver*, Jonas is chosen at twelve to begin taking in the memories that have been hidden from the rest of his community because he is able to see things differently than the rest of his peers. Because of this sight, he becomes exposed to the truths of the world and can no longer pretend—he knows that the color red exists, that elephants once were alive and humans murdered them, that his father is not as benevolent as he once believed. The boy decides he must do something. At first, he plans to free the society, to break the system.

In the end, the boy just runs away.

The first time I ran away from home, I was five. I announced my intentions over breakfast and my parents helped me with a packing list. I stuffed a collection of pennies, a nightgown, a book, and some clean underwear into a little cinch sack. My father used a bungee cord to strap my favorite stuffed dog to the back of my banana seat and cheerily waved goodbye.

I didn't know until years later that as soon as I turned the corner, he hopped in the car and took up position at the other end of our block where our suburban neighborhood intersected with the William Floyd Parkway, a four-lane highway that hosted extravagant accidents at least a few times a month. My friends and I were all allowed free range for a three-block radius, but none of us were allowed on the highway—this was the rule. My father sensed, though, that whatever spark of independence was driving me to run away and believe that I had the capacity to survive on my own might also drive me to believe that I could—should!—cross the highway.

He was right. I immediately pedaled up the third block to the metal barrier that bordered the four-lane parkway. I stood with the small blue bike packed with my possessions between my legs, a few feet from the cars whizzing past. I don't remember how long I stayed there, watching. My father remembers being in agony, hiding behind the tall shrubs of a house on the end of the block, torn between trusting me to make the right decision and not being able to catch up to me quickly enough if I did not.

Finally, I put my feet on the pedals. But instead of trying to cross that highway, I turned my bike around and coasted back into our neighborhood. My father returned home, expecting me to pedal up the driveway any minute. I did not. Instead, I spent the afternoon tucked on the edge of a neighbor's lawn a few blocks away, screened in by some bushes. I read my book, played with my stuffed dog, ate one of the peanut butter sandwiches I'd brought along with me. But after some time, I realized I had no place to brush my teeth or change into the nightgown I'd packed. I went back home, and I never ran away again.

The first time I tried to leave the farmhouse, I took the children to my parents' house. After hushing them to sleep upstairs, I joined my parents on their big leather sofa in their perfectly appointed living room. I told them I did not want to go home.

My parents listened quietly. When I was finished, they put on the tea kettle. We sipped tea into the night while they explained that I could not stay. That I had to go back to that house and my husband. That I had to return with my children.

If you stay here, they said, *you'd just be running away. That's no way to leave.*

It had never occurred to me that they would not let me stay. Instead, two days later, they helped me repack my bags and load them into the car. They watched as I clipped my children into their car seats and backed out of their driveway. This time, my father did not follow me.

For years I didn't understand. But now that the boys and I were liv-ing in our castle, with an arboretum as our backyard and our own

health insurance and a CSA box we picked up from campus every
Thursday, I understood.

Running away is different than leaving.

When my father plays chess with my children during his visits to
our apartment, he is impressed that they know about castling. He
counsels them to use this as part of their opening strategy, to play
defense before offense. My youngest parrots him, calling the move
crucial.

My father never taught me how to play, but he brings a travel
chess set when he comes to visit so he can play with his grandchildren. He teaches the boys how to lose, how to shake hands over
the board. He teaches them how to think three steps ahead. He
teaches them how to protect themselves. Sacrifice, I learn, is sometimes the best strategy.

My friend Brandy comes to visit us with her son, and we show
them the Amish market and the dog run and the playground
on the college campus. Though Brandy was one of my closest
friends and had been for more than fifteen years at that point, we
hadn't seen each other much because R. did not like her. As with
many of my friends and family members, I'd cut off contact, the
pain of not talking to her being easier to take than what I would
have to endure otherwise. I was so grateful when she was still

there after it all, waiting patiently, happy to hop in the car and come check on us.

We sipped coffee in our stone house before she had to get back on the road. While our boys played Pokémon in their room together, I asked what she really thought of the place.

"I think you should open some blinds," she said. "You don't have to live in the dark anymore."

About five months after moving to Lancaster, I was back on the job market again, since my position was only secure through the end of the school year. I graded papers into the night and juggled freelance work, barely sleeping, though I still felt that I could burst with joy each time I opened my kitchen cabinets and saw my glasses and mugs stacked the way I liked them to be stacked, their mouths open in a small hopeful chorus.

One morning, I noticed a raised red circle on my stomach. I went to work as usual, but it was still there when I got home. Within days, my body erupted in small red dots. Any cloth on my skin felt like a hair shirt.

I went to the doctor. He looked sadly at my stomach, at the red dots. I'd already diagnosed myself with scabies, with bed bugs, with shingles, with fungus. But it turned out I had something called pityriasis rosea. *Pity what?*, I'd asked. It was a skin condition that doctors know little about, except that it seems to go away by itself after a while and is not contagious. There is no medicine that seems to work for everyone, and the rash usually disappears after six months.

"Six months," I blurt.

"Yes," he continued, sympathetically. "But this rash is kind in some ways. We don't know why, but it doesn't creep above the neck or onto your hands or feet. It is a mystery!" So long as I wore long sleeves and pants, no one would even know I had it. He suggested using Head & Shoulders as a body wash to try to curb the itching. I asked what might have triggered this if it was not contagious.

"Have you been under any stress lately?"

His eyes had already flipped to his next chart. That morning, in his waiting room, I checked "Separated" on the little form for the first time, wrote down my mother's name as my emergency contact, feeling seventeen again. I shake my head. "No more than usual," I say, and start getting dressed.

I laugh when I am back in the parking lot. I'd infected myself with pity.

❧

In the classroom, my students write about their own families in their nonfiction work, the ways their families ended. One promising student disappears for a few classes and when I chase him down he apologizes, says that his father had been badgering him to sign a form releasing him early from child support payments. The man started calling his son multiple times a day, all through the night, until he finally threw his cellphone out the dorm window. My student's face was puffy from lack of sleep and too much drink as he confessed this in my office, but it was his resignation that frightened me the most. He wasn't asking for help or sympathy. He just needed another day to clear his head before he could get back to work. He still had the handwriting of a child.

Later, he wrote a powerful, gutting essay about the late-night phone calls, what it felt like to listen to his father's slurring. When we workshop the essay in class, he is asked about his mother's part in all this. She's not at school so she can't be in the scene, clearly, but his readers want to know about their relationship.

In class, he waves his hand dismissively and juts out his chin. "She can't protect me anymore," he says matter-of-factly. "She did for a long time, in ways I never knew until now. But that's over."

He does not include her in his final revision.

When my next job comes through, it is a bittersweet relief. The new position holds the promise of tenure, and will take us to Long Island, closer to friends and family. And yet, we've grown to love Lancaster, and none of us wants to move again. We are all tired of leaving. But time is still elastic. I continue to mold our world and our truths to make them softer, gentler for the children. I'm not sure how much longer I will have this power, but for now, I wield it gratefully.

In *The Giver*, Lowry writes, "The worst part of holding the memories is not the pain. It's the loneliness of it." In that stone castle, we rebuilt our story. Together. We shared the same memories. We loved our schools and the market and the rounded walls of the playroom. But stability meant more than comfort to me now. "We gained control of many things," Lowry writes of the society's choice to mute emotions. "But we had to let go of others."

By the end of the year, I knew the names of all the chess pieces and what they could and could not do. I watched my children's strategies on the board, tried to understand their minds through the ways they moved their pieces. For much of their lives so far, I'd seen them as a unit. This year, though, they'd begun to differentiate, from one another, from me. One prefers vanilla, while the other only eats chocolate ice cream. One loves bright colors and pattern, while the other will only wear plain shirts. One reliably opens each game by castling early, while the other hangs back, saves the move for later.

One afternoon, my youngest has me cornered on the board. We are playing our game on top of a moving box, one of many spread throughout the stone hall of our apartment. Sound becomes more echoey with each item we pack. I castled early in the game, but now I am in trouble, my king under attack, and so I castle again.

My son yelps, tells me I can't do that. He explains that once you move your rook out of castle, the protection disappears. It's like a magic spell that has been broken.

"The castle is gone," he says with such certainty. "You can never castle again."

Looking around at all our boxes, the finality of his statement makes me want to cry.

❧

On one of our last mornings, a small voice cuts a jagged line into the quiet of daybreak. My body reflexively lifts out of bed, finds its way over the piles of tiny cars and books and socks, through the stone darkness of our apartment, what will now simply be our first without their father. I steer myself into the bedroom the boys share, see it is my oldest who is awake, find his bed, crawl in.

"Mama," he repeats, softer this time. His eyes are wide and staring. "What's inside my bones?"

His body is taut beneath his duvet and the nightlight hollows his eyes grey. He is five. He loves ABBA, the beauty of photosynthesis, the number zero. He is small for his age, can't yet tip the old brass scale past thirty-eight pounds at swim lessons. He is sharp-edged, ungraceful; holding him feels like putting my arms around a folding chair. I murmur about minerals and marrow, picturing the mealy silt sealed inside his spindle legs.

My hand rests on his sternum, thrumming with his heartbeat. He lightly moves it away. He weighs what I've given him, half-remembered fragments about blood cells and tissue.

But it's enough, for now.

His body relaxes beside me and his breathing goes hard, like his brother's across the room. I stare at him as the light shifts through the blinds. The translucent skin on his eyelids gives a faint ripple, the thin purple branches of blood vessels pulsing like a secret between us.

What's inside your bones, sweet boy?

I am.

The Stone Boat

I KNEW ABOUT THE PAINTING from the beginning.

"I started a portrait of the boys," he'd said one afternoon, leaning over the car, his paint-smeared forearms propped atop the roof in the sun. This was during the period before we were able to name what was happening between us, this splitting, this terrible tearing apart. Every other weekend, I drove the boys, our two sons, three hours from our new home on Long Island to our old home in Pennsylvania, where their father still lived.

We were in the middle of our dirt driveway in Pennsylvania when he said this, perched over opposite sides of the car, the kids strapped into their car seats, ready to start the drive back to New York. I reminded him that we'd agreed a long time ago to not even share photos of the kids on social media; their likenesses in paint on a canvas felt the same for me. At two and five, they were not old enough to consent. We'd agreed images of our children were off-limits until they could have some sort of say.

"I'm painting it for myself," he assured me. "It's private, just for me, because I miss them." This stung. I'd taken the boys away, moved us from the farmhouse when I landed a new teaching job, searching for a stability that kept eluding us. All he'd wanted when we lived together was to be left alone so he could paint in peace in his studio. Now that we were gone, he seemed unmoored without our presence to push against.

Painting was the way he processed. I understood this, it was like writing for me in this way. It didn't seem fair for me to take their image away from him, too. I was glad he was working.

Still, there was something unsettling about the conversation. As I drove home, shuffling the discs of our audiobook in my lap, the idea of the portrait troubled me. It was unlike R. to offer up any information about his work. His painting studio had become off-limits to me; it had been years since he discussed a work-in-progress with me, invited me into his process. Something struck me as off-key. Was it his words or his face? He had not been asking permission, but his eyes still searched mine for approval as he spoke, testing a boundary, pushing against an invisible fence to see how much give was really there. But we were already late, with a long drive ahead of us, so as the boys clamored for juice boxes and puzzles behind me, I filed the unease to be further dissected later.

I usually loved R.'s work, even if I didn't always understand it. Along with portraits, he painted dense natural landscapes, half-dead clutches of tulips, moody cityscapes with an abstract style I might call a kind of exaggerated expressionism. He'd been a full-time artist since we'd first met more than a decade earlier. Back then he worked with a heavier brush. When he didn't have money for canvas, he'd paint on board, and some of his earlier paintings could get centimeters thick, creating a sculptural effect. When people came to his studio for the first time in those days, they'd usually say the paintings reminded them of Chaim Soutine. But as his work matured and he gained confidence in his voice and drawing with the paint, the thick layers dropped away. His brush was still loaded; he never went in for that slick stuff, like Elizabeth Peyton or Alex Katz. More recently at studio visits, people often referenced Van Gogh and Alice Neel. I think he wished people would say Lucian Freud, but mostly it annoyed him that they mentioned any other artists at all in reference to his work. He took it as a slight, as if they were deriding his work as derivative, rather than simply lining something up in their minds.

A critic once noted that R. uses his subjects like props, simple vehicles to express his obsession with color and pattern. Another writer, after sitting for a portrait by R., described the discomforting sensation of being surrounded by the other portraits in the barn studio as akin to being in a cabinet of curiosities rather than a painting studio; that the faces in particular had the look of animals doomed to extinction.

Some of his paintings were so beautiful they became terrible. A portrait of a dancer and choreographer, Stanley, was nearly grotesque in its vulnerability. Splayed open-legged on a couch covered by a salmon-pink chenille-dot coverlet we'd found in an old trunk at the farmhouse, Stanley sat bearded and shirtless with one arm slung over the back of the couch, looking into the corner of the room. His torso was like a child's, except for the sparse chest hair.

His arms were junkie-frail, his green jeans with pastel pink roses garish. We took to calling the painting "Stanley Green Jeans."

From Stanley's 2019 obituary, I learned that he was born in 1970 in Dexter, Iowa, and moved to New York City at nineteen to attend Juilliard. He built his own performance group and became known in the downtown dance world. In his last ten years, broke and battling addictions, he could no longer afford studio space and held rehearsals in McCarren Park, around the corner from his apartment. He modeled for money, which is how R. started working with him. At the end of one of our cocktail parties in R.'s Great Jones Street painting studio, at 3am, Stanley gave a private performance, bleary-eyed and perfect, his spine twisting as he lunged across the dirty floor of the painting studio. There was no music, and the few of us left were silent in awe as his bare feet shushed against the wood. He crashed into one of the walls, knocking into a painting, but recovered, and ended his performance on the floor, panting, his body and face contorted, before walking out the door and into the night.

When I look at this painting of Stanley in his green jeans and roses, painted years before his death, I see all of this. It is disturbing and glorious and prescient and awful, all at the same time.

A poet who once sat for R. called the experience *hauntological*. He went on to explain that the image itself was not haunted, not in the classic way of a ghost obsessed with the past, but that it was as if the person sitting had been painted into their future, "a certain future," he'd written. This was the haunting, this certainty, knowing the sitter's fate couldn't be stopped. As the paint dried on his portraits, it was as if the sense of inevitability also became locked in and could no longer be scrubbed away or changed.

❧

I've never had a formal art education, but I know what I like. In my senior year at Vassar College, I signed up to audit the storied Introduction to the History of Art and Architecture course, but I kept falling asleep in my hard-backed squeaky auditorium seat the minute the lights went off. My parents did not have much art in the house growing up, but the act of making art was respected. My mother's mother painted beach scenes on the smooth insides of clamshells during summers at the seashore. My father's mother had also painted, mostly birds and flowers on pieces of slate or small canvases, and her sister, my great-aunt, churned out similar works that she showed and sold out of her country barn. My father's sister was a photographer for the local Vermont newspaper where she was also a beat reporter; after she died at forty-seven, a local art gallery showed her black-and-white prints of local life. But fine art? That only lived on the walls of museums like the MOMA and the Met and the Guggenheim, places we visited on family trips before filling up on hotdogs or pretzels from the street vendors outside.

I was afraid to go to R.'s studio the first time. I didn't think I was capable of liking him if I did not like his art, because what is someone's art except themselves, displayed? I was relieved when I saw the rows of strange deflated tulips on the walls. The canvases all shared the same size and subject, but each told a different story; strung along the wall like that, they reminded me of prose poems or a collection of Shakespeare's sonnets, leaping from *the dull substance of my flesh* over to *brass, nor stone, nor earth, nor boundless sea,* stanzas separated by the space of white wall between them. He'd never studied color theory, but there was something sensual in the muddiness of his canvases, and the depths he was able to conjure through sable brushes and palette knives seemed to promise a care and attention to the world around him.

Living with a painter was its own kind of art education. In an old journal, I listed the exotic-sounding names from the Winsor & Newton paint tubes crinkled and crusted on his glass-topped paint table: bismuth yellow, purple madder, scarlet lake, indanthrene blue, alizarin crimson, mars black, permanent rose. He kept a small library of heavy used art books, pages stained and wrinkled, mostly full of the work of other male artists. He explained (in lay terms) the reason grid paintings were considered fine art, demystified the meaning of the numbers at the bottom of art prints. He corrected me when I referred to Joan Miró as a woman.

I took on some of his likes and dislikes. Cedric Morris, Marsden Hartley: good. John Currin, Damien Hirst: bad. This was not unusual. For a period in my early twenties, I had a habit of assuming some of the characteristics of the men I dated. During my first month with the bass-playing son of a famous musician, we went to Sam Asch together and I bought a cherry red Ibanez guitar. He wrote out the music for Bob Dylan's "Isis" in black Sharpie and showed me how to move my fingers. I played the cut from the *Desire* album over and over and practiced the song on my couch in my apartment in Astoria even after we broke up a few weeks later, though I sold the guitar to a friend after a few months. When I started dating a hairdresser who bleached his hair white blond and wore black leather silver pyramid–studded belts, I let him bleach white stripes into my own hair and we wore each other's clothes. We broke up while he cut my hair in Tompkins Square Park one summer afternoon; a section of my bangs broke off a few weeks later from bleach damage. I still have one of his belts.

I've collected things from these relationships over the years, incorporating different aspects of these men into my own body, my own practices. I no longer play bass, but Austin changed the way I listen to music. I no longer wear studded belts, but I still think of Matt's South Williamsburg basement apartment that he shared with six roommates, his freezer full of cigarettes and Milky Way bars. One morning, I apologized for having to get up early to go to my office job, and he rolled over from his mattress on the living room floor to look at me with an uncharacteristically serious expression. "Don't apologize," he said sternly. "You're our hero. Don't you realize you're the only one of us with a real job?" I hadn't, before then.

As a writer, I intuitively enjoyed shouldering into someone else's coat for a period, stretching my arms out and testing the fit. Profiles were my favorite form to write for magazines, allowing me to ask intrusive questions and understand how a person came to be. Everyone else always seemed like fully formed beings, while I felt like more of a magpie, collecting scraps from others to wallpaper my nest. I preferred the role of the observer, the chronicler—I liked to leave a little room in myself to pour someone else in.

A profile is a kind of portrait; a prose poem is more like a tiny landscape. R. never painted from imagination. He only painted what was in front of him. Together we deemed him a nonfiction painter.

❧

After our first few years together, I began to sit for R. regularly. The process had lost most of its romance. I understood he painted me only when he had no one else to paint, not because he wanted to paint me, specifically. When I was in front of him, I became a jumble of spheres and cubes, no different from any other model who sat for him. Once he started painting, everything else disappeared anyway.

One winter, a year before we were married, I perched on a cold metal chair in his cavernous studio, a sprawling 2,000-square foot rectangle with arching wooden beams and wide plank floors. The old mill building where he'd had his studio in Williamsburg for the past ten years was being turned into million-dollar condos, and they'd moved him out of his upstairs unit to the ground floor; no views, but more space. A red light gleamed from a plug-in ceramic space heater.

It is difficult work to be looked at so intently, for so long, not being able to move, like one of Nabokov's pinned butterflies. I wore a heavy cable-knit sweater and sat, sulking, holding my pose by staring at the slow-moving hands of the clock on the wall while working out an essay in my head due for a class later that week.

After an hour or so, when my hands and feet were numb and I was too cold to continue, we stopped. He snapped a Polaroid to work from and then I did some jumping jacks and poured a hot cup of Bustelo from the percolator to warm up my hands. We probably went for fish tacos at Bonita afterwards. Then I went on to my graduate classes or my evening shift at the Brooklyn bar I tended and he went back to work on the painting.

I didn't know it would become my favorite painting of his. I didn't know he would capture something in my face—the drawn mouth, the unfocused side gaze, a general cold discomfort—that would be more recognizable to me than any mirror or photograph could ever reflect.

In the farmhouse where R. and I lived together the last few years of our marriage, our bedroom window looked out at the long dirt driveway and old dairy barn on our property. He'd moved his Brooklyn art studio into the barn, another structure with hefty wooden beams and warped plank floors. The sharp tang of turpentine and the heavy mineral scent of oil paint hit the nose as soon as he opened the studio's glass-paned doors, and the floors were covered in sawdust and strips of trimmed canvas. After we opened the bookshop in town, he hung a cherry red bucket swing from one of the barn beams using two heavy chrome chains. If I were at the shop and the babysitter had to leave early, he'd plop one or the other son into the swing facing out the door and push. This way he didn't have to leave the studio.

With the bedroom lights out, I could sit up in our bed and see the barn glowing like a punched tin lantern as he worked into the night. Often, he'd stay in the barn all day and most of the evening, coming in only for meals or ice for his coffee. People would come over, sit for a painting for a few hours, or drink some beers, or stare at his work on the walls. It had been a long time since I'd sat for a painting; I'd tried a few times when my first child was still a baby, desperate for him to look at me, but once my second child was born, I just couldn't find the uninterrupted hours he would need from me to pose. So, he painted others.

Sometimes his walls would be full of portraits, making it hard for me to stand in the studio, with so many eyes staring hard. I always appreciated that his portraits were not sunny or sweet, showing instead the way a face turns down when a person is asked to sit in stillness and silence for hours. But when there were multiple portraits on the walls, the studio felt like the hallway of a jail or insane asylum, each portrait a cell, with everyone looking at me, hoping I could help them escape.

When my eighty-year-old great-aunt, who was also an artist, saw an image of my cable-knit sweater portrait on his website, she slapped him. "Is this what you see when you look at her?" she demanded. She said I looked sorrowful, vulnerable, so incredibly alone, all the things everyone always says about the people in his portraits. He tried to laugh off her reaction, and I tried to explain that I found the painting an eerily accurate representation of the way I see myself.

"If that's really how you feel, dear child," she said, arching her thin eyebrows, "you should consider your company."

That painting was now one of hundreds in the barn, slotted into a rack in a back corner. Many nights, I stared out at the candle-glow of the night studio, thumping beats from the '70s rock radio station drifting up to me if the windows were open, wishing he would come to bed. But when the light would finally snuff out and I would hear his boots clomping up the porch, then his socked feet on the stairs, then the groan of the mattress as he climbed into his side of the bed and stayed there, the heavy smell of linseed oil wafting from his body, I found myself wishing he'd just stayed in front of his paintings. I'd regulate my breathing and keep my eyes closed and wonder how he could study the human face for so long and not be able to see the one closest to him.

When we first tried to make a garden in the farmhouse's front yard, we turned up rock and rock after rock. Our area was named for them; the locals joked that they were rock farmers, and taught us how to haul our harvest with something called a stone boat.

I was intrigued by the sound of those words together. I imagined a small, smooth, hollowed-out boat made of stone, small as a child's hand, like the paper boats I used to make as a kid. Except, I wondered, wouldn't a boat made of stone sink? Virginia Woolf came to mind, walking into the River Ouse, pockets full of little stone boats, clinking in her overcoat like coins.

A stone boat, it turns out, is made of wood. It is a simple sled, just a few planks strapped together. If you wanted to get fancy, you could chamfer the edges, but most of the neighbors just threw together some used wood planks and attached a length of rope in triangle formation. Popular on farms throughout the Northeast where they needed ways to clear stones and stumps from their land, stone boats were often pulled by cattle or ox in the old days, though now most of the men seemed to use tractors or an ATV. Just roll the stones on and slide them away.

There was always extra wood in the painting studio; R. built his own canvases using pre-made stretchers or two-by-fours. He had chop saws and table saws, chainsaws and an air compressor, an entire workshop there in the barn. He made his own stone boat one afternoon and proudly zipped back and forth on his riding lawnmower, ferrying rocks from one side of the yard to the other to make space for the garden.

The winter after we made the garden, and each winter after that, the frost would push more rocks up to the surface. The snow would melt and there they would be, a whole new crop of rocks. The kids and I picked as many as we could from the dirt, making a quaint grey ring around the garden. R. dutifully hitched up his stone boat and ferried more rocks over to the forest, but each spring the boys and I picked less, and he ferried fewer and fewer, and soon our garden closed in on itself, twenty rows of zucchini and lettuces and corn and garlic shrinking to twelve rows, then five. In the end, all that was left were two single rows of garlic and row after row of rocks. When I finally left, the stone boat lay abandoned at the back of the barn, wood planks silvering, rope fraying in the breeze.

It started with a simple message asking if I'd looked at R.'s Instagram account lately. I hadn't; in fact, I didn't even have an Instagram account, hadn't logged into my own Facebook page in more than a year. Still, it only took a few quick clicks to find the images.

There on my screen were my children's faces slathered onto canvas in R.'s thick, sculptural style. Not just their faces, but their bodies. They stood, next to one another, arms hanging limply by their sides, in a life-sized full-frontal nude portrait.

There were multiple shots of the painting; different close-ups of their faces, their feet, a hip and a hand. One wide studio shot was all Instagram-perfect north light and golden barn beam, their little red bucket swing down in the corner, chain curled like a snake. In this photo, a canvas I guessed was about six feet across held their complete naked bodies. A swipe of grey and blue between their legs hung sadly against their thighs, each toe on each foot a tiny round pebble. Their sweet faces were rendered slack in R.'s awful, hauntological hand.

I slammed my laptop shut at my dining room table 100 miles away. I barely made it to the bathroom and retched into the toilet, a response that still threatens as I type these words onto my screen.

It took a few days before I could call him. In that time, other people reached out. He'd posted the images on Facebook, too. It took another week for Child Protective Services to call.

Years later, I had a long phone call about parenting and art with my friend Rachel, a playwright and director in Lancaster. When we first met, she was married to one of the good ones, lived in a colorful townhouse in the city with a Tibetan peace flag strung across the porch, and had a rambling red house in the country with a wall of books, a cupola for star-gazing, a piano in the living room. Our older sons were the same age, were in the same pre-K class together. One day, on the Montessori playground, Rachel's husband spoke earnestly to my son about the beauty of the number zero for nearly thirty minutes. He was a brilliant mathematician, an athlete, was funny and handsome. Rachel had just given birth to their second child when her husband began a destructive disappearing act into addiction. I couldn't make sense of what he became, and neither could she. So, she made art out of it instead.

On the phone we talked about defining boundaries as an artist parent. I asked her to describe her process in creating an experimental play she wrote and put on in Philadelphia. There were multiple stations, and audience members interacted with the actors at each one and could only stay for a certain amount of time. "The uncertainty of not knowing what to do became a shared experience," she said, describing the performance's interactive nature. The show was organized around three stories: "The Ghost of Mediocrity," "The Body That Wouldn't Be," and "Papa's Done Gone Crazy." They were all about her husband.

She worked to make the live performers at each station vulnerable in some way, usually by asking them to do something that didn't create a power dynamic with the audience members. "My son's station was really cool because you could see how comfortable people became when they realized they would be interacting with a child; his vulnerability was built into his identity so he didn't even need to do anything." She had her son sit at a table with a chessboard and invite audience members to play a game with him. "They would immediately smile when they sat down. It gutted me how incredibly kind these strangers were to a little boy."

By this point, her husband hadn't visited their sons for more than a year. The audience members were at each station only for a short time, a minute and a half or so before moving to the next station. Her son would reset the pieces on the chess table each time.

While Rachel's son was fully and enthusiastically engaged in his part in his mother's play, he did not explicitly know what the play was about. His part was very task-based, not personal, and allowed him to feel comfortable and confident and safe. "Part of what I was playing with by using the different stations was about encountering different parts of our life with his father," Rachel said. "Playing chess was something my son loved to do with his father. What every audience member had to do was leave him."

Rachel was essentially retraining her child to have a different relationship with being left.

By the time we spoke on the phone, three years had passed since Rachel lived with her husband. Her son enjoys theater and has performed with her a handful of times in different plays. Since she is a theater professor, it is a convenient way for them to be together more often, especially in the absence of his father. "I find it tricky—it is wonderful and beautiful to share that with him, but really important to me to not take up so much emotional space that he doesn't have any. I don't want him to have to live my stories."

We were quiet for a moment on the phone with each other. I wondered if her last point is truly possible, regardless of whether a child has artists for parents or not. I've told her about the painting; she is one of only a handful of people I've been able to speak about this to without the words disintegrating in my mouth like sawdust. She understands. She says her play was so abstract because it is a story she needed to tell and a story she didn't want people to know at the same time.

After we hang up, I think about the difference between a play and a painting. Rachel's son will never be able to view the play; there is no record of it, for better or for worse. Anything he thinks about it will be based on what he remembers from when he was very young. But a painting? Or a social media post? These are indelible; archival evidence.

And what about words on a page?

Later that evening after the phone call with Rachel, as I played Magic: The Gathering with the boys in the living room, I thought about the way I could hear in her voice how much she still loved her children's father. She hadn't made the play to destroy him. And she made sure not to destroy her son in the process. He left them first, but through the play, she taught her son and herself how to leave him.

When I left with the boys, R. retreated to his easel, to the place that felt the most familiar, where he was in charge of the color and the context, the foreground and background, the narrative.

And, if I'm being honest, it's where he belonged. Part of me could understand his drive to make a painting of his children. No part of me could understand his making the painting he did, nor sharing it.

———

When I finally called to confront him about the painting, he seemed most concerned about finding out who had told me that he'd posted the images. He kept saying that I knew about the painting all along and he didn't get what the big deal was about it.

My voice took on a shrill quality unrecognizable to me.

You painted a life-sized full-frontal nude portrait of our children! They are naked! And then you posted it on the internet! With their names!

He talked more about how much he missed them, how he'd wanted to capture what he called their last moments of innocence, and then he returned again to my knowing about the painting all along, didn't I remember that day at the car?

I did remember that day. I asked if he remembered promising that day that the painting was private, that he had no intention of ever showing it to anyone.

Yes, he finally said after a long pause. *I remember saying that.*

I waited for him to say he'd forgotten his promise, or that a painting is different than posting photos of your kids on Facebook, or that I was stupid, that I just didn't understand art.

Instead, he sighed into the phone.

But the painting was just so good.

The Child Protective Services investigation that ensued focused on whether or not the painting could be considered child pornography. It also focused, as any CPS investigation must, on the safety of the children in the home. My home. The investigator came to my apartment, counted my smoke alarms, looked inside my refrigerator, my cupboards, as if that would somehow magically tell her something integral about our family. Does my store-brand cereal make my children less safe?

As the CPS people talked about child pornography and sex offender registries, it all sounded too ridiculous. This was a soap opera I was watching on television, I told myself, not my actual life. I pinched the soft flesh of my thigh beneath the table to try to wake myself up as the investigator went over her notes and handed me pamphlets about nearby safe houses, lime-green cards with domestic abuse hotline numbers.

The painting was problematic, sure. But the problem was self-ishness. Lying. Putting one's art above one's own children. The problem had nothing to do with my husband being a sex offender. I may have laughed at my dining room table, that first meeting when the investigator explained things to me, the children safely up the hill at their suburban school, our shoes all lined up perfectly by the door, the way they never were otherwise except that I didn't know how else to prepare for her visit but by tidying.

We don't really know how to handle a painting, the investigator admitted to me. *We don't have rules for this.* If the image were a pho-tograph, she explained, there were clear-cut definitions and pro-cesses. Fine art did not compute.

The investigator visited every week. She asked invasive ques-tions, about my future plans, about whether I would file for divorce soon, and if so when.

I needed to think about myself now, she counseled. I needed to imagine how this would look in court, if it came to that. What kind of mother continues to allow someone access to her children who has a history of violating them? She interviewed my pediatrician to see if I'd kept up with their well visits and vaccinations, my therapist to see if I had Stockholm Syndrome, if I could be trusted to keep the children safe from their own father.

She scheduled a visit for when my sons would be home. She sat the children on my couch and asked if their father had ever painted them. He had, they confirmed. *How do you know?* she asked my older son.

He showed me the painting.

I was a few feet away, holding my breath. This I had not known. *What did you think of the painting?* The investigator kept her voice light, sing-songy. *A little weird*, my son whispered into his lap. He explained that it was weird because he and his brother had no clothes on.

There was silence for a moment as my heart caved in on itself.

It's okay, he said suddenly, brightly. *That's just how painting works. Dad told me. The clothes go on last.*

He saw himself as a paper doll.

The investigator left us alone after that.

I try to untangle these complexities in my mind, see the situation in some neutral way. My mind flips naturally to Sally Mann. Not a direct comparison, but for her third book, *Immediate Family*, Mann had photographed her children at nearly the same ages, four and six, though in the rolling rural backdrop of Virginia instead of Pennsylvania. Her previous book, *At Twelve*, had also featured naked images of young girls, but these were not her own.

"It's hard to know just where to draw that stomach-roiling line, especially in the cases when the subject is willing to give so much. But how can they be so willing?" she questions in her *New York Times Magazine* essay, "Sally Mann's Exposure." "Is it fearlessness or naivete?" Or, I wonder, is it simple trust? Why would you expect your own child not to be willing? The CPS investigator explained slowly one afternoon that even if R. had not intended anything untoward with the boys, the next time they are asked to take off their clothes for another adult to look at their body, they will be primed to say yes, because they've already done it. It's like a cork that you cannot replace. Something had been broken, and I hadn't even realized.

Mann argues that what her detractors failed to understand was that "taking those pictures was an act separate from mothering." The photos were art, not real life, she charged.

"The fact is that these are not my children; they are figures on silvery paper slivered out of time." The photos are simply a representation of a moment, an idea, Mann continues. "These are not my children at all; these are children in a photograph."

Paper dolls, I think.

I don't know if his father really told him that, that the clothing gets painted on last, or if he made it up himself.

Is it worse to be seen? Or not to be seen at all?

When I looked at that painting, every awful fear I had about

my children was swirled into their sallow faces. The asylum of portraits lined up in the barn, the terrifying tragic beauty of Stanley
Love. In the same way that I can recognize that Mann's photos are
stunning works of art, I understood what R. meant when he said
the painting of the children was so good; the brushwork, the colors, were all lovely, powerful. But if I wandered into a gallery one
Saturday afternoon and stood in front of this enormous canvas of
these life-sized child bodies, as a mother, I would still recognize
their need to be held, covered. Perhaps this was what he was trying
to capture—the vulnerability of children, his own heartbreak and
loss painted into every inch of their bodies. Even if they were not
my children, I would need to look away.

But they are my children. I cannot pretend they are not.

After a very long and tumultuous year, Child Protective Services
finally cleared R.; we were relieved, but by that time the CPS
investigation almost seemed beside the point for me. During this
period, when I looked at R., that canvas was all I could see. His
freckled hands were the hands that painted those brushstrokes and
clicked *share*, his soft brown eyes the same eyes that studied them
and turned their bodies into spheres and cubes. And each time my
children stood next to one another—on the playground, waiting in
line at the movie theater, standing in the doorway with backpacks
on getting ready for school—the painting cracked in front of my
vision like lightning. I could not exorcise it from my mind.

I think about this need to show someone, the element of art
as communication, that it exists as part of a conversation which

requires a viewer. Am I not simply painting my own portrait? As I write these words, am I not unearthing this horrible moment in our personal history, shining light on it the same way their father hit *share*? Showing my version of the world through my own limited and biased point of view, building a narrative around it, turning it into a metaphor? Placing art above parenting?

When I viewed the painting, I thought I saw R. for the first time as a parent. I saw, for the first time, the parent R. could never be. With some critical distance, I have come to understand that this painting is not representative of R.'s fatherhood. To R., the painting is a painting, and the models are like any other models. It does not reflect his parenting or how much he loves the boys or how much the boys love him. This is not a family portrait.

I think instead of an afternoon that he sat on the hill above our garden near the farmhouse. R. is leaning back on his arms, tired from pruning the apple trees, his legs out in front of him in the shape of the number 4. The pruning shears are across his lap, the long arm of the tree branch lopper with its scissored head at his foot. My younger son is in my arms; we are standing, and my oldest is sitting next to R. on the grass, munching on a cookie. He has on brown corduroys and they are tucked into his favorite blue rain boots; R. is wearing workpants and the sleeves of his plaid flannel shirt are rolled up to his elbows, the freckles on his muscular forearms giving the illusion that he is somehow tan in March. My son edges closer to him until he is nestled in the crook of that number 4 his father is making with his legs, leaning easily into his body like it is an extension of his own. They are both smiling and R. ruffles his hand gently through his son's soft hair. It is nearly nine years to the day as I write this. I know these things in such detail, because, like Mann, I took a photo.

This essay is just a portrait, one of many. I tell myself that I've taken care to cover my children's bodies here on these pages.

After our phone call, R. hung up and wrestled the giant canvas that held the painting of the boys out of the barn. He fashioned the canvas into a stone boat, hauling it half a mile up the hill face down on the ground before dousing it with lighter fluid and striking a match. I don't know if he was silent or if he screamed. I don't know if the portrait took a long time to burn, or if the mix of gesso and oil paint on linen made the fire spit and hiss. I don't know if he watched or if he closed his eyes, if he stayed until it was finished. But I do know that when he sent me a photo later, seeing the skeletal remains of the fire-scarred stretcher bars was almost worse than seeing the image of their naked little bodies to begin with.

In his effort to preserve his children, to preserve his attachment to them, to the family we had been together, he instead destroyed the painting. "Nostalgia is a sneaky curator," wrote the essayist Leslie Jamison. "But without interrogation," she cautions, "it can also obscure the root systems of pain lurking beneath the romances of memory." R. is, after all, a nonfiction painter. We looked at Stanley's portrait, saw his torture, plain on that canvas, and simply appreciated its beauty, didn't try to help the flesh-and-blood man outside the painting. I recognized the truth in my own face when he painted it. I understand now that it wasn't their nakedness, but the prescient root systems of pain he painted into our children's faces that were the hardest for me to look upon. They looked so alone in the world. R. had painted my deepest fear of what my decision to leave would do to my children. And seeing it, rendered life-sized and in full color in his hauntological hand, I feared there was no way we could ever escape it.

His words still ring in my ear.

But it was just so good.

It was. And now it is not.

Imaginary Friend

She is a woman whose desires stand
at the bottom of a cracked pitcher, waiting.

—CAROL SHIELDS, *THE STONE DIARIES*

WHEN MY CHILDREN WERE VERY LITTLE, they invented imaginary friends. My youngest's imaginary friend was named Oaken John; my oldest, in classic Psychology 101 textbook territory, named his Bad Guy. Oaken and Bad Guy went with us on car trips, required seats at the dining table, extra scorecards at mini-golf.

My children are eight and ten now, and Oaken and Bad Guy are no longer a consistent presence, but they still appear every so often. Last week, I heard my sons discussing where they thought they'd gone, what Oaken and Bad Guy had been up to since they'd last visited. My oldest said, "Oh, Bad Guy? He's been on a loooong vacation." I thought back to the days when Oaken and Bad Guy were daily visitors and I would sometimes have to push them on the tire swing in front of our old Pennsylvania farmhouse. Back when we still lived in that farmhouse, when we still lived with my sons' father.

I wondered where imaginary friends might vacation. I thought of my own imaginary friend, who was tall and lean and blond. I'd named him Heathcliff, because I thought of him as part *Wuthering Heights* character and part Michael Penn song, a Romeo in black jeans.

My younger son called me back to reality, back to our small suburban kitchen the three of us like to crowd into while I am cooking. I turned on the stovetop—*click, click, flame*—I pictured all of our imaginary friends, vacationing on a beach somewhere, relaxing and enjoying their time off together until we needed them again: Heathcliff, Bad Guy, and Oaken John, staring out to sea, their hair sandy, salt crusting along their sunburned necks.

I also named him Heathcliff because that was pretty close to his actual name.

In real life, he and I were together from our sophomore through senior years in college. He was the first man who could make me sigh just by watching him walk across the cafeteria at our school's Sunday brunch. He was tall, very tall, and thin, and had a sort of relaxed amble whose slowness made me blush. He had long, spindled fingers and a delicate mouth. On the soccer field, he was fast and graceful, and I loved watching him walk home to me after practice. I would sit reading a book on a bench in front of his dorm and wait for his return, his blond hair darkened with sweat, cleats slung over his shoulder, a slow grin breaking across his face as he drew closer and closer.

One time, we both had the flu and spent two days hiding

under a quilt in his dorm room. The edges of the world were soft but solid and we moved by sound and smell and feel. I remember sharing an orange under that quilt, delirious from fever, both real and cabin, his thumbnail sliding under the skin of each segment, popping the fruit's small, juicy membranes. Our skin smelled like citrus for days.

After college, we kept in touch the first few years, but then he disappeared. By the time my children conjured their own friends in the Pennsylvania woods, I had not seen or spoken to him in a decade. Although he worked in the tech industry, he had no digital presence, no Facebook page to stalk. He hadn't stayed in touch with mutual friends. He always held a space at the edges of my mind, but in an ephemeral more than corporeal way.

Finally, at our fifteenth college reunion, after a long and boozy night of reminiscing with friends and him not showing up again, I returned to my dorm room and swayed over my laptop. The plastic give of the single mattress, the dark whorls on the scarred wooden desk, the chemical smell of the industrial shower curtains, the verdant Hudson Valley air steaming through the window screen— each sensory detail made me think of him. I found him, of all places, on LinkedIn, and hit *send* before I could think much about it. By the time I peeled off my clothes and climbed into bed, he'd sent a response.

For the next three years, we communicated through boxes: the black rectangle of my iPhone, the square glow of my computer screen, and, a few times, a secret PO box in my small town. Our conversations were intimate but chaste, detailed and serious, never untoward. Not once. And yet, I told no one about him.

Mostly, we emailed in a weekly, sometimes daily, volley. We talked about work, about his boss, about my bookshop and job interviews. About his soccer team and his Bunker Hill neighborhood, about the hemlocks and wild turkeys on my property, my son's obsession with his blue rain boots. He wasn't married, or it didn't seem like it, though we were careful not to ask too much about those details. It took me a year to work up the courage to ask if he had any children. No, he said. Not yet.

My marriage had been fraying for years by that point and now, rereading these hundreds of emails, I recognize the quality I missed most dearly from my relationship with my husband at the time. The emails are full of a congenial camaraderie, an everyday knowledge and shorthand of our hopes and fears, cheerleading and soothing and propping one another up. This was the kind of talk I used to have over the coffeemaker in the morning or in the last moments before sleep at night in the early days of marriage. It had been so long since someone seemed genuinely excited to hear from me, who wanted to know what I felt and thought and did during the day, who wanted to make me smile. I felt a slow burn throughout my body, embers fanned and flamed.

I was running a small bookshop and raising two children, and I collected things to tell him throughout the day. I was also making preparations to leave my marriage, and my home. I never explicitly said to him that I was in the middle of this rupture, because we'd tacitly agreed that was off-limits, but he was my constant companion through it all, through the job interviewing, the boxing up and closing down of my bookshop, the search for a new apartment in a new city, the breaking down one life and building up an entirely new one.

I used our correspondence as a stage upon which to create a character. Instead of sharing the money insecurities or the terrible final months of late-night kitchen arguments or the crippling self-doubt, I built a narrative of survival. I chose my details carefully, crafting a story that starred a plucky fighter whose independence and verve were her defining features, someone on the cusp of flight, rather than the crash-landing failure it mostly felt like. I liked this version of myself, and the idea that I was building her for me, a kind of totem or trouble doll I could pull out from under my pillow anytime I needed her. She almost became a separate imaginary friend all on her own.

I liked that he gave me space to imagine myself this way, the confidence to build myself up. I told myself I deserved this kind of relationship, that I needed the strength it brought me, the brightness of his humor and kindness. The reminder that I could be a person with whom another person wanted to exchange humor and kindness.

But I knew what I was really doing. I was wooing him.

At nineteen, I'd also pursued him. Hard. I'd returned early to campus my sophomore year for a student government orientation; he'd returned early for soccer. I heard about him before I met him, from a girl who'd hooked up with him the weekend before. She was an athlete, an extrovert, with dark hair and big flashing dark eyes, my opposite in every way.

I wound up on a shopping trip with her at Kmart, to buy craft supplies for an orientation event. She gushed about him as she flicked through carousels in the underwear department, piling cheap thongs in bright colors into the crook of her elbow. I remember thinking this was important, this detail, that she was a girl who bought sexy lingerie at Kmart. As if sex were a commodity as common as a box of cereal, a new water bottle.

Her desire was contagious. I listened to her breathlessly rhapsodize about her feelings for him, how much she wanted him, and I wanted that: those feelings. I had a boyfriend at the time; he was away at Williams for the semester, and I liked him very much, but I'd never felt like that. There was an urgency, a physicality to her want; she was flushed just thinking about touching him again. So, I co-opted her desire, and its object. And I bought a pair of emerald-green nylon string-bikini underwear.

When we were nineteen, it took a week. A week of observing both him and the girl, of testing, of finding fissures, of holding back just enough to see if I could catch his eye during a party while she went out to smoke a joint. Then I just had to speak quietly so that he needed to lean down to hear me over the music, to touch his back lightly, bring him closer into my hair, near my neck. Meanwhile, I was clinical in my rationalizing; this girl was not right for him, she'd quickly find someone else, she was confident and this would not really hurt her, plus we were acquaintances, not really friends. I justified every inch of it, but I knew exactly what I was doing. And I did it anyway.

At the end of that orientation week, he and I found ourselves in the back of a van with a dozen other people; another soccer player had driven the van to campus and now it sat parked in front of the senior townhouses, a kind of outdoor cabana. Slowly, the van emptied out. We stayed. When we finally kissed, it felt inevitable.

That we'd fallen into such an easy epistolary rhythm almost two decades later was no surprise. In fact, it had kind of been our thing. Nearly half of our college relationship had been conducted long distance. Our junior year, I'd gone to school in London, while he stayed stateside. Phone calls were too expensive, cellphones didn't exist yet, and there was nothing like Skype or FaceTime available. Once a week, we'd use the library computers to sign into a UNIX program that allowed us to communicate real-time; the screen was black, the text electric green, and you had to type commands like TALK to start a session. And we would write and mail letters to each other, pages and pages of letters. Letters, I realized, I still had.

My storage boxes were stacked precariously in a corner of the dairy barn that also functioned as my husband's painting studio. Battered and musty, these boxes had sat untouched for years; books from college; souvenirs from my traveling years, trips to Thailand and Vietnam, Germany and Egypt, Israel and Spain; two small albums of photos; a Doc Martin boot box of mix tapes. I had an entire shoebox dedicated just to his cards and letters.

Turns out, he'd kept mine, too.

On days when the boys were napping or sufficiently engrossed in a cartoon and their father was out, I'd stealthily make for the barn. I would open the box and sometimes just stare at the hand-writing. The way he looped his H, the pressure of his pen and per-fect spacing of his words. I liked taking the letters out one by one, feeling their multipaged heft, not even opening them, just trailing my fingers across the sandy brown envelopes, the red *Par Avion* stamps. On days I didn't receive an email, or even on days I did, I liked to hold the pile of old and weathered looseleaf paper in my hands, blue lines translucent as veins, proof that I hadn't simply imagined him.

That year in college we quickly became a couple, one of those annoying hand-holding campus couples that people roll their eyes at behind their backs. Although my desire for him was initially sec-ondhand, it quickly caught hold on its own. I was very physically attracted to his body, but also his person; he was brilliant and kind, a physics major who loved music and drawing and his mother. We met each other's families, became friends with each other's friends, made promises.

One summer, I flew down to Texas to visit him. He picked me up at the airport and drove directly to a small field. He pulled his car over and led me into a forest. He'd scoped out the spot before-hand, planned it out step-by-step: on the way home from the air-port, so our timing would not be suspicious, private enough to ensure complete seclusion. It was the first time I'd ever experienced sex with such urgency, sex that had been pre-planned so meticu-lously. I liked imagining him imagine it—the place, the positions, the logistics, down to him packing a beach towel for my knees.

I'd also planned a surprise. When his parents and sister went to run errands a few days later, I unearthed a pale peach silk teddy I'd borrowed from my roommate. The color washed out my own, and I am certain I looked like a middle-aged housewife from the '80s. I'd never before worn a teddy—nor have I since—and its awkward construction was not conducive to the efficiency required, but we managed to make it happen over our laughter, first on his bottom bunk and then again in the shower.

Holding those letters in my hand so many years later, though, it was not the sex that kept me returning to that space between the past and what I'd started to think of as my possible future. I'd had plenty of friends use social media to revisit and reignite affairs; could there be a more banal cliché than cheating through Facebook? Those interactions seemed tawdry and cheap, dime-store underwear territory. But this was different, I told myself, as I crouched quietly in the corner of the old dairy barn, surrounded by my husband's paintings and the old Pack 'n Play sprouting cobwebs in the corner. There was substance here. This was real.

Wasn't it?

As I got closer to leaving my marriage and tensions in my house ticked up, I started planning. One afternoon, I packed a box with the things I cared about most—things I wouldn't want smashed in a fit of anger or lost if I had to leave quickly—and placed it in the back of my car under some scarves and a blanket. Hidden inside beneath a layer of old maternity clothes: a small Depression glass vase a friend had given to me on my twenty-fifth birthday, a vintage Vassar paperweight, favorite hand-knit baby hats and tiny cloth shoes the boys had outgrown, a photo album, a collection of Mass cards. And the shoebox of letters.

The next morning, in the preschool parking lot after dropping my children off at their church basement Montessori class, I carefully moved the box from my trunk into a friend's. She was one of the few people I'd shared details with about my marriage. She said she'd hide the box in her house, underneath a pile of sewing scraps, until I planned out my next move in more detail.

"I promise not to even look in," she'd said at the time. "I'll just keep the box in the craft room and forget about it until you need it."

For the next few years, while I took apart one life and built another, I refreshed my email hoping to see his name. We traded photos— of old threadbare t-shirts we'd stolen from one another and kept, of his new office after a promotion, of a vintage typewriter that made him think of me, of my homemade Hula-Hoop. And then, we also reminisced.

Remember sledding across Joss Beach on the cafeteria trays?
Remember mushrooms at the farm?
Remember stargazing after the bonfire?
Do you remember?
I remember.

In our emails, we did not talk about our senior year or our breakup or how things were supposed to have turned out. But I thought a lot about those things.

I always told the story the same way—on dates, to my friends, in therapy offices. Having spent our junior year apart, while I was in London, the next summer we both took on-campus jobs so we could live together. On steamy August evenings, we'd laze on the two single mattresses he'd moved to the floor and talk about the future.

I was torn between California and New York. I planned on going to law school, but wanted to work for a year or so first. I sort of wanted to work at a nonprofit, or maybe in politics. Or join the Peace Corps. I was the first in my family to go to college, and part of me imagined leaving campus on a kind of golden cloud that would simply steer itself.

Meanwhile, the physics major lolling in bed next to me was a realist and a planner; on top of his summer employment, he'd signed up to assemble circuit boards in his room at night, mailing the electronics back to the company and getting paid per shipment, saving money for our life together after graduation. I asked where he wanted to live, and he answered that the place would be based on the opportunity.

What he said next: *Well, my grades are higher, so I'll probably have a better shot at getting into graduate school. We should see where I get in and then you can just get a job in that city.*

What I heard: *I'm smarter, I matter more. If you stay with me, you will always just follow. I will take care of you, but you will need to make yourself smaller.*

I felt something lift out of me in that moment, circle above us in the churn of the box fan, and slip out the window into the night. As hard as I tried in those next few months, I couldn't find what I had lost.

Twenty years later, I wished I could reach into the room and shake myself. *Listen!* I wanted to scream. *Really listen!* This was a boy trying to do the right thing, showing his love by taking care of me in the best way he knew how. Neither of us had secret trust funds or rich uncles or a unicorn rent-controlled apartment in the Upper West Side.

His comment was not elegant, and it was, admittedly, a bit tone-deaf, but it should not have been a deal-breaker. He wasn't trying to control me, he was trying to take care of me.

"Or maybe he was trying to do both," my therapist added last week.

Or maybe he was trying to do both.

Imaginary friends fade as childhood fades. They are situational. After divorce, the years of my marriage seemed like a kind of childhood, a time when I still believed in things that I now know are not true, were never true. As children move out of that country of imagination into the real world, they gain a kind of critical distance, inhabiting a state in which they know their imaginary friends are not real, and yet they hold on to them anyway.

We'd been emailing for almost three years when a major snowstorm pushed into the Northeast. I'd left the farmhouse two years earlier, for one and then another new home, and the town I'd recently moved to got hit with an unseasonable three feet. I started shoveling at 5:30am and continued every half hour. In my email to him that morning, I described the blue haze and the quiet of the falling snow, made light of my not being able to keep up with it.

What I didn't tell him was that after I finally completed hours of backbreaking work clearing out my driveway, rushing back and forth between the shoveling and tending to the boys inside or bundling them into snowsuits and peeling them back off again, the plow came along and edged a two-foot-high wall of ice against the lip of my property, effectively sealing us in and ruining all my work. I didn't tell him that I sat in the snow and cried in defeat, then got up, dried my tears on my scarf so the boys wouldn't see, and walked up the block until I could flag down a pickup truck of local guys with a snowblower in back who finished the job for some cash and cookies. Instead, I told him about taking breaks and making "lying down snowmen" with my sons, wanting to spike my cocoa. Bright! Sunny! Verve!

He responded in his normal way, just a few hours later, in an email with the subject line "Snow Big Deal," talking about his plans to ski, his busy work schedule, his permission for me to go ahead and spike that cocoa. At the end he wrote: *Stay warm and safe and have fun with all that snow. It really is a wonder when it's quiet and crisp and the light is just right as you described it so well.*

And then I never heard from him again.

I won't write about the emails I sent in the weeks and months that followed, until I finally understood that he was gone. It took too long, but eventually, I got it. I didn't understand it—maybe he got married? or died? or maybe a girlfriend stole into his account and blocked my emails? Or maybe he decided to focus his time and attention on a real human instead of a blinking name in a box?—but I got it. By then, I'd steadied myself with my new life, made friends and stabilized my credit score and had drinks with colleagues. I was no longer drowning; I'd built my own life raft and was used to sailing solo. I missed him, and his absence shook me deeply. But ultimately, losing his steady presence was like losing a crumpled map to the wind; I'd stared at it long enough. It didn't change where I was going.

A few months ago, a plain brown box arrived at my door. When I saw the return address label, I realized it was the stash of belongings I'd given my friend for safekeeping, the box of the things most important to me that I'd planned to pick up over and over again, but never got around to. The past years were a blur of hustling for jobs, for security, for normalcy; there hadn't been much time or money for travel. I could barely remember the items the box contained. Except for one: the shoebox of letters.

That night, after the kids were asleep, I sliced through the packing tape quietly. The maternity clothes were there on top, just as I'd left them. Underneath that layer of subterfuge were the impossibly small baby shoes, the purple and blue Depression glass vase, the paperweight, cool and heavy in my palm. It's strange, the things you think to grab when your house is burning down around you.

I found the shoebox on the bottom. It had been more than a year since I'd last heard from him, and he was no longer in my daily thoughts. Still, my hands shook as I brought the letters out of the box and into my lap. Seeing my name in his handwriting undid a knot of hope I hadn't known I was carrying in my chest.

When I was finished looking, I set the shoebox on a top shelf in my bedroom closet, next to a red silk bag full of foreign coins from all the countries I'd visited when I was younger and a box tied with a blue ribbon full of all the baby teeth my children had lost. I thought about why that shoebox had been so important to me, about the boy who wrote those letters and where he had gone and why I'd been so drawn to him, why I'd wanted him so desperately.

I hadn't known the shape of my desire, so I used another girl's to conjure my own. In college, I didn't trust that a relationship could be free and wild and solid all at the same time, so I ran away. I didn't have imagination enough to see myself happy with another partner again if I left my marriage, so I built evidence out of our correspondence, out of our past. But it was all just a bunch of old paper in a box.

Desire is simultaneously as invisible and real as an imaginary friend, as ephemeral as hope.

Every so often I take these things down from their shelf and try to make sense of them—the teeth, the coins, the letters—and of my past lives. The teeth are impossibly tiny and jagged, the bloody roots turned black in the hollows of each shiny, brittle shard. Could they ever have truly lived in my sons' rosebud mouths? I sift the money through my fingers, trying to recall each coin's origin as I trace the raised crowns, cut-out centers and squared edges. I cup my heavy palm to my nose, breathe in the coppery smell, try to remember a time when I might have known their worth, what any of the markings meant, to which country they belonged. Recently, I added my old wedding ring to this pile of metal, and the plain worn band clinks brightly against the other foreign currency. When I open the shoebox, his handwriting still collapses me. Sometimes I open the envelopes and unfold the letters, but more often I do not.

I tell myself, *I am the tooth fairy.* I tell myself, *These countries will continue to exist even if I never see them again.* I tell myself, *He was real.*

These things are all true.

These things were never true.

Suspended Animation

A S A CHILD, I OFTEN watched my traveling-salesman father sit down in his old blue armchair after coming home from a day or week on the road. It amused me that, after so many hours of sitting in a vehicle, he would want to just sit in his chair for the night. His body would sag into the cushions, and he would stretch every so often, rolling his neck and flexing his wrists. I could tell he was in pain by his eyes, the way they were narrowed and unfocused, a band of tension stretching across them like a mask. He kept bottles of pain relievers in the cupboard next to the coffee, by his bed, in the cupholder of his car. His pain seemed workaday, just part of his routine.

My pain is also ordinary. It isn't even particularly painful, just dull, distracting, frustrating. Relentless. Each morning, I stumble downstairs and start my ritual: open the kitchen blinds, measure out four heaping scoops of dark roast, pour in four cups of water, click the silver button. Then I reach into the cabinet above the coffeemaker and pull out the jumbo-sized bottle of Costco-brand ibuprofen.

I see that same mask I used to see on my father's face on my own face these days, in a photo snapped without warning by my seven-year-old son or if I catch my reflection in a store window by accident. If I'm paying attention, I can spot it on my fellow drivers as we stop at a light, the other mothers at the playground, or the students in the classroom where I teach. A darkness across the brow, a cinched look, a strain that isn't quite erased by a smile: the pain may be different, but the mask is the same.

My migraines, which started when I was thirteen and have gone through dormant periods, recently became debilitating again. I had been treating them with a combination of Excedrin Migraine and Amerge, one of the common triptan medications used to break a migraine cycle by narrowing blood vessels around the brain. When the headaches returned, I was a few months into a new teaching job on Long Island, and just over a year into living on my own with my two small sons after leaving my husband, who'd remained in our house, in another state, while we were separated. Neither of us had filed any official papers yet, but we hadn't lived together in over a year; I didn't think I ever wanted to live with anyone aside from my sons ever again. I wasn't sleeping or eating very well, and it was around this time that my therapist asked what I did for fun. "Work?" I replied meekly. It was no surprise that I'd become submerged in a sea of headaches during this period, but this battery of migraines felt different.

Returning to the suburbs was wearing on me; I'd grown up on Long Island, but I was a South Shore kid. My hometown had been improvisational and a bit wild, a jumble of old bungalows on cement slabs surrounded by wild clutches of honeysuckle and sand dunes dotted with thorny rose hips. Here on the North Shore, I felt like I was moving through a pneumatic tube, sealed off from everything. Nothing smelled, nobody yelled, even the dogs barely barked. It was like eating a store-bought apple after having picked them off your own tree your whole life; clean, but tasteless, and a little bit mealy.

My migraines always arrive with an aura, a kind of shimmery lake of silver that starts as a tiny pinhole and expands over the course of an hour across my entire field of vision until I am completely blind. Although being blinded can sometimes be inconvenient— when I'm driving, or standing at a blackboard with another two hours of teaching ahead of me, for example—it rarely frightens me anymore. The aura stage is strange, but painless, and I've grown to enjoy it. I know that for at least forty minutes all I can really do is sit quietly. I can't read. I can't grade papers. I can't check email. I also know that the discomfort is temporary, that it will end.

The blindness throws off my other senses so that smells become magnified and sounds are difficult to process; I have a hard time determining if I am whispering or yelling, so I can't return phone calls or hold a conversation. Instead, I just sit and watch the silvery stars pulse across my line of vision, let them expand, wait for them to recede. The sensation is quite beautiful, really; I imagine the experience similar to looking at a droplet of mercury under a microscope. Exposure can kill you, but its shine is no less alluring.

I've grown to feel grateful for the aura because it acts as a warning
bell and gives me time to gulp down some caffeine and get to my
pill bottles in an effort to dull the extraordinary pain that is on its
way. The aura is like a tornado warning, giving me plenty of time
to get underground.

But during this new wave of migraines, these auras sparked
across my vision and then . . . nothing. I still got the headache-
hangover that follows a migraine, like a full-body charley horse
that lasts for two or three days. But the worst part—the excruciat-
ing pain like a tourniquet twisting around my skull—was missing.
It was as if the headache was being polite and holding itself back,
as if it knew I'd had enough pain these past few years after watching my marriage fall apart, packing up and moving multiple times,
parenting on my own, job hunting and trying to keep my sons and
myself afloat on my teaching salary. It was hard enough to make
sure I ate at least one meal a day and combed my hair, brushed my
teeth. My world was a precarious balance of cutting everything
close: the time between my last class and picking up the kids, the
time between my next paycheck and rent, the time between visits
to the gas pump. I always had a dull, widespread ache across my
head and body these days, but the migraine was being merciful,
holding back the full-blown crushing pain that would force me to
retreat to a dark room for at least a day.

I was relieved for this small clemency. But then, after this happened a few times in a month, I became concerned. What if this
wasn't mercy? What if this wasn't even a headache, but some kind
of stroke or brain tumor instead? I popped more Excedrin and
made an appointment with a neurologist.

❦

I'd had aura without headache during only one time period in my life before. Pregnant with my second child, I had a few of these episodes at the end of the first trimester. I was living full-time in rural Pennsylvania at the time, and unlike my first pregnancy, with ob-gyn visits in Manhattan that were all technology and blood tests and charts, for my second pregnancy I was under the care of a country midwife. Sometimes during appointments she just rubbed my belly and asked how I felt. She thought the painless migraines were perhaps hormone-related, and might ease up once I got past that first trimester.

The auras did eventually stop, but not until the tail end of my second trimester. They were then replaced with early contractions. Instead of feeling my skull crushed by a migraine, I would sit in bed and watch my swollen belly tighten and lift, squeezing the little body it held inside. It was as if the tourniquet had moved down my body. At first I thought perhaps these were Braxton Hicks contractions, but I timed them and kept logs in a little notebook, hash marks breaking down the number of contractions per hour as if I were deciphering a secret wartime code. Like the painless migraines, these pregnancy auras heralded painless contractions—I felt a tight pressure, and terrible worry, but the actual pain never came.

The midwife prescribed flower essences. Another alternative healer friend gave me tissue salts. When I looked up the remedies online, I was confused—both seemed aimed at anxiety and stress, not pregnancy or hormones or anything contraction-related. I

ended up in the hospital overnight a few times, the contractions
monitored by a belly band. The hospital room, with its clockwork
staff, quiet humming machines, and antiseptic smell, was the only
place I could sleep for more than thirty minutes at a time. I didn't
have work, I didn't have a toddler to feed and entertain and mon-
itor, I didn't have a husband whose frustrations were spilling out
and splashing across every corner of the house. Pregnancy was a
particularly potent time, with our house alternating between fiery
rages and a cold silent chill. I'd explained away his anger during
the first pregnancy by hanging it on the stress of beginning a family and tight finances. When we found out about the second pregnancy, the move to the country had been an attempt to assuage
some of these stresses, but being isolated out in the middle of the
woods was just like producing the same play on a smaller stage,
everything close up and heightened.

At the end of each hospital stay, when the nurse told me it was
safe for me to be discharged and return home to my toddler and
husband, I felt like crying. I just wanted to stay where things were
peaceful, and calm, and where nurses smiled when they offered
me tiny boxes of cornflakes and lunchbox-sized cartons of milk.

In a gleaming medical building of glass in suburban Long Island,
I sat on the exam table and followed a penlight from right to left
as the neurologist gave me instructions. After a quick check, she
said I was not having a stroke and she saw no evidence of a brain
tumor, but she did notice I had very little range of motion in my
neck. It was true that I'd had a hard time turning my neck to

check for cars when changing lanes, though I hadn't connected it to my headaches.

"Here's what I can do," she said. The neurologist was in her early thirties and had her fingers laced over her pregnant belly, rings sparkling amidst the medical-grade steel in the room. When I told her I had two sons and was currently living apart from their father, she blinked for an extra beat before smiling broadly again, as if erasing my last comment. "Well, we can try medication, or we can give physical therapy a shot first and see how that works for you. And in the meantime, if the headaches change or the pain returns, come back and we'll reevaluate. Okay?" She blinked again and I understood I was dismissed. I took my prescription and went back to work.

I imagined physical therapy would be a kind of guided workout in a gym. I dug out my ratty old sports bra and yoga pants and bought new red sneakers on sale from Amazon. I also imagined I'd be in a gym-like setting with injured athletes and other middle-aged people with problems, like me. I was surprised when I was the only person under the age of seventy sitting in the waiting room, except for some of the patients' health aides.

I was called into a small room with wraparound curtain walls. I was confused when they handed me a hospital gown. "I'm here for my neck," I explained. The assistant nodded and repeated that I should get undressed from the waist up, leaving only my bra, with the gown opening at the back.

A few minutes later, the owner, a man with soft hands named

Dr. P, entered the small space and drew the curtain. I sat in a vinyl office chair in front of a hospital bed and watched him cover a rubber donut with a mesh hairnet and tear a hole in the middle for my nose and mouth. He motioned for me to place my head in the donut. I did so, stretching my forearms awkwardly across the bed, hospital gown splayed open, leaving my back naked. I realized my hands were balled into fists.

"Relax," Dr. P whispered in his Eastern European accent, clucking slightly. He squirted cold jelly along my spine, promising it wouldn't stain my clothes. With his finger, he drew a square on my back along the edges of my open gown. "This is the only place I will touch you," he promised.

I felt silly then, like a child at a doctor's office, being calmed for a procedure. I thought of my sneakers, the red too bright, so clearly new. I hadn't realized I would need to undress and be touched. This felt unnecessary, invasive. *I'm not afraid of him*, I told myself, but I still couldn't seem to unball my fists the entire time he rolled his palms and forearms against my shoulder blades and up my neck.

When he finished the massage, Dr. P used a towel to wipe away the jelly, which reminded me of pregnancy ultrasounds, before leaving me to put my shirt back on. He said in a resigned voice, "Okay. Maybe you trust me next time." A female assistant led me through some stretches, and after an hour I left.

Afterwards, I could still feel Dr. P's hands on me. His touch lingered, and I caught myself balling my hands as if I were still stretched out on that hospital bed. I finished work, picked up the kids and got them through homework and dinner, bath and bed, cleaned up the kitchen and made lunches for the next day, did some more work on the computer at the dining room table. I was just sinking into sleep myself when I realized why his touch unnerved me so.

It had been nearly three years since I'd been touched with any care. Sure, my children constantly pawed at me, grabbing and climbing and stretching out on me. One of the most surprising parts of motherhood for me was the sheer physicality of it, the constant press of my boys' bodies on mine. But to them, my body was like a piece of furniture, just there to support them, transport them, to curl around them and offer comfort.

It had been so long since anyone touched me without asking anything in return, touched me to release pain, touched me with softness and intention. Over the past years, my body had become a machine with parts: feet to drive a car; legs to get me to class on time; fingers to type; shoulders to hold my bookbag, two child-sized backpacks, lunch boxes, the extras bag with sunscreen and towels and wipes and oranges. My back to hoist one child on, my hand to hold on to the other. I didn't exercise, didn't have the time. It had been so long since I'd thought of my body in its own right.

Dr. P's touch had activated something, brought my body back to awareness, and in that process I realized I'd stuffed my connection to my physical self under the bathroom sink next to the makeup bag that held my old caked mascara, a half-empty lipstick tube, and my engagement ring.

At my next physical therapy appointment, a different man entered the room and swept the curtain closed behind him. He wore

pink drugstore glasses, light blue baggy jeans, and a fleece vest.
He introduced himself as Jose and his hands went directly to the
tight places in my back and neck without me directing him. He
asked about the headaches, how long I'd had them, how I combat-
ted them. I confessed about the bottle of pain relievers above the
coffeemaker, that I decided to try physical therapy because I don't
want to take prescription drugs.

Jose was quiet for a moment, digging into the tight straps of
tendon running from my shoulders up the back of my neck.

"But how is taking ibuprofen every day any different?" He
sighs. He looks me in the eye as he speaks quietly. "If you keep
coming here, you shouldn't need to take those anymore. You tell
me if you still need them, okay Professor?"

I nod. As he continues to massage me, his hands gentle and
firm, fingertips padding across my spine like a piano player, my
fists unfurl.

After a few weeks, I felt like a regular at the rehab. I recognized
the health aides in the waiting room, left my bag in the car under
my coat so I just needed to carry my phone and car key. Some days
Dr. P appeared in the room, looking quickly at his little card before
tearing the hole in the hair mask and asking me to put my head in
the donut. Instead of asking me how I feel, he asks me about my
school, or the weather, or the election. Each visit, I hope for Jose
instead, and when he walks in the room, I'm relieved. He is always
trying out some new pair of glasses or gadget, like wireless head-
phones. He tells me he has never had a massage in his life. I ask him
why and he says he doesn't really like people touching him. "But

you don't mind touching other people?" I asked. He just shrugged and smiled.

We developed an easy banter. He talked about his wife and his children and his home country and soccer. He told me he saw me walking with another patient of his, that he is glad we are friends, that I need friends. He reminded me to repeat the exercises at home. "You are a mommy," he liked to remind me. "You have to be strong for your boys." Without ever asking directly, he seemed to know that although I was there to fix my migraines, it was more than my neck and head that was locked and tense.

If he had asked me, I would have stumbled over my words. I wasn't divorced, but I wasn't married anymore. I usually just said we lived apart, or explained that my husband was an artist and he needed space to paint, more space than we could afford in New York. Not that many people asked; I spent most of my time shuttling between my classroom and my children's school. During the time between my appointments, I'd store up things to say to Jose because often my physical therapy appointment was my only adult interaction, not counting my phone calls with my mother, my classes, and time on the playground with other harried moms. Physical therapy was the only time when someone asked how I was feeling and waited for me to answer.

R. and I were expressly not talking. Before I left the farmhouse with the children, there were glimmers here and there of the man I'd hoped would be my partner, but I slowly came to understand that although they sometimes flamed gloriously, those glimmers had become the aberrations. I missed the camaraderie that comes with marriage, the everydayness, that feeling of being in it together, but I didn't miss being married to my husband. And I didn't quite know what to do about that.

The year stretched on, and I continued physical therapy. One semester ended, another one began. R. and I celebrated a strained Christmas together at the farmhouse. In our new town, the boys and I settled on our favorite pizza place, the best spot for ice cream. The auras had stopped and I could turn my head to check traffic behind me while driving, but my face still felt locked in pain, my jaw tense and eyes narrowed. I never quite felt the relief Jose had promised.

Then one day, Dr. P stood in front of me and announced that I felt better. I thought about this, and while it was true I hadn't had a migraine for months, I didn't actually feel much better. When I said this, Dr. P dismissed me with a wave.

I looked at the yellowing newspaper clip of Dr. P next to the rehab's front door. In it, he wore a unitard, fit and strong even in his sixties, a competitive wrestler. With my head back down on the papered donut, he told me I have tension headaches, not migraines, and ignored me when I disagreed. I have heard him through the curtains with other patients who try to explain their pain to him— what hurts most today, how it has changed since last time, or how it alters with the weather, or their diet, or exercise. And I heard that same clucking he gave me during my first session, the chiding, the derision. *What do you know about your own body?* this clucking says. I am reminded of couples therapy sessions with my husband, when I would attempt to share my feelings. "When you say or do X, I feel scared/mad/frustrated," I would try, following the coaching of the therapist. "No," he would respond. Just, no.

I submitted to Dr. P's massage as best I could, then got dressed again. I didn't schedule my next appointment on the way out that day.

One late afternoon a few weeks later, as I walked into the university club dining room after talking on a symposium panel, I blinked to clear a sunspot from my eyes. But it wasn't a sunspot. Within minutes, I knew, I'd be blind, and stay blind for the better part of an hour. I popped some pills, made a quick circuit around the buffet, and found a seat next to a colleague who I knew wouldn't judge my squinting. I sat aiming my fork at the food on my plate with varying accuracy as the silver blinded me completely and then began to recede. Once the shimmer was gone, I rushed to my car and drove home, hoping to finish my commute before any crush of pain began.

But the headache was still holding back. Three more auras followed that week, and my body was seized in what felt like a permanent endorphin rush, an unrelenting charley horse from the top of my head to my hips. The auras hit me in waves, crashing over me, but between my teaching schedule and my children I couldn't get back to physical therapy for another week.

When I finally returned, Jose stepped into the room, took one look at me, and stopped. "Where have you been, Professor?" he asked. "You are in pain again," he observed, shaking his head sadly.

It was true. My shoulders were hunched to my ears and I could feel the tightness in my eyes. I did not have an active migraine that day, but felt shipwrecked from the battery of headaches and headache hangovers the past few weeks. Everything hurt. I complained for a bit, sounding like a petulant child. *I've been coming to rehab for months already! Shouldn't this be fixed? When will I be able to stop? How much longer do I need to come for this to work?*

Jose looked at me gravely. "Your headaches will never go away," he chided. "You have to be friends with your body and make your headaches a part of you. Figure out what they are trying to say. Don't try to cut them out or dull them. Move with them. Listen. They are trying to help you."

Jose gave me my usual massage and then suggested we try something new. He had me lie on my back on the table and cupped my head in his hands. With small movements he manually stretched my neck while sitting at the end of the hospital bed. After a few minutes of silent stretching, he started to speak near my ear. "My nephew got a divorce last year. The divorce was so quick, it was like camping. They took everything apart so fast, like pulling down a tent and packing everything away. Poof. You finish camping and there is nothing left."

I sat quietly, eyes closed, as he moved my neck slowly. He continued.

"You know, Professor, marriage is like a table. You need four legs. If one leg is gone, the table can stand for a while, but if you lean on it the wrong way, it tips and crashes to the ground."

The tears began to well beneath my closed eyelids.

"You need a man who will stand by you for one hundred years, Professor," Jose said softly.

And he laid my head gently on the exam table, leaving with the gentle whoosh of the curtain before the tears slid out, staining the paper cloth beneath me.

I filed for divorce the next day.

Like so many people around me, I still have that tightness in my eyes that just doesn't seem to disappear, and I still see the shadow of the pain mask across my face when I catch an unexpected glimpse of myself in the mirror. After ten months of rehab, my head and neck feel better, but I know now my pain will never go away. Pain just isn't like that.

When people ask me about my husband now, I still fumble for words. His new art studio is in the city, he is still painting portraits, and his voice still clenches at the mention of a bill. I still call him my husband even though we are going through a divorce. Both words make my head ache a bit when I say them, but it is so much better than not saying them at all.

I am still alone, but I am no longer lonely. I've started walking on the beach or on the trails at the nature preserve near my house. Sometimes I take these walks with friends. My children take chess and tae kwon do, they laugh out loud during playdates, and they see their father every other weekend. I signed a three-year lease on my apartment, and I let my hair grow long and my house is always full of music. Instead of oil paintings, my walls are full of children's drawings and postcards and family photos.

And yet, the incessant suburban drone of the leaf blowers, the toned upper arms of the PTA moms, the pungent smell of ozone emanating from the miles of manicured sidewalk after a morning

rain in summer: they all set my teeth on edge. I miss the way the
frogs and fireflies come out at the same time in the country, my
own short film playing just off my porch every night; or in the city,
I miss the way the bottoms of my feet ache and burn at the end of
the day, and how my roommate Jenny and I would come home
after work to our third-floor walk-up on Spring Street and take
turns standing ankle-deep in a cold bath while the other perched
on the closed toilet lid, chatting about our day. In the suburbs,
everyone's grass is the same color, everyone's garbage can clearly
labeled with their house number, everybody simply waves at a safe
distance. The street lamps click on at the same time every night
and there is no darkness, there is no light; it just is.

I wake up in the morning, turn on the coffee, my NPR. I reach
for the bottle of pills in the cabinet or I don't. My headache, like
me, is suspended in midair. We are waiting for something to happen. When it does, instead of pushing it away, I'll cup the mask to
my face and try to see the world through it, like looking at mercury under a microscope.

Finding Home

THE FIRST TIME I CONFESSED aloud to being a single mother, I was talking to Rebecca Solnit. She'd come as a guest speaker to my university as part of our MFA reading series and we met before her event so I could interview her for our literary magazine. We'd spent an hour together, first examining the old black-and-white photographs on the walls in the austere conference room, laughing conspiratorially about the ratio of men to women in the images. She recounted some esoteric historical fact about Holland, because she is Rebecca Solnit, and we sat down at the glossy lacquered table, the kind I'd recently grown accustomed to in my divorce lawyer's offices, the same impenetrable glaze atop the same piss-yellow wood.

The room grew dark as we sat. Solnit is passionate in thought but not diction; her answers came out in full, potent sentences, forming perfect unhurried paragraphs straight out of her mouth. Her casual brilliance is intimidating, as much for her meteoric intelligence as for her all-in-a-day's-work air.

She is insanely prolific, and though I called myself a writer, the

truth was I hadn't filled a page in a very long time. I'd wanted so
desperately to impress her, to feel some camaraderie, but at that
giant table I began to feel like an imposter. I ruffled through my
notes, suddenly hating all of the questions I'd so painstakingly pre-
pared. The feeling was uncannily similar to the way I often felt at
the same god-awful table at my lawyer's firm, the bloodless copies
of court papers in front of me.

This was my second year teaching at the university, and I'd
spent most of it trying to hide my slowly disintegrating home life.
I was working toward tenure, and the last thing I wanted was to
become a red flag; divorce signals disaster case, and I preferred
them to see me as a calm, sure thing.

In that conference room, Solnit and I talked about the essay
and literary maps, the notion of hope and whether we had any.
"I've been thinking a lot, lately, about boys," I began, hesitating,
seeing Solnit's eyes flicker to her watch. "I have two young sons,"
I continued. She smiled blandly at this, and I suddenly hated the
navy blue gabardine pants I'd chosen to wear, and the bed in my
suburban Long Island bedroom I'd laid them out on that morning, my bright bird-patterned pillowcases suddenly seeming
childish and fey.

I kept going. "The thing is, I'm a single mother—"

Solnit's eyes flickered with interest. She drew herself upright,
to attention, leaned forward and said with feeling, "*Good* for you."

We finished the last fifteen minutes of the interview sitting
with our knees almost touching, talking about boys and our hope
and their possibility, the struggle of raising good ones. Then we
walked next door, joined in the tepid buffet line, filling our plates

with salmon and rice pilaf, and moved with the rest of the professors and deans to the auditorium.

Good for me, I repeated to myself later, sitting in the audience and listening to her talk about mansplaining and Trump and protest. She'd said it as if we were talking about a raise, or a decision to quit smoking. *Good for you* also means: *You are moving in the right direction*, or *Keep going*, or *You're on the right track!*

And a little door opened up in my heart. If this were a math problem, she'd shown me that breaking up my family was not simply subtraction. By taking away, I could be creating room for more.

Was there a moment you knew you wanted to end your marriage?
This is the question everyone always asks, the still-married ones, after one too many glasses of wine at the PTA fundraiser, at the ladies lunch after chaperoning the first-grade aquarium trip, in the corner of the patio at the neighborhood Fourth of July party, alongside the dance floor at weddings. After a while, I came to understand that they were really asking about themselves, matching their experience with mine, pulling a measuring tape around my ribcage and then circling their own to see how close the numbers fell.

I'm sure I've given a different answer every time I've been asked. The most honest one is this: You never *know*.

Divorced people don't ask me that question. Once, in a makeup store, I asked the woman behind the counter for help. "I've been wearing the same color lipstick for twenty years," I explained. "They discontinued it, and I bought the last two from your other store on Broadway last year, but now there are none left, and I guess I really should just try something new, but . . ." I trailed off, inexplicably close to tears as she stared at me dispassionately. Here was this gorgeous, unblinking woman in front of me, with flawless skin and glossy lips and creamy brown cheeks, unafraid to experiment with her makeup on the daily, unafraid of change. *But a person can only take so much change,* I wanted to tell her. The store was empty and it was just the two of us. I bit my tongue to keep from crying and decided I needed her to understand. I cleared my throat and tried again. "The thing is, I'm going through a divorce, and—"

The woman put her warm hands on my shoulders, looked into my eyes, and said soberly, deeply seriously: "Congratulations."

I felt inducted, into a world unseen by the marrieds, into a world I never wanted to see when I was a married.

The pain of divorce is different for everyone, but it is also the same. I hate this. I hate that the books I read early on in the process, the therapists I spoke to in person or listened to on podcasts, the friends who'd been through it, were all right. I feel like I walked into a one-street town called Divorceville and the only storefronts I could see were those cheap trick psychics, one after another, offering to read your palm or your tarot cards for five dollars. They all said the same boring things.

And they were all right.

Decades ago, in my twenties, I used to run the numbers in my journal, betting against my friends. When I was thinking about getting married, I tallied up all the married people I knew. I would look at my two best friends from college, both married to men they met at the same college, and smugly reassure myself that my odds were pretty good.

What an asshole.

❧

They say the most stressful life events are divorce, the death of a loved one, and moving. This list always confused me. Leaving a marriage is another type of death, of course. You are killing the person you were, the person you'd hoped to be. You are killing off the version of the future you'd once believed in. But moving? There is so much agency in the act of moving, so much implicit hope in a new home.

I am not a child of divorce, though my parents both went through divorces before they married each other. So many friends who are children of divorce tell me that as adults, they now understand why their parents needed to separate, are grateful, even, that they did.

But when they say this, they all set their jaws a certain way. It doesn't mean they are happy about it.

The pain of divorce is really the pain of grief. You grieve for the death of the fantasy you believed, you hoped for, the one you so desperately wanted to be true. And everyone can smell it. The inescapable stink of failure that the newly divorced emit is the worst thing, no matter how much sex or money or food or Tough Mudder races they stuff into themselves. It is the smell of abject sorrow, of the pain of being so completely, utterly, undeniably wrong. It is also the cold-sweat fear that if you could be so gloriously, dumbly, incredibly wrong about your choice of life partner, you could never trust yourself to be right about anything else again.

Time passed. My still-husband still lived apart from us, but now in Manhattan. We put the farmhouse up for sale. I enrolled my kids in public school, in tae kwon do, in chess. Picked a new pediatrician. Hired babysitters, got library cards. *Will we ever live with Dad again?* my older son would ask every so often.

Let's make our summer list! I'd respond. Or, *Do you think the ice cream man will come tonight?* Deflect, deflect, defend, just like I'd watched his little body do every Tuesday and Thursday afternoon, tied tightly into his white tae kwon do uniform like a box of fancy cookies.

I was like a woman closing her eyes the moment before her car crashes, willing the situation to stop or simply disappear altogether. I did not have this luxury. Each week my time was split between my work at the university, my writing, and my children. And each week, one invariably fell by the wayside. I drew myself into my own body, moving quickly and efficiently through my days. Some weeks the boys would complain—*All you do is type, type, type*—and other weeks I'd be consumed with volunteering for the elementary school book fair and playdates and calls with my lawyer and midterms in my own classes. My children, my students, my lawyer; sometimes, it felt like they were all sitting on my chest.

My own writing, meanwhile, was like a distant song, something I heard the woman next door singing to her child. I didn't have time to think about where I might have heard that song, much less try to sing it in my own voice.

That year, I took up running. I preferred to run alone, in the woods, in the nature preserve near my apartment. The trails were soft, sandy dirt, shaded with a few gentle hills, interspersed with vistas overlooking the waves crashing on the rocky beach below.

I liked to run two circuits through the trails and come out on the downhill slope leading to the waves. The rickety ramp onto the beach had a kind of shipwrecked look, and the sand was always littered with cement pilings and rusty boat rudders and whatever other beach detritus happened to wash up on the shore. One April weekend, I dragged my children out to that beach for an Earth Day cleanup activity. We were given gloves and plastic bags and told to tally up the different types of garbage we collected. There were the ubiquitous straws and fishing line and bottle caps and beer cans, along with a disturbing number of tampon applicators. I steered my children away from the rotting horseshoe crabs they'd been lining up along the shoreline, and when my oldest made a move to retrieve a condom from the thorny underbrush along the dunes, I announced it was time to go home.

On the weekends, or at school functions, or in the supermarket, I'd watch the other families. Some had two adults, but most had just one woman with children trailing behind her. *Was she a single mother,* I'd wonder, *like me?* We looked the same. Just another tired mother trying to keep one child from dropping their ice cream cone down her shirt as she hoisted them onto her hip, hold-

ing another one by their hand or sleeve or collar. Mine were no longer toddlers, but I still tried to keep them within reach, one hand
attached to each boy at all times.

What did single mother mean, anyway? The math felt off; the
term smacked of being diminished, when taking care of children
without a partner only inflated every responsibility. Each time I
said those words, I felt like it somehow identified me as less than. I
wasn't a mother, I was a *single* mother. I was somehow not whole,
never could be. The term made me feel like half a person, even
though everything in my life had expanded.

Paradoxically, I found parenting infinitely easier as a single
mother. Parenting was now marked by no longer having to fight
against another person day in and day out to establish a structural
sanity. If I wanted something done, I did it. And if I didn't feel like
doing it, I only had myself to answer to. One of the starkest differ-
ences, though, was the sheer absence of time alone. Forget about
personal time; even attending an evening PTA meeting meant
finding and paying a babysitter. I couldn't ever just zip to the grocery store to grab a gallon of milk if I ran out; this involved two
children peeing and packing snacks and snapping them into their
car seats and then loading them into a shopping cart, herding them
around a store, adding sixteen other items to the basket along with
the gallon of milk including a Matchbox car and a certain type of
squeeze yogurt their friend at school had in his lunchbox and cookies for being good and two packs of gum and a spiky fresh pineap-
ple they promised to try when we got home and then wouldn't.

When I did find myself alone with an hour ahead of me, I ran.
On my running days, I'd get to that sandy beach and slow down,

catching my breath as my feet shuffled heavily in the sand. I'd make my way to a particular boulder the size of my dining table and hoist myself up on it. I'd stare out into the sea, what I thought might be the low curve of the Throgs Neck Bridge just visible to my left, and then I'd stretch out on the dark rock, like a sunning turtle, letting the rays dry the sweat from my shirt. Sometimes the rock was burning hot, and I leaned my shoulders back into that hard heat, searing the soft flesh just behind my armpits and on the backs of my thighs. I liked feeling that pain, the rock hard and solid against my skin. Sometimes I think I just liked feeling.

When I'd moved into our new apartment on the north shore of Long Island, I was consumed with filling the house with bright, happy things. Maybe I thought if I filled it with enough color and fancy the boys wouldn't notice the absence of the other body. Even when he was with us, their father's attention often seemed else-where, thinking about the painting on his easel or who would be modeling for his life drawing class that week. But it was impossible to ignore his physical absence.

I bought plants, and hung paper birds from the ceiling and the children's art everywhere. I think I was also hoping they wouldn't notice our furniture was a collection of cast-offs. The TV console was a craft table from their old Montessori preschool. The tele-vision on top of it was from my parents' guest room. Our dining table had been given to us by a generous neighbor, who looked at me quizzically when I said the round wooden table would go per-fectly in our eat-in kitchen. "But you know it isn't a dining table, right?" she'd asked. She patiently explained that it was for a living room, the kind of table that goes next to a piano and upon which you put a runner and family photographs. I did not have that kind of living room, and didn't think I ever would. I told her the table would be perfect for us. And it was.

We sat at that table on some vintage 1950s Shelby Williams chairs I'd bought in my twenties when I wrote for home design magazines and had time to scour eBay for such things. The ruddy red vinyl seats were still in pretty good shape, and it occurred to me that I could probably sell them and make a little money—the holidays were coming and money was tight. I was making more money more reliably than I ever had, but my expenses were also higher than they'd ever been, and I supplemented my paycheck with a constellation of freelance writing gigs, making use of balance transfer offers on my credit cards, and waiting until the treads on our sneakers wore completely away before replacing them. Around that time, I saw a message on the local parents listserv offering a set of black wooden dining chairs for free. *Perfect!* I thought. I secured the chairs with an email and set off to pick the kids up from school.

A few days later, we drove up the hill, to the affluent part of our Gold Coast town. We pulled into the empty driveway and I spotted the chairs on the porch. "Just wait here, guys," I said to the boys in their booster seats behind me.

I carried two of the chairs back to our car, opened the hatchback, and stuffed them in. The boys craned their necks to watch.

"What are you doing, Mama?" one or the other asked.

"The family who lives here got new chairs, and they don't need these anymore," I said in my world-explainer voice. "So now, we get new chairs, too."

"But we don't need new chairs," my oldest said.

"Well, I was thinking we could use these chairs around our dining room table and sell the other ones," I said. I left the hatch open, figuring I could fit one more chair in, but would probably have to come back for the rest.

I wrestled the first two chairs into the car and noticed my older son's shoulders shaking. I got back in the car and was surprised to see him crying. I thought he was hurt, that his little brother had maybe reached over and punched him. "What on earth is the matter?" I asked, turning my body into the space between the driver's seat and the empty passenger seat. He just kept crying, there in the driveway with half the chairs in the car.

As we drove home, he did his best to calm himself long enough to speak. He finally said loudly, "But I like our chairs!" I stared dumbly at him in the rearview mirror. His small face was deadly serious. "You can't sell our chairs! They are *our* chairs!"

I hadn't even realized he'd noticed them.

Once, when I was newly pregnant with my second son, I visited a medium. She had a British accent, curly dark hair, and a face long and sculptural like a Modigliani. Her floral perfume was the only spark of texture in the staid midtown Manhattan corporate apartment where she saw her clients.

The medium talked for nearly forty minutes about my career, about family and friends, about the past. At the end of the hour, she asked if I wanted to know anything else. I asked about my relation-ship. *Oh, he's not the one*, she said quickly, easily. I fingered my wed-ding ring awkwardly under the table. *He's not*, the medium said sharply. *And you know this.*

I asked next about motherhood. I hadn't told her I was preg-nant, and she hadn't seen my toddler or the child in my belly in the reading. *You will become a mother one day*, she said with certainty. *And you'll be a good one.*

She softened for a moment. *But it will take you a long time.*

❧

Louise Glück once wrote, "We look at the world once, in child-hood. The rest is memory." I knew from the stories of many friends and the essays of so many of my college students that the moment you are told your parents are getting divorced is seared into your memory. The act of divorce takes such a long time that I had the luxury of stalling—separating is different from filing for divorce is different from finally getting a divorce, which in our case unfurled across many years. I practiced my words in therapy, thought about the best place and time to do it. One friend forever hated the family couch after her parents' announcement; another could never eat a certain kind of cake her mother had put out alongside her news. In the end, after all my attempts of controlled burning, it bubbled up spontaneously one afternoon during homework at the dining room table.

"Families are all different," I started, lamely. I continued to fumble into the idea that some parents live together, others live apart. The boys had a few friends in their elementary classrooms whose parents were divorced, but I wasn't sure what was discussed at school or how.

"Do you know what the word *divorce* means?" I waited for the flicker of fear in their eyes, but they were still just half-listening, coloring their maps or practicing their multiplication tables. My oldest rolled his eyes.

"We *know* what divorce is, Mom." Okay. That was a surprise. But a helpful one. Now the next hurdle. I took a deep breath. I told them their father and I were getting a divorce.

After a beat of silence and stillness—no pencils scratching, no waxy crayons coloring—they returned to their tasks at hand. I asked if they had any questions.

"No," said my youngest carefully.

"It's just . . . ," my older son continued. "We thought you already were."

I kept thinking that if I could get to the other side of this divorce, or if I could get a tenure-track position, or get more pages written, or run one more mile, or could get new furniture, I'd be all right. I'd be closer to home, or to some made-up idea of home I'd assigned to myself.

What I kept forgetting was that I was already home, because this moment is what will mean home for my children. Their childhood and memories of family and home will not wait for me to construct them. They already exist. The sound of my type-type-typing all the time, our kitchen dance parties, picking through the horseshoe crabs on beach cleanup day, the three of us laughing in my suburban Long Island bed with our heads on my bright bird-pattern pillows on lazy Saturday mornings, the bottom of the bed covered in our dog-eared books. Night after night, we will sit on our old ruddy Shelby Williams chairs at our secondhand non–dining room table, the three of us, and be home. It's not how I imagined it. But now I can't even remember how I once imagined it.

Still Life 3: The Suburbs

INTERIOR OF A SILVER VOLVO WAGON, back-door pockets stuffed with Candy Ring wrappers, pencils, and rocks; I am looking in the rearview mirror or over my right shoulder into the backseat, my left hand on the wheel, right hand on the seat back next to me. Two small boys, both with eyes the exact color of my own, stare back at me, pleading or explaining or demanding or questioning or laughing or crying or sulking or fighting or trying to hide. The car smells vaguely Cheerio-like. No matter the music, the soundtrack is chatter and the rhythmic kicking of a seat back.

There is almost never a front passenger. On the rare occasion we need to ferry a guest, I must first clear out the pile of student papers and Amish Country ticket stubs and grocery receipts and emergency snacks and half-empty cans of spray sunscreen. For a period, the seat was nicknamed Mom's Mobile Library because of the person-high pile of books that lived there. On the drive to their elementary school each morning, we'd get halfway down our block before the car beeped urgently, warning us that the front passenger was not buckled in, until one day it occurred to me that I could simply plug in the seat belt around the books and, *voilà!* No more beeping.

I am in the driver's seat, but I don't always know where we are going. I am in the driver's seat, but it is my father's car on paper until the monthly payments I send to my parents' mailbox in envelopes my mother has pre-addressed and pre-stamped add up to say otherwise. I am in the driver's seat, but the wayback is full of things that are not mine, including a broken umbrella, a roll of flattened paper towels, extra sweatshirts, hats and gloves, car blankets, a half-filled-out book of Mad Libs, a picnic blanket, a Frisbee, footballs, and, on Tuesdays and Thursdays, two violas.

We love the car, and depend on it, hard, even though it keeps trying to teach us we shouldn't. The skylight motor stops working, skylight half open. The dashboard likes to flash threatening alerts that I know not to be true, like *Lift Open* or *Washer Fluid Low*. We get flat tires everywhere, it seems. On a deserted country road in Pennsylvania, where the tow truck operator tells me he only has room for one child in his cab, not both. On a street corner in Brooklyn, where the tow truck guy knows a guy. In the town of Lancaster, where we once lived, where I wait for the tow truck while my friend Rachel rescues the children, ferrying them off down the road in her maroon sedan, their faces unrecognizable against the glare of the sun as they turn to wave from the backseat. The boys know not to panic, know where to find the AAA card, know what it feels like to be rescued, to need rescuing.

———

When their father lives two states away and we drive three hours each way every other weekend, we listen to the following audiobooks on loan from the library: *Magic Tree House Collection: Books 1–8; Magic Tree House Collection: Books 9–16; Magic Tree House Collection: Books 17–24; The Penderwicks; The Penderwicks on Gardam Street; The Penderwicks at Point Mouette; The Penderwicks at Last; A Wrinkle in Time; Dragon Rider; Little House in the Big Woods; Charlie and the Chocolate Factory; Charlie and the Great Glass Elevator; Fantastic Mr. Fox; The Hobbit; Harry Potter and the Sorcerer's Stone; The Mysterious Benedict Society; Midnight for Charlie Bone; Charlie Bone and the Time Twister; Charlie Bone and the Invisible Boy; Charlie Bone and the Castle of Mirrors; Charlie Bone and the Hidden King; Inkheart; Where the Mountain Meets the Moon; The Magician's Nephew; The Lion, the Witch and the Wardrobe;* half of *The Horse and His Boy,* until the scary part.

When their father moves to Brooklyn and the drive is only fifty minutes long, the three of us sing along to pop songs on the radio instead, changing as many lyrics as we can to the words *fart, butt,* and *toot.* From the backseat, they make a rule that I cannot dance while driving; in response, I ordain them the Little Mormons.

The creases of the seats in back are at once gummy and sandy. I fish out mini-golf pencils, half-melted M&Ms with the Ms rubbed off, pennies, army men missing limbs, and disintegrating cheese puffs from the space beneath the seat-belt clips, imagining myself brave like Flash Gordon in that movie when Timothy Dalton forces Flash to stick his hand inside the beast tree. Feeling industrious while waiting in the elementary school car line one afternoon, I try to get out bits of granola bar from the 12-volt cigarette lighter in the center console whose cover is long gone. I unfold a paper clip and begin to tweeze out the sticky clumps of oats until I give myself a shock, like in a game of Operation. The center console USB port never works again.

One morning, the three of us go out our front door in a flurry of backpacks and coats and feet stuffed halfway in sneakers. We get into the car, snap into our seat belts and wait for the clock to flash to life to see how many minutes we have left to get to school before the first bell, but the car doesn't start. We quickly deduce that one or the other son forgot to close the back door all the way after coming home from chess club the day before (*It doesn't matter who! It's not about fault!*). I try the ignition again and again, but pretending doesn't help, the battery is dead. We get out of the car and stand in the driveway. Their small faces are looking at me, like I will know what to do.

And suddenly I do know what to do. Or at least what to do next. I push down the worry about how to get a jump and whether I still have the cable kit my father gave me somewhere in the basement and how much this is all going to cost me since I don't get paid until next week. I switch on a bright smile before turning to them and slapping my hands against my knees. *Okay, my Little Mormons. Let's get walking.*

At the end of our block, I turn back and can no longer see the silver glint of the car in our driveway. But I know it is there, a quiet and unmoving block of steel, as the three of us continue on our way up the road, hand in hand. What begins as adventure quickly turns tiresome, and in another two blocks my older son's bookbag is slung over my shoulder and my younger son rides on my back. We have a long way to go, most of it uphill. We certainly won't make it by first bell. But we'll make it.

End Papers

W HEN THE CALL CAME IN, I was at the playground, standing in the shade of a giant Norway maple and wondering
why trees in the suburbs don't seem to smell. I saw the PA area
code and I knew the call would be about the farmhouse.

I looked out into the elementary school field for the shapes of my
sons and debated answering. I wasn't sure I would be able to handle
the phone call right there, in public, the other mothers so close. For
strength, I put my hand to my lapel and rubbed the hard edge of my
grandmother's pin I'd attached to my blazer that morning.

A few years after my grandmother died, my parents passed
along a small white box of costume jewelry, a collection of vaguely
Elizabethan fake-pearl necklaces, chunky medallions on garish
shiny chains, clip-on earrings with glass rubies nested in rows of
cubic zirconia, none of which I ever recall my grandmother wearing. Mostly, my children and I used them for dress-up living room
parties. But this strange little pin had become a favorite: a scraggly
silver-plated donkey with a single green stone for the eye. It was
terribly ugly, but I fancied it.

I took a breath and answered. The broker's voice was chipper on the phone. The paperwork was ready, everything was in place. The couple buying the house wondered if they could keep some of the tools and flat files in the barn, maybe some furniture. I told her she'd have to talk to R. about that; I hadn't taken any of the furniture from the house when I left three years earlier and didn't plan to take any now. They could have everything, as far as I was concerned.

The air brakes grunted behind me as the row of afternoon school buses began to rumble by. We agreed to touch base in a few days and hung up. The boys were still in the field with their friends, playing some bastardized version of football or soccer or both. In that moment, I wanted to call off the whole deal, yank the house from the market, just stop the whole process. Most of my thoughts about the house had been focused on finances—paying off what was left of the mortgage, recouping the cash I'd put in as a down payment twelve years earlier, figuring out how to split the rest equitably between my soon-to-be ex-husband and me. I hadn't really let myself think about the place itself.

Until that moment, I hadn't really thought about not being able to stand on that porch again, or the reality of that spot, that view, belonging to someone else.

That house was where I'd been my happiest. My loneliest, my most isolated, but also my happiest. When I say that to my mother or to friends, they look at me strangely. To them, I was just a ghost in those years. I was absent, out of touch, lost out there in the woods. I missed birthdays and weddings and baby showers, stopped answering the phone when family called. This is not the mark of someone happy.

Maybe a better description would be that this house was where I felt closest to the possibility of finding happiness. Walking the trails around the old farmhouse, I'd found the kind of cellular belonging that I hadn't had since I was a child playing in the wildlife refuge at the end of my block. Inside that house, I was shrinking, erasing, disappearing, but outside, it was as if the whole world belonged to me, every curving cattail, every sweet blossom of honeysuckle. It wasn't quite that I was happy, but I felt, in some alternate timeline, I could be.

That country was nothing like the sanitized suburbia where I now lived, where packs of children were the most feral things in the streets and the trees had no smell and all natural sound was drowned out by the thrum of the street cleaner. Sometimes, the blocks in my town reminded me of cardboard boxes of Shake 'n Bake stacked in a row at the food store, one after another after another. But I'd grown to prefer the safety of that uniformity. It irked me at times, but I was happy—actually happy—to feel safer than I had for a long time, my sons and I just one family in a crowd of many others, tucked gratefully inside our own little box of Shake 'n Bake.

I lifted my arms to wave the boys in from the field, but they ignored me. I was suddenly impatient, annoyed at the playground's sour-smelling wood chips poking through my sandals. Why did these splinters of dead trees at my feet have a stronger smell than the living ones in front of me?

I'd already marched halfway across the field to collect the boys when I realized the donkey pin was gone. I checked my pockets, retraced my steps, enlisted the kids to help me look. I'd paced around the playground during the phone call, so we split up and searched, bent close to the ground like bloodhounds, hoping to catch a glint of the imitation silver or green eye. Another mother came over and offered to help, asking what it was we'd lost.

"A pin," I said. "It's a little silver donkey," moving my hands to show her the approximate size. She looked at me as if I'd told her we were searching for a piece of chewed gum. "It was my grandmother's," I added.

"Oh! Was it very expensive?" she asked.

No, I said, shaking my head.

But it was mine, and I'd pinned it over my heart that morning, and now it was gone.

⁓

A month later, I pushed my foot on the gas as the car crested a hill. We were a week away from closing, and I wanted to visit the farmhouse one last time, pick up a few remaining books and odds and ends before R. finished packing. My pulse began to race and my stomach lurched the closer I got to the house. I still knew exactly when to push the gas pedal and where to brake, where to watch for tractors on the road and when to watch for deer. As the car climbed the last long incline, the road curved and gave me a view of nearly the whole valley. I made the last turn before the pavement gave way to gravel and took it slow, nodding to the empty spot in the line of pines where I'd crashed my car seven years earlier.

Someone had finally planted a replacement.

꘡

I'd already made the decision not to attend the closing in person. It was just too painful. I knew I couldn't sit in the same basement conference room of the same small-town bank where we'd first closed on the house twelve years earlier. I couldn't sit next to R. in that small windowless room while we signed away the one place in the world either one of us had ever felt was truly ours. I also couldn't sit there without him.

Our first divorce hearing had happened earlier that month. When we arrived at court, neither of our lawyers were there yet, and we said an awkward hello as we tried to figure out what to do, where we were supposed to be. I was dressed in a blue suit and had blown my hair straight, put makeup on. R. was in his usual uniform of jeans and a white t-shirt, though he'd buttoned a plaid shirt over it for the occasion. We found some photocopies on a podium; R. was never good with forms, so I tried to fill one out for us both, but neither of us knew our case number or our lawyers' addresses. We stood together behind the weird knee-high wooden fence that separated the judge and lawyers from the rest of the room until we were able to flag down a clerk. When I asked if I was filling out the right form, the clerk gave me a strange look.

You don't know your case number and you don't know if it's the right form, he scoffed. *What is this, your first time here?*

I felt my face grow hot and stammered that yes, actually, this was my first time here.

The clerk looked from me to R. and back to me again. Under-

standing washed across his face and he touched my wrist apologet-
ically. *I'm so sorry, I thought you were a lawyer.* Now it was his turn to
stammer. He gestured at R., in his jeans, and at me, in my heels. *I
thought you were* his *lawyer.*

I assured him it was fine. We all laughed conspiratorially and
he told us we were in the right place and to just wait until our
lawyers got there and they'd know what to do. The man started
to walk away and then turned and gestured at me with a gotcha
expression on his face, pointing his finger at me like a gun. *Are you
sure you're not really his lawyer?* Guffaw, guffaw. Once the door to
the judge's chambers closed behind him, I turned to R. and rolled
my eyes, grateful for the break in mood, ready to laugh together.

His brow knitted and he wasn't looking at me. He seemed
embarrassed.

Why didn't he think that maybe I was the lawyer? he asked quietly
to no one in particular, genuinely perplexed.

R. remained perplexed about the entire process. I think at each
step—as I moved out, and then filed for divorce, and then agreed
to put the house on the market—he believed I would change my
mind. Sometimes I thought I would, too. Nothing I said seemed
to penetrate. He constantly asked me, *Why are you doing this?* For a
few years, I tried to explain to him in different ways—in late-night
talks, in letters, in couples therapy, in the answers I scrawled on
worksheets in our save-your-marriage books—but nothing seemed
to compute. He was certain I was seeing someone else, certain my
birth control pills were messing with my brain, certain my parents

were controlling me, certain there was something I wasn't telling him. I told him everything. He just couldn't hear it.

But I love you, he would say angrily, like an accusation. As if I had broken a rule, as if I hadn't also broken my own heart.

A few years into our marriage, R. lost his wedding ring in one of the fields behind the farmhouse. He often took it off to paint or mow, and one day he put it in his pocket and it must have fallen out. He took an old metal detector out into the field, found a bunch of nails and other junk, but not the ring. He never replaced it.

One night near the end of our marriage, while making dinner, I took my engagement and wedding rings off and placed them on the windowsill above the kitchen sink before plunging my hands into a bowl of cold raw meat. After dinner, I washed the dishes, lining them up in the dry rack while staring out over the hill. That night, I did not put the rings back on.

This is how a marriage ends. Slowly, piece by piece, and then all at once.

Later on that day in the courtroom, when we were seated with our lawyers at separate tables, the judge called us the plaintiff and defendant instead of by our names and I was told to stand.

Raise your right hand.

The stenographer, a middle-aged woman with moussed-up curls and tan pantyhose, taptaptapped a few feet in front of me.

Do you swear to tell the truth, the whole truth . . . my ears suddenly felt funny, like someone had put earmuffs around my head. Everyone's eyes were on me. It was my turn to speak.

I do.

I do. There was only one other time in my life that I'd stood in front of an official of the court and said those words. Once the tears started, they wouldn't stop. The judge pushed forward as I stood there crying, gulping for air.

He asked me to list my address for the court. All of the street numbers of all the homes I'd ever lived in floated across my brain. They looked like one of those color blindness tests you take at the optometrist. 5. 89. 532. 15. 70. I'd lived in my apartment on the north shore of Long Island for three years by that point, but my brain couldn't fish out the right house number.

The stenographer had stopped typing. She stared openly, hands frozen above her little keys as I wept. The earmuffs were getting tighter.

Where is your home, Miss?

I kept sobbing. My lawyer nervously shuffled papers in his briefcase beside me.

Where is your home?

I finally made it to our road and took the left fork, hearing the creek before I could see the little bridge. The air always got cool as the road dipped down here, the brambles on the sides of the road giving way to the waving hands of fern. We were the first driveway on the right. As I drove up the long stretch of grey shale marked by a middle stripe of grass, the red metal roof of the barn came into view first, the white siding of the house just beyond. *This is not your house*, I told myself. *This is not your house.*

At the barn bar down the road, the men had told us that when Old Man McGarry first came to these hills, he dug a kind of mud hut along the creek, and that's where the family lived while they built this house. They cut down trees by hand, building the farmhouse and barns with the timber. The rock walls lining the paddocks were built after McGarry and his family cleared the fields of rocks.

I looked at the house and forced myself to imagine other people living there. The couple who'd bought the place were from Philadelphia, I knew. When our real estate agent told us their name, I looked them up online. They were barely retirement age, with adult children in their twenties. I found photos of the house in Philadelphia they were leaving to come to this one. It was stunning. Another old beauty, that one made of stone. The house was three stories with lovely gardens and charming old details. There was a piano and a little library. The wife's art studio was on the top floor. I fantasized for a moment about buying their home, about trading lives, until I realized that they'd had to sell their house in order to buy ours and so it already had new owners.

I asked our real estate agent why the couple was leaving such a beautiful place. *They lost someone,* she said. *I think maybe the house is too sad for them now, too many memories.*

Recently, I was standing on a city street with a different man. He zipped across the road while I stayed on the curb, waiting for the light to change. A car came around the corner, too quickly, and I yelled out to warn him. I yelled my husband's name.

I'd yelled that name more than any other over the past fifteen years, that single hard syllable; I'd yelled it out of frustration, fear, love, anger, caution. His name will always be in the back of my mouth, circling that upper left molar I cracked a corner off while eating popcorn. The dentist said she could replace the corner with porcelain, build the tooth back to its original four points. "But there's really no need," she continued, wiping her gloved hand on my blue alligator-clipped bib. "It would be so much easier to just smooth out that sharp edge. You only need three good points on a molar."

You just need three.

I told her to go ahead, just smooth the sharp bits. But often I'll find my tongue worrying that spot, testing, expecting to find four when there are only three, reminding myself it really is gone.

When R. comes to pick the children up every other weekend now, he rumbles down our tight suburban street in his blue pickup truck. I am usually in the kitchen, packing small bags of carrot sticks for the ride that I know will go uneaten, will just come back to me, stuffed in the side pocket of their travel backpack they keep their changes of clothes in, and on Sunday evening I will take out the dirty underwear and socks and t-shirts, the small bag of dried-out carrots, like bony brittle fingers, pointing. *You did this*, they say. *You*. And every time, I take them out, stuff them in the trash.

When his blue truck pulls up, the children will run out of the house and pull open the heavy back doors, hike themselves into the truck like they are climbing up on a horse. He keeps the trailer hitch on the floor in the backseat, a dense bar of metal with a ball attached that I imagine becoming a weapon in a car crash, launching itself into my children's smiling faces, a two-for-one, double-whammy death. On the weekends they are with him, my brain does this. I think of all the ways they might be dying that very minute. Even while I sleep, I dream of them sliding down sewer grates, stepping out into traffic, being crushed by a branch while on a bike ride in Prospect Park.

But that's all after they drive down the block. While they climb in, I'll watch from the kitchen window or the top of the driveway. R. might have paintings wrapped up and ready for delivery, or stretcher bars, or his French easel rattling around in the truck's bed. I know the radio will be playing '70s rock. The cab of the truck has a vaguely chemical smell, grease and turpentine and maybe fast food from old wrappers the kids have stuffed in the doors in the back. He might need a haircut or a new coat, and I know what his neck would smell like between his hairline and the lip of his white t-shirt, likely smudged somewhere with oil paint. Some days it takes everything in me not to walk down that driveway, open the passenger door, get in.

After it became clear to him that there would be no reconciliation, we eased into a kind of strained détente. Phrases like "visitation schedule" and "shared calendar" became part of our new lexicon. One afternoon, as I pushed a cart full of Boboli pizza crust and Pirate Booty around a Costco, he called my phone. I picked up, staring straight at the fluorescent tube lighting above me, already trying to blot him out. He was having another heart attack, he said. It had been more than ten years since his last one, but he'd stopped keeping up with his pills and annual visits once I left. He was at the hospital, waiting for a room.

He needed another stent, maybe two. He gave me the address of the hospital in Scranton. He'd be in for a few days. I told him to be strong, to hold on, to keep me posted. Then I hung up and finished shopping.

It took a few days before I understood that I had no intention of going to the hospital. I stayed in contact with friends who visited, who went to the house and packed a bag with a change of clothes and a sketchbook, brought it to the hospital for him. I sent flowers. Children were not allowed in that wing of the hospital, and we agreed we wouldn't want the children to see him like that anyway, we didn't want to scare them. I said I couldn't take time off from work, I couldn't figure out childcare. The hospital was two states away, I didn't have money for a hotel. Every time he asked when I was coming, I batted it away. *I'll talk to you tomorrow*, I said. *Let's see what the doctor says.*

But the truth is, I knew that if I returned, if I saw him in that hospital bed, I'd never have the strength to leave again.

When I finished packing my car, I walked around the house one more time. This is the bluestone slab where I once wrote all the words my son could say in brightly colored chalk. This is the apple tree that always blooms first every year. This is the milkshed our friends helped us clear the fox nest from. This is where we split the wood. This is where the wild rhubarb grows. This is the grounding wire for the lightning rod on top of the barn. This is the peach tree we couldn't save. This was the house where I became a wife, a mother, a bookseller. This was the house where I wrote my first book, cooked my first Thanksgiving turkey, baked my first loaf of bread, my first pie.

I knew there was no way to find my way back to the home I missed. I wasn't sure it ever truly existed in the first place.

At the end of the long driveway, even though I promised myself I would not, I stopped the car and looked back. The buildings were still standing and I had not turned into a pillar of salt. I looked one last time at the red metal roof, the silver glint of the aluminum chimney. I knew where the bluebird was buried that I'd found dead in the woodstove one morning, I knew where the tree stump was that we'd carved all our initials into. And I knew that in a few months' time, the garlic bulbs down in the garden would begin to send up their thin green sprouts, but for now, they were just small ears curled beneath the ground, waiting.

I never did find my donkey pin. I like to imagine a child picking it up, pocketing it during recess and secreting it away in a shoebox beneath their bed, among buttons and acorns and strange-shaped stones and shells from the beach. More likely, though, it is buried on the edge of that field somewhere.

A few weeks after I lost the pin, bulldozers moved in and tore the entire playground apart to build a temporary road for trucks to get to the back of the elementary school's property for a construction project. The PTA held fundraisers, and after the construction was finished a new playground was built in place of the old one, the plain metal slide traded for a spongy ergonomic playset with big bright plastic parts, black nylon ropes in place of wooden ladders.

My kids prefer the old playground. They don't understand how grown-ups could spend so much time and money and manage to produce something worse than before. Sometimes, after school lets out, I'll push them on the rubbery blue swing set in the corner back by the fence. One afternoon, they dangled their skinny legs, surveying the new plastic pieces in front of them.

One or the other said with a sigh, *I miss the way it used to be, Mama.*

I think of the old silver slide, and my donkey pin, and the family hidden up on a blue hill, the father at the easel, the mother at the sink. I think of the way these ghosts haunt us, how they sometimes seem more real than the very objects in front of us.

The boys grip the chains tightly with their small fists, legs pumping, flying forward and going nowhere at the very same time. The clouds shift and the sun warms us; a hawk with a nest nearby circles above us in the sky. I look at their heads of soft hair, glinting in the sunshine, ruffling in the wind, and I can feel the small knobs of their spines against my hands as my palms meet their backs. My tongue goes automatically to my cracked tooth, three points instead of four.

"I know," I say to them, smiling, though they can't see me there behind them. "Sometimes, I miss the way it used to be, too."

I push them away from me and they return, their gravity a beautiful, sure thing.

ACKNOWLEDGMENTS

When a book takes more than ten years to build, it goes through many lives. One person has been a constant throughout: my literary agent, Anna Stein. Thank you for your loyalty, your friendship, your honesty, and your lion's heart.

Thank you to Jill Bialosky, who is my dream editor, terrifying in her brilliance and talent. You saw what this book could be and patiently guided me along the path until I could see it, too. Drew Elizabeth Weitman made sure the wheels never came off the bus; thank you for sticking with this project for the long haul, from your first read to the last, and for your kindness in visiting my classroom. My gratitude extends to the entire W. W. Norton team, including Erin Sinesky Lovett, Michelle Waters, Grace Shum, Rebecca Munro, Jodi Beder, Lauren Abbate, and Gabrielle Nugent. I am grateful for the advice of Louise Carron and Edward Klaris. I am honored by the beauty of Richard Ljeones's cover design. Thank you to everyone at W. W. Norton and ICM.

Thank you to the following entities for support: Hofstra University, Humanities New York, The Bread Loaf Environmental

Writers' Conference, The Katharine Bakeless Nason Endowment, The Port Washington Public Library, and The Virginia Center for the Creative Arts. During the pandemic, Caity and Todd at the West Kill Cabin gave me space and the luxury of privacy when it was most needed. And to every independent bookstore and public library: Thank you for the work you do and the lives you save, including mine, over and over.

Thank you to the many spectacular editors who have guided me across the life of this book, including: Thomas Beller at *Mr. Beller's Neighborhood*, Jill Christman at *River Teeth's* Beautiful Things, Jonny Diamond at *LitHub*, Guy Trebay at the *New York Times*, Jenisha Watts at *The Atlantic*, and Robert Wilson at *The American Scholar*, as well as Sandy M. Fernandez while at *The Washington Post* and Sadie Stein while at *The Paris Review*. The book would not have found its way without Michelle Wildgen.

It's been my good fortune to be able to lean on many generous mentors, workshop pals, first readers, and smart artists and critics throughout the years, including: Beth Ain, Andrew Blauner, Andrea Efthymiou, Michele Filgate (I owe you a Disney Cruise), Gina Frangello, Sam Freedman, Kabi Hartman, Artis Henderson, Sheena Joyce, Laura Joyce-Hubbard, Margot Kahn, Taylor Larson, Richard Locke, Phillip Lopate, Katie Machen, Martha McPhee, Padmini Mongia, Honor Moore, Judith Mueller, Leigh Newman, Patricia O'Toole, Christina Sirabian, Kerry Sherin Wright, and Jennie Yabroff. Thank you to my entire Ad-Hoc Tenure Committee at Hofstra, especially Dr. Craig Rustici and Dr. Karyn Valerius. Thank you to all of my students, who give me so much hope.

Thank you to dear friends, present and past, including Katharine Brown, Nina Burleigh, Alison Green Myers, Jen Wood

Kiesendahl, Meegan Murray, Heather Hogan, Micki Lazar, Crystal Ketterhagen, and Pennell Whitney. Thank you to Bill Anton & Paul Ludick and Laura & Jim McManus. Thank you to Amy Benson, Sonya Chung, and Sam Lipsyte; thanks too late to Leslie Woodard, and there will never be enough gratitude showered upon the amazing Dorla McIntosh (missing your wedding remains one of my deepest regrets). Thank you to Cindy Bass, Melissa Connolly, Dardana Geller, Meghan Getting-Straesser, Jen Shapiro-Lee, and Jill Vegas. Thank you to Marci Nelligan and to Rachel Anderson-Rabern, who shared the hardest parts and helped me understand my own. Thank you to all of the caregivers who helped me across the years, and much gratitude to the many single parents who showed me that family doesn't have just one definition.

Thank you to my home team: Megana and Jinnah Hosein, Brandy and Mike Keenan, Margaret and Ben Parker. And to John Spagna: Thank you for stealing Emily Dickinson and for saving my life, again and again; Coco: Finish that story! To Dr. Carrie Diamond, whose questions have made me a better writer, parent, partner, and person: Thank you for helping me find my way out of the monkey house.

Thank you to my Noah, who told me so. Please don't ever stop—at least, not for the next 50–200 years.

Thank you to my parents, who taught me to do the right thing, not the easy thing, and who have helped me in every way possible. I am grateful for your love each day.

Finally, thank you to my children, my whole heart: This is my story, but this is not the only story. I cannot wait to watch you go out into the world and make your own.

A NOTE ON SOURCES

The events in these essays are portrayed to the best of my memory, experience, and research. The bibliography below includes some of the most pertinent books and sources I used while working on this project, but is by no means exhaustive in terms of what I read or what should be read on the topics.

Home Fires

Most of my sons' books were paperbacks and hardcovers saved from my own childhood, but *Roxaboxen* was new to me and quickly became a favorite of ours. Marian and her friends reminded me of my own childhood, building worlds of forts and empires in the Wertheim National Wildlife Refuge in Shirley, Long Island. Tina was our Marian, and we all worked hard at playing adults. I love the darkness of this book, the precarity of the world the children build, that only they can access.

While researching collective memory in postwar countries for my undergraduate thesis work, I studied Benedict Anderson's *Imagined Communities*, my first primer on constructing a shared identity through imagination and memory. In *The Future of Nostalgia*, Svetlana Boym focuses closely on Russia, but her ideas are applicable beyond and share with Anderson a similar mix of anthropology, psychology, and history, while layering in more space for romance and longing. Leslie Jamison's gorgeous coronavirus essay utilized Boym's work to excavate our obsession with returning to normal, which became an instrumental read of the work for me.

Anderson, Benedict. *Imagined Communities: Reflections on the Origin and Spread of Nationalism*. Verso, 1991.

Boym, Svetlana. *The Future of Nostalgia*. Basic Books, 2016.

Jamison, Leslie. "The Past Year Has Taught Me a Lot about Nostalgia." *The New York Times*, March 11, 2021.

McLerran, Alice, and Barbara Cooney (ill.). *Roxaboxen*. Scholastic, 1994.

Intrepid

Along with my various personal experiences with the ship over the years, I made use of the Sea, Air & Space Museum's comprehensive resources to build this essay. I've long been obsessed with the place. When my first book came out, the *Intrepid* had just left its pier and I missed it dearly, writing for the Powell's newsletter about the way it reminded me of the difficult days of writing my first book, when I was paralyzed by writer's block, stuck deep in the sludge, just like the ship. In 2016, *Newsday* asked me to interview the astronaut Mike Massimino about his book *Spaceman: An Astronaut's Unlikely Journey to Unlock the Secrets of the Universe*, a fantastic memoir of a blue collar, Long Island kid's meteoric rise within NASA. The spaceship that landed on the moon in 1969 was built on Long Island, sparking

Massimino's boyhood dream when he first learned this. I love the way these lumbering machines lodge in our childhood memories and become part of our stories.

After 9/11, I became part of a study run by a British organization interviewing people who were near the disaster site that morning. Nearly five years later, I sat with the interviewer in a small office downtown, telling him where I thought I was standing, what time things felt like they happened. He asked me question after question. *Did you see the airplane parts?* No. *Was the smoke very bad?* No. *Were you having trouble breathing when you were standing on the corner?* No. *Was there metal on the ground?* No. I felt like I answered the questions all wrong; I told him I was on the 1 train, but I meant the C. I told him I thought I was east of the towers, but he showed me on a map that I must have been on the north side. While I'd studied the fracture of memory that occurs after war, I knew nothing about the effects of post-traumatic stress on memory yet, the way time and space often collapses in on itself in these moments. I remember worrying he wouldn't believe I'd actually been there that morning and I remember feeling so disoriented I questioned it myself. That is, until after the interview, when I went to the corner where the interviewer thought I must have been standing and found the fire hydrant, stood in that same spot and knew it, even though nothing else surrounding it remained. I wrote about this interview for MrBellersNeighborhood.com and used those notes as a source for this essay.

I still have a hard time reading anything about that day. When I tucked into Elisa Gabbert's mesmerizing collection, *The Unreality of Memory and Other Essays*, I reflexively threw the book across the room upon opening to the page with the photo of the jumpers. As it was for many readers, E. B. White's timeless *Here Is New York* was a balm for me after 9/11 (even with his prescient line about "a single flight of planes no bigger than a wedge of geese can quickly end this island fantasy"), and this, along with Colson Whitehead's mournful and joyous "The Way We Live Now: 11–11–01; Lost and Found" ("We can never make proper goodbyes") helps me move through the early hours of that morning every year.

Gabbert, Elisa. *The Unreality of Memory: And Other Essays.* FSG, 2020.

Massimino, Mike. *Spaceman: An Astronaut's Unlikely Journey to Unlock the Secrets of the Universe.* Crown, 2016.

White, E. B. *Here Is New York.* Harper, 1949.

Whitehead, Colson. "The Way We Live Now: 11–11–01; Lost and Found." *The New York Times*, November, 11, 2011.

"His Wife Once Bit His Hand to the Bone"

Along with my own experience sitting for paintings, I interviewed artist models and artists about their relationship to the process. I also sat for the artist Felicia van Bork, and she kindly allowed me to pick her brain before and after she painted. I am grateful for that experience, as it realigned the process and power dynamic in my head—I was reminded that being painted by someone else can feel warm and wonderful, and I was glad to enter my final revision with that reminder.

As additional research, I read what I could find on Jo, including parts of Hopper historian Gail Levin's giant *Edward Hopper: An Intimate Biography*, Elizabeth Thompson Colleary's *My Dear Mr.*

Hopper, and Sara McColl's luminous essay, "Jo Hopper, Woman in the Sun." The author and literary critic Gaby Wood's penetrating review of one of Hopper's shows gave me deeply important insight. A Hopper retrospective is up at The Whitney as I write these notes, and includes three of Jo's watercolors on the walls, though her presence is everywhere in the show, from her likeness on her husband's canvases to her meticulous notes cataloging his sales to her commentary on his paintings. One of the small placards beside her piece *Back of E. Hopper* includes her quote, "I paint what he doesn't." I'd like to imagine a world where she wasn't forced to choose.

Colleary, Elizabeth Thompson. *My Dear Mr. Hopper.* Whitney Museum of American Art, 2013.

Levin, Gail. *Edward Hopper: An Intimate Biography.* Knopf, 1995.

McColl, Sara. "Jo Hopper, Woman in the Sun." *The Paris Review*, February 26, 2018.

Wood, Gaby. "Man and Muse." *The Guardian*, April 25, 2004.

Cycling

Along with news accounts, the shows and film mentioned in the essay, and the internet, the book *Indian Larry: Chopper Shaman* provided insight and background. This essay sat unresolved for years until I mentioned my sidecar memory to my parents. I thought at first my misremembering meant the undoing of the essay; then I realized it was the entire point.

Nichols, David, and Andrea "Bambi" Cambridge. *Indian Larry: Chopper Shaman.* Motorbooks, 2010.

The Cow

I didn't recall the use of the term "freemartin" in Huxley's *Brave New World* until I began researching the subject. I used multiple internet sources, including TheCattleSite.com, and fact-checked this essay with my resident livestock expert and 4-H matriarch, Brandy Keenan, though any mistakes are my own.

Huxley, Aldous. *Brave New World*. Vintage, 2010.

The Ghosts in the Hills

The opening of Truman Capote's book *In Cold Blood* is one of my absolute favorites. I reread this book every few years and have watched both *Infamous* (2006) and *Capote* (2005) multiple times, as referenced in the text. The isolation of the Clutter home struck an eerily similar note to the red house down the road; we had no idea what was happening in those woods.

While at the Virginia Center for the Creative Arts in August 2021, the artists Jonathan Adams and Bug Carlson generously included me in a conversation about heterotopias. After that, I fell deep into the wormhole of heterotopia, reading some of Michel Foucault's scholarship on the subject, along with others. Specifically, I found Foucault's essay "Of Other Spaces: Utopias and Heterotopias" helpful in my thinking about Rock Lake, along with Knut Åsdam's "Heterotopia: Art, Pornography, and Cemeteries" and many other resources on Peter Johnson's Heterotopia Studies website.

In searching specifically for resources on the relationship between heterotopias and maps, I was delighted to find my Hofstra

English Department colleague's forthcoming (at the time) book, *Against the Map: The Politics of Geography in Eighteenth-Century Britain*. I interviewed Adam Sills further and we discussed everything from sweatshops to yacht rock.

Also helpful in writing this chapter: Janisse Ray's *Ecology of a Cracker Childhood* and Sarah Smarsh's *Heartland, The Wayne Independent*, and various gardening books picked up over the years.

Åsdam, Knut. "Heterotopia: Art, Pornography, and Cemeteries." Heterotopiastudies.com.

Capote, Truman. *In Cold Blood*. Vintage, 1994.

Foucault, Michel. "Of Other Spaces: Utopias and Heterotopias." *Architecture /Mouvement/ Continuité*, October 1984.

Ray, Janisse. *Ecology of a Cracker Childhood*. Milkweed, 2015.

Sills, Adam. *Against the Map: The Politics of Geography in Eighteenth-Century Britain*. University of Virginia Press, 2021.

Smarsh, Sarah. *Heartland: A Memoir of Working Hard and Being Broke in the Richest Country on Earth*. Scribner, 2019.

Lessons from a Starry Night

I went through more than a year of Eye Movement Desensitization and Reprocessing (EMDR) therapy to be able to drive again. Initially skeptical, I came to relish the strange process of finger-wagging and free-associating. Those EMDR sessions crystallized the crash scene and cemented it into a sensory landscape I was able to walk around in; EMDR ultimately functioned as its own form of research.

Rachel Carson's *Silent Spring* is easily one of the most important books I've ever read in my entire life. Carson's essays and books, especially *Under the Sea-Wind* and *The Edge of the Sea*, remain in my Top Ten Desert Island Books list alongside Susanne Antonetta's *Body Toxic* and Terry Tempest Williams's *Refuge*. Linda Lear's biography, *Rachel Carson: Witness for Nature*, along with discussions during my time at the Bread Loaf Environmental Writers' Conference in Ripton, Vermont, were essential to this piece.

Carson, Rachel. *The Sense of Wonder: A Celebration of Nature for Parents and Children*. Harper Perennial, 2017.

Lear, Linda. *Rachel Carson: Witness for Nature*. Mariner, 2009.

The Leaving Season

It is unlawful to hunt on Sundays except foxes, crows and coyotes.

—PA GAME COMMISSION

The germ of this essay was born from a PA Game Commission mailing that came to the house outlining the—very—many hunting seasons and bag limits in our region and the rules and regulations that guide them. Deer season was celebrated and ubiquitous, but only through conversations with neighbors did I come to learn more about the intricacies of flintlock versus archery versus rifle, antlered versus antlerless, furbearer hunting versus big game, and more. These conversations and the materials from the Commission were invaluable resources in reporting for this essay.

As in my first book, *Welcome to Shirley: A Memoir from an Atomic Town*, I became keenly aware of the layers of class and belonging in this corner of Pennsylvania. Books like *A Small Place* by Jamaica

Kincaid, *Maid: Hard Work, Low Pay, and a Mother's Will to Survive* by Stephanie Land, *Dakota: A Spiritual Geography* by Kathleen Norris, and Smarsh's *Heartland* were important totems for me in this vein. Of particular note: Pennsylvania is one of the few states that does not officially recognize any Native American groups. Books like *Invisible Indians: Native Americans in Pennsylvania* and *Indians in Pennsylvania*, organizations like the Pennsylvania Youth Congress, and the Carlisle Indian School Project offer resources and research that actively push against this erasing. Joy Harjo, whose poem "Once the World Was Perfect" is excerpted in this essay, recently coedited a poetry anthology by writers of Native nations called *When the Light of the World Was Subdued, Our Light Came Through.* This collection features the poem "My Industrial Work" by an anonymous student of the Carlisle Indian Industrial School in 1914.

The original version of this essay was written for the anthology *This Is the Place: Women Writing about Home.* That anthology taught me so much about the nature of home, both as a four-letter word and as an impossible destination.

Anonymous Poet From Room 8. "My Industrial Work." *The Atlantic Magazine*, October 2020.

When the Light of the World Was Subdued, Our Songs Came Through. Edited by Joy Harjo. W. W. Norton, 2020.

This is the Place: Women Writing About Home. Edited by Margot Kahn and Kelly McMasters. Seal Press, 2017.

Kincaid, Jamaica. *A Small Place.* FSG, 2000.

Land, Stephanie. *Maid: Hard Work, Low Pay, and a Mother's Will to Survive.* Hachette, 2019.

Minderhout, David, and Andrea Franz. *Invisible Indians: Native Americans in Pennsylvania.* Cambia Press, 2008.

Norris, Kathleen. *Dakota: A Spiritual Geography.* HarperOne, 2001.

Wallace, Paul. *Indians in Pennsylvania.* The Pennsylvania Historical and Museum Commission, 2015.

The Bookshop: A Love Story

At The Wayne County Historical Society, one can visit the original Stourbridge Lion in the main exhibition room. The store Milkweed no longer exists, but Jim and Laura are still painting away in the nearby hills. The Honesdale I write about here is as far away in time as the bookshop, as disappeared as the room of books itself, though traces are still visible if you look hard enough. Philip Hone is widely considered one of the most prolific diarists of his time period, and his comprehensive and delightful journals were also remarkably helpful to understand just how little connection the man had to his namesake town.

When I first thought about opening the bookshop, I wrote to two dozen of the best readers I knew and asked them for their personal top-ten lists. This was how I came to stock some of the books I hadn't previously read, but now consider some of my own favorites, including *My Garden (Book)* by Jamaica Kincaid, *Mrs. Bridge* by Evan S. Connell, *Wolf Hall* by Hilary Mantel, and *Never Let Me Go* by Kazuo Ishiguro, some of which are included in this essay.

Hone, Philip. *The Diary of Philip Hone, 1828–1851*, volume 1 and 2. Dodd, Mead and Co., 1910.

Our Castle Year

It was during our castle year that Colm Tóibín's exquisite and crushing novel *Nora Webster* came out. I was asked to review the book and I can still remember clutching the giant galley at night under six layers of blankets in my cold little carriage house bedroom in the same way that I can still feel in my marrow the moment Nora stands at the edge of the cold sea, submerged in grief. In my review I wrote, " . . . she is vaguely aware that she should be there for her sons, but she simply cannot make herself available. For much of the book she remains a prisoner to her sadness, and it is only when she sees her sons beginning to seal themselves off in the same way that she begins to rouse." There are certain times in a reader's life when it feels a book has been written just for them. This is one of mine.

I also love watching Tóibín chart his beliefs about books in his criticism, as he is "an intense and moody thinker about books and writers," as the incomparable Dwight Garner wrote in his own *New York Times* review of *New Ways to Kill Your Mother*. Tóibín's mothers, in his fiction and criticism, have deeply impacted the way I think about my own mothering.

Lowry, Lois. *The Giver.* Houghton Mifflin, 1993.

Tóibín, Colm. *New Ways to Kill Your Mother: Writers and Their Families.*
    Scribner, 2012.

The Stone Boat

This essay, more than any other, would not have been possible without countless conversations and interviews, formal and informal, with dozens of parents and artists over the years. These conversations allowed me to pierce the dark swaths of anger that clouded every thought related to this experience and gain at least some semblance of critical distance from the subject, though I did my best to reflect honestly in the text when this was impossible.

I attempted to write this essay many times without including our experience with Child Protective Services. At first, I thought my reluctance was the result of shame, but it soon became clear that I was not including this part of the story out of fear—fear of disclosure and judgment, of course, but also fear of opening myself and my family to the possibility of that terrifying knock on the door again. I decided to include this experience here for exactly that reason—so many of the incredibly brave and brilliant parents I spoke to in researching this essay have been cowed by a system designed to make us think it is our families that are broken when, in fact, it is the system itself that requires repair.

Due to the sensitive nature of the subject, I've chosen to paraphrase sources I might otherwise quote or point to more directly if included in another essay, though I've listed some below.

Jamison, Leslie. "The Past Year Has Taught Me A Lot About Nostalgia," *The New York Times*, March 11, 2021.

Mann, Sally. *At Twelve: Portraits of Young Women*. Aperture, 1988.

Mann, Sally. *Immediate Family*. Aperture, 2015.

Mann, Sally. "Sally Mann's Exposure," *The New York Times Magazine*, April 16, 2015.

Imaginary Friend

To build this essay, I relied primarily on the boxes of letters described in it, as well as years of emails and my own journals. The topic of desire is one I found myself steeped in during the writing of this book since, during the last few years, I was simultaneously coediting a collection of essays on this very topic. Lisa Taddeo's groundbreaking work, both in her book *Three Women* and her essay for the anthology, were especially important in my thinking around the different themes in this essay.

Taddeo, Lisa. *Three Women*. Avid Reader Press, 2019.

Wanting: Women Writing About Desire. Edited by Margot Kahn and Kelly McMasters. Catapult, 2023.

Suspended Animation

Joan Didion could likely be listed as a source in every one of these essays, but for this particular topic there is no better essay on migraine than her gorgeous classic, "In Bed."

Didion, Joan. "In Bed." *The White Album*. Simon & Schuster, 1979.

Finding Home

The conversation with Rebecca Solnit during which we discussed single mothering and our hope for boys took place on March 27, 2017, and an edited version appeared in the literary magazine *Windmill*, which I produce with students at my university. The conversations with the children and my session with the medium are based on journals and memory.

During the editorial process, the copyeditor asked how I was able to see the Throgs Neck Bridge from where I lived. In attempting to fact-check that the bridge was, in fact, the Throgs Neck, I found that it now seems impossible, even though most of my neighbors, when asked, also believe it to be the Throgs Neck. Through maps and assistance from my public library, I've been able to determine that we are all likely looking at the Bronx, and the lighthouse that twinkles in the forefront of the view is on an island known as Execution Rocks, where British soldiers once chained their captives at low tide, and then waited for the rising water to drown them.

On a recent winter walk on this rocky beach, I looked again at this view, the ghost shapes stretching across the sky beyond the placid water, and thought of the Joy Williams line: "Memory is the resurrection." I'm not sure why so many of us believe we are viewing the Throgs Neck from this shoreline, but when held against the reality of staring into a watery graveyard, I surely prefer the hope and promise of a bridge in the distance.

"An Interview with Rebecca Solnit." *Windmill: The Hofstra Journal of Literature & Art*, 2017, issue 2.

PERMISSIONS

THE LEAVING SEASON

Kelly McMasters

THE LEAVING SEASON
Kelly McMasters

1. In "Home Fires," the first essay of *The Leaving Season*, Kelly McMasters describes a safety exercise she conducts with her young sons that involves imagining what they'd save from a house fire. "I also think of all the things I'd leave behind, the things I would let burn" (p. 4), she writes. Discuss the themes of safety and risk that recur throughout the book. How does this essay help to frame them?

2. In "His Wife Once Bit His Hand to the Bone," McMasters reflects on her desire for R. to paint her portrait early in their relationship, comparing him to a similarly enigmatic artist she meets years later at a colony: "We wanted her to help us see ourselves" (p. 35). Talk about her wish to be painted by her partner. How do romantic relationships help us to "see" ourselves? How do you think that connection differs from the typical, transactional relationship between artist and subject that she observes at the colony?

3. Early in her marriage, McMasters writes, "I'd gone from single and completely independent, financially and otherwise, with my own space, to a full-time working spouse and nursemaid" (p. 62). What effect does this change have on how she views herself and her relationship? What role do their respective genders play in how she and R. approach this period in their lives?

4. Describe the social and physical challenges McMasters and R. face upon moving to their Pennsylvania farmhouse.

Why does "the country [begin] feeling more real than the city" (p. 101) for the couple? What do they love about rural life?

5. McMasters writes that R. "has a feral quality that always made the city a bit difficult for him" (p. 118), and that allows him to fit in with their Pennsylvania neighbors even as he practices a vocation that is unusual for a man in their new community. By contrast, she recognizes that her "value [is] measured in pies and babies" (p. 76) by these neighbors. How is McMasters's self-expression hampered by what the neighbors expect of her?

6. The roles of wife and mother feel unnatural to McMasters when her children are small. She recalls, "I was not a cook, but I cooked. I was not a mother, but I mothered. I was not a wife, but I wifed" (p. 145). Are you used to women voicing thoughts like these? Why might mothers feel that their identities are at odds with the idea of a "natural care-taker"?

7. McMasters and her husband buy a bookshop, and she chronicles her life there in the essay "The Bookshop: A Love Story." Talk about why she loves running the bookshop. Were there any aspects of her experience that surprised you as you read?

8. Discuss the parallels between McMasters's choice to close the bookshop and her decision to leave her marriage. What are the factors that help her make up her mind?

9. In "The Stone Boat," McMasters writes about discovering a nude portrait of her sons, painted by her ex-husband, on Instagram. Mulling over how the painting might resemble her personal essays about the family, she asks, "Am I not simply painting my own portrait? . . . Placing art above parenting?" (p. 208) What do you make of these questions? What priorities must a parent weigh when

choosing to share information about their children, whether through published writing or through social media posts?

10. After her divorce, McMasters finds that many married people ask her: *"Was there a moment you knew you wanted to end your marriage?"* (p. 245) Discuss her answer. Does her observation that "leaving a marriage is another type of death" (p. 247) resonate with you?

11. How does the author's view of herself change after her divorce? How does she approach motherhood and her career differently after the end of her marriage?

Diana Abu-Jaber	*Life Without a Recipe*
Diane Ackerman	*The Zookeeper's Wife*
Michelle Adelman	*Piece of Mind*
Molly Antopol	*The UnAmericans*
Andrea Barrett	*Archangel*
Rowan Hisayo Buchanan	*Harmless Like You*
Ada Calhoun	*Wedding Toasts I'll Never Give*
Bonnie Jo Campbell	*Mothers, Tell Your Daughters*
	Once Upon a River
Lan Samantha Chang	*Inheritance*
Ann Cherian	*A Good Indian Wife*
Evgenia Citkowitz	*The Shades*
Amanda Coe	*The Love She Left Behind*
Michael Cox	*The Meaning of Night*
Jeremy Dauber	*Jewish Comedy*
Jared Diamond	*Guns, Germs, and Steel*
Caitlin Doughty	*From Here to Eternity*
Andre Dubus III	*House of Sand and Fog*
	Townie: A Memoir
Anne Enright	*The Forgotten Waltz*
	The Green Road
Amanda Filipacchi	*The Unfortunate Importance of Beauty*
Beth Ann Fennelly	*Heating & Cooling*
Betty Friedan	*The Feminine Mystique*
Maureen Gibbon	*Paris Red*
Stephen Greenblatt	*The Swerve*
Lawrence Hill	*The Illegal*
	Someone Knows My Name
Ann Hood	*The Book That Matters Most*
	The Obituary Writer
Dara Horn	*A Guide for the Perplexed*
Blair Hurley	*The Devoted*

Available only on the Norton website